Praise for *Sociometrics*

"In *Sociometrics*, Tian Dayton masterfully integrates principles of group dynamics and psychodrama therapies with insights into bodily states and feelings gained from contemporary neuroscience. *Sociometrics* infuses therapeutic principles in an intuitive and functional program that shifts the agent of healing from the therapist to the group. We learn that through sociometrics, the threads of healing are woven as the client experiences a reconnection with the inner self and a connection with others."

> —**Stephen W. Porges, PhD**, Distinguished University Scientist,
> Indiana University; Professor of Psychiatry, University of North Carolina;
> creator of the Polyvagal Theory

"With her decades of experience, taught by the masters, Tian Dayton has become one herself. In *Sociometrics*, she offers the clinical field another enriching, engaging book that clearly details how to work with the ramifications of trauma and addiction. Her detailed theoretical and practical descriptions of the use of sociometrics and psychodrama empower clinicians in all settings to create a space of safety and choice for the client. I have witnessed her work and seen the movement for those caught in the flight, fight, or freeze mode. Work that sometimes never gets resolved, or takes years, is readily hastened in these action methods."

> —**Claudia Black, PhD**, Senior Fellow at The Meadows and author of *Unspoken Legacy: Addressing the Impact of Trauma and Addiction within the Family*

"Having watched Dr. Dayton doing a psychodrama, I am gratified to read this clear explanation of the process and additionally to be exposed to the concepts of sociometrics. This book provides a roadmap for clinicians to approach patients with complex trauma in an evidence-based skill set steeped in solid aspects of neurobiology. Dr. Dayton provides a generous mix of the theoretical and clinically practical for practitioners to utilize in their work."

> —**Mel Pohl, MD,** Senior Medical Consultant, Pain Recovery Program,
> The Pointe Malibu Recovery Center and author of *A Day without Pain*

"Sociometry is a part of J. L. Moreno's triadic system of psychodrama, sociometry, and group psychotherapy. Dr. Dayton has spent her entire career adapting these methods for practical use in working with addiction and trauma. Sociometrics respect Moreno's theoretical roots, and in so doing, Dayton's adaptations have retained the creativity and spontaneity so core to Moreno's thinking while creating an approach that is tailored for use in treating addiction and trauma."

—**Daniela Simmons, PhD, TEP**, President, American Society of
Group Psychotherapy and Psychodrama (ASGPP), Founder & CEO
of TELE'DRAMA International

"Sociometrics get clients on their feet and engaging with each other in ways that give them new experience and practice at opening up. The process is the very opposite of isolation and withdrawal, rather it's one that fosters communal containment and connection. For teens and young adults who struggle with addiction, this is game-changing. It helps them to build the skills of emotional literacy so that they can self-reflect and share in meaningful ways with their peers. And these skills of resilience become portable as they take them into the futures they are building as sober and contributing adults."

—**Jamison Monroe**, Founder of Newport Academy/Newport Institute

"My father and Miriam's grandfather developed psychodrama and sociometry in turn of the century Vienna, alongside Freud. Moreno observed that words were too narrow to address what he felt was the human need for action and interaction. He thought that the body needed to be involved in therapy in order for healing to be fully realized. In his own words, 'the body remembers what the mind forgets.' With our current acceptance and understanding of neurobiology and emphasis on embodiment, his work has never been more relevant. Tian Dayton demonstrates a deep understanding of Dr. Moreno's work. Dr. Dayton's writing makes complex theory accessible and pleasurable to read. This book will help practitioners and those affected by trauma understand how psychodrama and sociometry in groups can provide unique, powerful healing of our deepest wounds."

—**Regina Moreno, MA,** author of *Words of the Daughter*, and
Miriam Zachariah, MA, TEP

Sociometrics

Sociometrics

Embodied, Experiential Processes
for Relational Trauma Repair

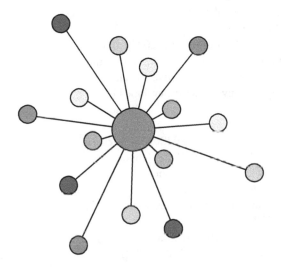

TIAN DAYTON, PhD, TEP

CENTRAL RECOVERY PRESS

LAS VEGAS, NEVADA

Central Recovery Press (CRP) is committed to publishing exceptional materials addressing addiction treatment, recovery, and behavioral healthcare topics.

For more information, visit www.centralrecoverypress.com.

27 26 25 24 23 22   1 2 3 4 5

Library of Congress Cataloging-in-Publication Data

Names: Dayton, Tian, author.
Title: Sociometrics : embodied, experiential processes for healing trauma
 and addiction / Tian Dayton, MA, PhD, TEP.
Description: Las Vegas, NV : Central Recovery Press, [2022] | Includes
 bibliographical references. | Summary: "Sociometrics is a therapeutic
 role-playing practice built upon the foundation of psychodrama and
 sociometry, the pioneering group-therapy concepts developed by
 fin-de-siècle Viennese psychiatrist Jacob Levy Moreno"-- Provided by
 publisher.
Identifiers: LCCN 2022012920 (print) | LCCN 2022012921 (ebook) | ISBN
 9781949481648 (paperback) | ISBN 9781949481655 (ebook)
Subjects: LCSH: Psychic trauma--Treatment. | Sociometry. |
 Drama--Therapeutic use. | Group psychotherapy.
Classification: LCC RC552.T7 D389 2022 (print) | LCC RC552.T7 (ebook) |
 DDC 616.85/21--dc23/eng/20220322
LC record available at https://lccn.loc.gov/2022012920
LC ebook record available at https://lccn.loc.gov/2022012921

Every attempt has been made to contact copyright holders. If copyright holders have not been properly acknowledged please contact us. Central Recovery Press will be happy to rectify the omission in future printings of this book.

Publisher's Note
This book contains general information about addiction, addiction recovery, trauma, mental health, and related matters. The information contained herein is not medical advice. This book is not an alternative to medical advice from your doctor or other professional healthcare provider.

Our books represent the experiences and opinions of their authors only. Every effort has been made to ensure that events, institutions, and statistics presented in our books as facts are accurate and up-to-date. To protect their privacy, the names of some of the people, places, and institutions in this book may have been changed.

Cover design and interior by Deb Tremper, Six Penny Graphics.

To Brandt

We don't say good-bye . . .

Contents

Introduction

When people connect over what matters to them, they have something very special to give each other. They are in the same place at the same time emotionally, psychologically, spiritually, and even physiologically. Whether at a baseball game or a treatment center, people can feel enlivened and part of something bigger than themselves when they're given a way to enter common ground. This is the relational power of what Stephen Porges calls "the social engagement system."

Sociometrics grow out of J. L. Moreno's triadic system of psychodrama, sociometry, and group psychotherapy. Inspired by my training, I designed processes that integrate neurobiology and concepts central to recovery with sociometry and psychodrama, which are more suitable for today's clinician and current treatment settings. Making experiential and embodied therapies useful in treating relational trauma and addiction is the core of my work and the subject of this book.

Thirty years ago, one of my trainees was struggling to deliver therapy to groups of thirty to thirty-five. In an attempt to help him, I tried something novel. I wrote various emotions on sixteen pieces of paper and scattered them all over the floor. I asked the group members a series of questions, and they walked toward the feelings that represented their responses. As they shared why they chose what they chose, the room came alive with chatter, laughter, and emotion. Difficult feelings were normalized, and people opened up. By finding common ground through expressing their shared experience, a kind of relational healing was spontaneously occurring. As with twelve-step programs, people were healing through identification, but they were moving, walking around the room so their bodies were part of the process; their limbic systems were warmed-up through motion so emotion flowed more freely.

Inspired by the efficiency and effectiveness of this approach, I came to the next group, with symptoms of PTSD, and I cautiously scattered the written emotions around the floor. Wanting relief from the lifeless PowerPoint, I took a chance that this process might teach challenging material. Once again, I witnessed the room energizing around shared concerns. Rather than me being responsible for bringing the material to life, spontaneous case examples started popping up all over the room, movingly embodied and articulated by the very people who were experiencing them. The subjects needing to be taught in treatment became immediately personal and relevant. Participants shared, listened, nodded in assent, looked around, down, teared up, and even cracked jokes. In front of my eyes, the process took on a life of its own as I witnessed what I now know to be the healing magic of co-regulation and the power of accessing the social engagement system through structured processes that facilitate relational repair.

These exercises were clearly sufficient for relational repair in and of themselves. But as I linked role play, two problems inherent in using psychodrama solved themselves. First, psychodrama is open-ended and can be hit and miss in the crucial function of providing the right container for the treatment of trauma. And second, its lack of structure can overwhelm clients, and for that matter, therapists.

Floor checks addressed these issues. Their continuity and structure made clients feel safe opening up. As they repeatedly moved through the process, two-thirds of their healing was already occurring. Role plays became focused; participants knew who they wanted to talk to and what they wanted to say, making dramas feel more manageable for clients and therapists alike.

Sociometrics offer a new way of doing therapy, an approach that reduces the role of the therapist while enhancing the healing power that is a natural part of any group. The clients are in charge of which feelings or symptoms they want to explore and how deep they want to go. Some group members model sharing material that matters to them, and that emboldens others to join them in entering deep states and co-creating a healing experience. Rather than isolating and running from painful issues, clients connect and communicate heart-to-heart, engendering feelings of closeness and mutuality rather than distance and alienation.

And it wasn't only the words they shared, it was their visceral experience of connection that was nourishing them. Participants became active agents in each other's recovery. The therapist's role became that of keeping the room safe and the process moving with a minimum of interruption and interpretation.

We learn our language of emotions slowly and over time, and we learn it in relationship to others. In a seamless, sensual, and intentional dance with our primary attachment figures, we learn whether it is safe to touch and be touched; to be ourselves; to feel, love, and need another human being; or if we need to self-protect.

When someone has been traumatized in intimate connection, they may develop layers of defense to keep from knowing how much they hurt. Then in therapy, they can be afraid of what might erupt inside of them if they let themselves revisit those hidden spaces inside themselves. But if they can't bring these hidden parts into consciousness and process them, they lie inside as emotional land mines waiting to be stepped on. Then clients are at risk of doing to others what was done to them; they pass on pain unconsciously.

That's why the healing vehicles we use need to feel welcoming and safe enough so that clients can let down their guard and feel the feelings they run from. And they need to be experiential and embodied, so that the body can disclose the tension, hypervigilance, or frozenness stored in its nervous system, and so that it can reveal the secrets it is holding.

Floor checks feel engaging, structured, and safe. Everyone is sharing real feelings, so emotions that might otherwise feel threatening come forward more easily through an intuitive, self-directed, communal process. Clients can revisit and revise unsuccessful attempts at connection that occurred in their past and skill-build in the present.

Sociometrics build resilience. Clients are on their feet, grounded, oriented in the room. Participants develop a *language for emotion* through repeated and structured encounters in which they get in touch with what is going on within them and search out the right words to describe it to others. Then *they* listen attentively as others do the same, organically enriching their emotional literacy and relational intelligence.

As I developed sociometrics over a period of twenty-five years as part of the Relational Trauma Repair (RTR) model, and tested each one as I went along, I learned that they work the same way wherever I use them, and they can be easily adapted for any population.

The shift in the mind of the therapist is that you will need to see yourself not as the source of knowledge but the facilitator of a process, to learn to mine the wisdom in the group and understand the awe-inspiring power of the human social engagement system to repair and rebuild itself.

Sociometrics require less training than psychodrama itself, while still providing the benefits of experiential, embodied therapy. They take the guesswork out of experiential/embodied work for therapists and focus the healing work clients need to do. And because they are processes that can stand alone, they can be easily incorporated into existing programming wherever an experiential component would invigorate healing. An additional benefit is that floor checks and timelines are psychoeducational. They turn the subject matter that needs to be covered in treatment into engaging experiential learning.

CHAPTER ONE

When Words Are Not Enough: Psychodrama as an Embodied, Bottom-Up Form of Therapy

By the group they were wounded, by the group they shall be healed.
—J. L. Moreno

We have to feel the stories of our lives to heal them. But the kinds of mental shutdown and dissociation that are part of trauma can cause us to relegate precious parts of ourselves into a strange and strained silence within us. However, these parts don't go away. If we don't feel them, name them, convert them into language, and reflect on them so they can be fit into the framework of ourselves and our lives, they sit somewhere inside, vibrating with unfelt life, holding pieces of our aliveness. They become part of our "unfelt known." We may recognize that our traumas happened; we can use words to step around them, to describe them just enough so we think we have unearthed and understood them, but we have not felt and comprehended them in the here and now. We can describe what occurred as a sort of story, but we cannot experience the sensations that are trapped inside the memories. Our feelings remain split off, fragmented, lodged in dark crevices of our mind and body. The past, then, still has power over us because of the emotional secrets it holds. The circumstances aren't necessarily unknown, but the feelings that are caught inside them are. We need to somehow enter the deep inner states that hold the real stories of our lives, and to do that, embodied forms of therapy are important.

A danger then, in any trauma treatment, is that clients may get stuck in a rigid or emotionally detached telling of a trauma story that does not easily incorporate sensation, emotion, healing, and growth. It is what we can tolerate sensing and feeling and what we allow to rise into consciousness that will let that mysterious trapdoor inside us fly open, so that we can see who we are on the inside.

Trauma can make us strangers within our own inner world.

Psychodrama and **sociometrics** can rewrite that story.

Psychodrama is all about bringing the *then* and *there* into the *here* and *now*. Healing—in fact life itself—happens in the present. PTSD leaves us with an emotional and psychic residue. Moments, or relational dynamics, from the past replay their contents over and over again in our present, intruding on our peace of mind and compromising our ability to live in the here and now. By lovingly placing these moments and interactions from the past on the psychodramatic stage, we can re-experience, rework, and reframe them, and in so doing, their power to pull us backward is lessened.

I have witnessed miracles occur when using **role play**—spontaneous slices of life, little human tragedies, moments of joy, and reconnection so vivid that they took my breath away with their authenticity. I have seen my own life flash across my mind and heard the same from others. Embodied role play, it seems, has the power to reproduce moments along our own developmental continuum that literally give ourselves back to ourselves—that let us reunite with forgotten or discarded parts, haul them out of cold storage, and get our hearts pumping again. It is, at times, like the most incredible theater you could ever see, though as a psychologist, I'm probably not supposed to say that. It is raw feeling or longing for action, quivering with unspent energy, unedited emotions, unspoken resentment, withheld love, craven urges, or exalted passions. It is people letting their humanity and vulnerability show, revealing a kind of inner truthfulness that can just knock your socks off. And it happens over and over and over again, these moments of recognition and reconciliation, of loss and redemption—this meeting of ourselves, entering the dark night of the soul, and letting light in.

Genuine trauma healing emerges in layers, and in the body as well as the mind. We do not understand the full meaning of our experience at any magical point in time; rather, that understanding is ever evolving. Clients continue to amend and refine their interpretations of relational dynamics and moments that shaped them as more pieces of the puzzle come into view and they sense themselves more fully as present in the moment. As they learn to shift body states that drive meaning and behavior—from anxious and defensive into more relaxed, engaged, prosocial states— they can revisit these dynamics and moments voluntarily, reframe them through new insight and understanding, and come to see them differently. They can get to know themselves in a new way.

We humans will forever be incomplete. We will continue to grow and change, ever reaching for that bit of new understanding, that new sliver of light. That's the beauty and the artistry of life and of the healing arts. Being able to bring the deeper layers of the self onto the stage in body as well as mind—where they can be experienced, played with, cried for, laughed at, and generally met in all their various forms—is the true work of psychodrama used for the resolution of PTSD.

Another aspect of healing from relational trauma is to re-engage the social engagement system and to recognize and make use of the healing power that is inherent within the group itself. Sociometrics access the deeper layers of self and relational interactions through structured and repeated moments of meaningful connection in which feelings are shared, heard, and witnessed and the body is in motion, in other words, participants are free to move at will.

One of my goals as a therapist is to be a part of facilitating a connection with the self and with others, and sociometrics are designed to do just that. The long-term effects of trauma grow in isolation; just walking in the door of a communal, relational, therapy-oriented space begins healing. The combination of sociometrics such as floor checks, the trauma timeline, and focused, simple role plays in service of a structured, relationally focused vehicle for healing is what this book is about.

Why Words Don't Heal: Moving from an Events Focus to a Relational Focus In Healing cPTSD

Healing **complex relational trauma** (cPTSD) can be confusing because there is not necessarily a clear event or specific moment in time that we can point to. It feels illusive, so we dismiss its significance and discount its impact. We may search for events that explain our chronic inability to know or accept ourselves and to connect at deep levels with others. We cannot necessarily find ourselves in questions such as "Were you physically abused as a child?" "Was there sexual abuse?" and so we discount our lasting hurt. But the drip, drip, drip of feeling dismissed, unseen, unwanted—of watching those from whom we long for love the most roll their eyes, make comments below their breath, or get irritated with our little attempts to connect—can impact our ability to live comfortably within ourselves and our close relationships. It can lead us to shut down our own feelings of neediness and dependency in an effort to feel safe and whole.

As children, in order to avoid the pain of feeling unseen or unaccepted for who we are, we may develop the habit of disconnecting with parts of ourselves that feel injured and dismissed. We withdraw from deep connection both with those inner parts and intimate connection with others. We learn that needing or even loving hurts, and it's better to go numb, dissociate, or withdraw.

Because we relegate these hurt inner parts to a state of unconsciousness, they can feel far away from our day-to-day lives; we barely know they are there. So later in life when these children, now adults enter therapy, they have a hard time bringing these memories or inner states into view. The sheer intensity of reexperiencing them can feel frightening. Or they fear that they might be grabbing only segments of memories—*Did this really occur?*—or be seen as making things up, as overstating their case.

If we grow up or live with addiction, with all of the denial and rationalization done by family members, our experience is even more confusing. The altering of reality, the gaslighting to make circumstances more palatable or less embarrassing—"Your mother has the flu" (read: She is not hung over), "Your father is outgoing; he just loves people" (read: He is not on his way to getting very drunk), "I have a sniffle" (read: I was not crying . . . again), "You don't really feel that" (read:

I cannot bear the truth of your pain)—can make us start to question our version of things. Reality has become blurred and indistinct; we've rewritten it so many times that we cannot find it underneath the many erasures.

Years later, when a therapist sitting comfortably in an upholstered chair says, "Tell me about your trauma," or asks how we felt at the time, we may draw an emotional blank. When asked to reenter those disparate splinters of personal experience and drag them from their hidden world into comprehensible, well-ordered sentences, we feel anxious and put on the spot. Where do we begin? What are we supposed to say? It was so long ago, and it feels so very far away. We feel tongue-tied at best and stupid at worst. Or, sadder still, we look to someone else to tell us what we're feeling because we can't come up with a version of our own.

Recalling this kind of imagery, body sensation, and emotion can make us feel a bit crazy or stirred up inside, so we try *not* to recall it. But our pain is still there. We want to find the right words to fix it. But words don't fix it. The problem is that we're being asked to describe our trauma, when, in fact, the language part of our brain wasn't functioning properly at those times when we were frightened or terrified.

"For a hundred years or more, every textbook of psychology and psychotherapy has advised that some method of talking about distressing feelings can resolve them," as Bessel A. van der Kolk puts it in *The Body Keeps the Score: Brain, Mind, and Body in the Healing of Trauma.* "However, as we've seen, the experience of trauma itself gets in the way of being able to do that. No matter how much insight and understanding we develop, the rational brain is basically impotent to talk the emotional brain out of its own reality" (van der Kolk 2014).

When we're feeling terrified, whether from facing a woolly mammoth, an attacker, chronic rejection, or a drunk and raging parent, the thinking mind shuts down as our limbic system revs up. We become supercharged with extra adrenaline and blood flow to enable us to flee for safety or to stand and fight. Or we freeze; we stand there in body but we disappear on the inside. We hide in plain sight, like a little fawn in the tall grass. We wait for the danger to pass and for a caring presence to return so we can breathe again.

But even though the thinking mind has gone off-line, the limbic system has revved up to enable the fight / flight / freeze, and it continues vigilantly doing its job of processing emotion and collecting sensorial data. It busily absorbs sense impressions—the smells, sounds, sights, and textures. The thinking mind, however, is too stunned and immobilized to organize these impressions and sensations into a recallable, coherent picture. It's as if a camera came loose while filming and pulled in bits of the ceiling, corners of furniture, and muffled conversation. We have bits and pieces of experiences, but not the complete picture.

Then, occasionally we'll recall a moment with crystal clarity, or from an odd angle almost outside ourselves. The fragments of memory and the feelings attached to them remain floating or numbed within us. When we try to recollect them, they are foggy and indistinct. In this limbic swirl, feelings start to fuse with sensation and imagery—for example, fear with the color of a bright blue sky, the smell of grass with sexual abuse—so when we recall one, others come flooding in with it. A sound or a smell can trigger a cascading set of body/mind "memories" from our past that intrude into our present, but we don't really know how they got there or exactly what they're showing us. These bits and pieces of personal experience and overlapping imagery exist within us without a story line because the part of us that makes this kind of meaning was temporarily off-line. These **frozen moments** remain pulsating with life but are lacking in thought and understanding. They were simply never elevated to a conscious level through language, processed, then filed away into the overall framework of *us*. Because we do our best to block out traumatic moments, it seems that we recollect them in parts. We catch glimpses of them, but their real and visceral content is locked away and out of reach, so our personal narrative has big blank spots in it. Then the narrative becomes a sort of story, but many of the pages are blank.

Van der Kolk recounts, "I am continually impressed by how difficult it is for people who have gone through the unspeakable to convey the essence of their experience. It is so much easier for them to talk about what has been done to them—to tell a story of victimization and revenge—than to notice, feel, and put into words the reality of their internal experience. Our scans had revealed how their dread persisted and could be triggered by multiple aspects of daily experience. They had not integrated their experience into the ongoing stream of their life. They continued to be 'there' and did not know how to be 'here'—fully alive in the present."

This is why being able to bring the body into the therapeutic milieu is so important: the felt sense, the emotional and sensorial residue of trauma, often arises in the body as sensation before we can describe it in words. We need forms of therapy that allow the body and mind to feel and sense their way along the associative mind-body pathways that will lead us toward these discarded parts of ourselves. Entering those dark rooms within the self—entering the "there" and gathering up and integrating those pieces of our personal experience so that we can be "here"—is the work of therapy. Through psychodrama we can embody and encounter ourselves in concrete form and viscerally experience our various parts and relationships before we're asked to reflect on them. This is what **bottom-up therapy** offers: we aren't asked to talk until we've experienced.

Bottom-Up, Embodied Therapy

"Show us; don't tell us" is the dictum of psychodrama. Psychodrama allows the body to find its footing in space and time, to embody and investigate inner dynamics in concrete form and use the space and stage to make the inner world more explicit, to structure and see "Where am I in relation to this, to you, to the system?" Through simulated role plays, both personal and interpersonal, dynamics emerge spontaneously as the past comes alive in the present moment; the *then and there* is brought into the *here and now*. The process of self-discovery is reversed from that of talk therapy:

it begins with the embodiment and **enactment** of a role relationship in space and time and ends with verbal communication or description.

In psychodrama, we talk *to* rather than *about*. We revisit relational dynamics that were either cherished or despised or both, which is particularly useful in treating trauma. Psychodrama allows for natural movement and role interaction to stimulate memories; it lets the body as well as the mind come alive and tell the story. Not only dreams, as Freud felt, but the body, it turns out, is another "royal road to the unconscious"; it holds the emotional and sensorial thumbprint of our experiences.

The client exploring trauma-related issues may come forward tentatively, searching for words to describe feelings that they can barely bring up to a conscious level, frightened of retaliation for even thinking what they may perceive to be disloyal or even subversive thoughts. Feeling what they have never fully felt, or revisiting parts of their inner world that they have assiduously avoided, can feel dangerous to them. These frozen moments live within us, silenced and unavailable. These are inner spaces that we got lost inside of because no one saw us there, and eventually we could not even see ourselves. We need to find those places, feel them, and speak from there, in our real voice, however muffled and indistinct. Simply saying the words that were never spoken without shutting down, acting out, or self-medicating can be deeply healing for the person who carries frozen or denied pain. Soon enough, the feelings come pouring forward; phrases flow from the heart; the body comes to life and speaks; sounds, gestures, and words make the air shake; and one has the sense of watching a perfect moment on stage, searingly real and alive.

Then the group identifies and finds the words to describe what came up for them while witnessing these sacred moments. After **sharing** with moving clarity about something that they have long held in silence, group members often say things like "Did that make any sense?" or "I feel like I'm babbling" or "I know I'm taking up too much time." Quite the contrary; those listening are often riveted, sitting on the edge of their seats as they quiver with identification and emotion. This kind of "aha" moment is healing not only for the one sharing or doing a drama, but for all those watching who suddenly see that they too may have such eloquence and intelligence somewhere inside them.

Do, Undo, Redo

Psychodrama allows us to bring interactions onto the psychodramatic stage where we can unpack and process them. "The psychodramatic method rests upon the hypothesis that, in order to provide patients, singly or in groups, with a new opportunity for a psychodynamic and sociocultural reintegration, 'therapeutic cultures in miniature are required'" (Moreno 2019, 52).

According to J. L. Moreno:

> Because we cannot reach into the mind and see what the individual perceives and feels, psychodrama tries, with the cooperation of the patient, to transfer the mind

"outside" of the individual and objectify it within a tangible, controllable universe. It may go the whole way in the process of structuring the world of the patient up to the threshold of tolerance, penetrating and surpassing reality ("surplus" reality), and may insist upon the most minute details of episodes in physical, mental, and social space to be explored. Its aim is to make total behavior directly visible, observable, and measurable. The protagonist is being prepared for an encounter with himself. After this phase of objectification is completed, the second phase begins; it is to re-subjectify, reorganize, and reintegrate that which has been objectified (in practice, however, both phases go hand in hand) (Moreno 2019, 52).

Here Moreno is referring to his shorthand of "do, undo, redo," in the "reobjectifying" or re-embodying of a scene so that the **protagonist** can experience it as he or she wishes it might have been. They can enrole **re-formed auxiliary egos** to represent more ideal versions of those in the scene and "redo" the moment moving those in it into new positioning and more desired constellations of relationships or proxemics.

Do, Undo, Redo as Paths to Greater Co-Regulation

Polyvagal theory (Porges, 1995, 2011) provides a window into understanding how the nervous system recalibrates itself in relational exchanges that don't feel safe and nourishing into a "braced for danger" state. Embodied healing is all about shifting that "braced for danger" state into a more co-regulated, mutually nourishing one. It's a simple, direct, bottom-up path of healing. A problem with a "narrative" is that it is often detached from these body states. It is simply a story, and a story doesn't necessarily have the power to heal, particularly if it is a rigid or fixed interpretation of events. A primary goal of psychodrama is to increase spontaneity and creativity. Moreno observed that there was often a rigidity in thinking, feeling, and behavior that was part of mental illness. He sought to change that through an experiential form of therapy that allowed the body to be a part of the process of healing.

"The undo and redo," as Stephen Porges, PhD, the creator of polyvagal theory states, "are integrated processes of separating the narrative/justification (as a search for meaning) from the feelings. The 'healing' effect is seen in the redo, when the 'visceral' feelings are no longer driving and perpetuating behavior through a narrative driven by physiological state (feelings)" (Porges, personal communication, 2022). There is, as Moreno says, "a new opportunity for a psychodynamic and sociocultural reintegration" (2019). Through a polyvagal lens, the "do, undo, redo" process restores the protagonist to a state of neural regulation.

In the "do" phase, the presenting scene is embodied. When we've been traumatized, we often make meaning based on our physiological state in those moments. If we're feeling "braced for danger," for example, we try to explain to ourselves why we feel anxious and shaky based on that upregulated state; we tell ourselves a story to justify why we feel the way we do.

In the undo and redo phases of a drama, we can rework those relational dynamics that caused us to brace for danger and move toward more comfortable states. Then the feelings that drive the behaviors can grow out of a more regulated and co-regulated physiology.

This is why keeping the process of psychodrama contained, uninterrupted, and safe enough so that they protagonist can shift from an upregulated state to a more prosocial state is so important.

Doubling and **role reversal** are techniques that help to shift states both with the self and in relationship to another. Judiciously applied, they allow the protagonist to get in touch with their own inner states and also gain understanding and empathy both for themselves and the other person. Porges noted, in our work with Helga in Chapter Three "Psychodrama Through a Polyvagal Lens," that the double can feel like a reassuring, witnessing presence. I would add that thoughtful role reversal stimulates co-regulated feelings if it remains within the framework of the protagonist. By this I mean that not all role reversals will be free of stress. For example, if a protagonist is reversing roles with a bullying parent and "showing" us what those interactions looked and felt like, the feelings triggered will be a reflection of the body states we experienced at that moment in time. But if we keep it real and authentic, those feelings will be processed, felt, named, communicated, and seen differently. The scene, or status nascendi, which was seen through the eyes of a frightened, helpless child will now be read through the eyes of a more mature adult. They can see things differently—not, for example, through the frightened or disempowered eyes of a child, but through the mature and empowered eyes of the adult they are today. The meaning shifts as new awareness and information emerge. It almost happens naturally: Protagonists feel so relieved from no longer having to keep their hurt a secret. They feel the support of the double who can say things like "don't you know how this hurt me?" almost as an inner voice, and they can finally be witnessed in their pain and let it dissipate. As role reversal unfolds, a protagonist may also receive doubling while standing in the role of the "other," e.g., their bullying parent. The double may be something like "I feel so lost, so inept, so alone." Slowly, light begins to dawn as the protagonist sees the parent, who once loomed so large, shrink in size, become human and flawed. And meaning continues to shift as the protagonist reverses back to themself—now seeing the parent differently—less triggered into hate and vengeance, and perhaps feeling compassion, and even open to remembering the parts of their parent they loved.

When we have been traumatized and left with physiological state that's "braced for danger" or "upregulated," we all too often move straight from feeling to action once this state is experienced or triggered. We have trouble experiencing, reflecting on, and thinking about what we are feeling and may project our feelings of anxiety, shame, or hurt onto whoever is triggering us. In this way, we recreate past pain in present relationships. We layer yesterday's meaning on today.

This is why bottom-up therapy works. The protagonist isn't asked to come up with a story to explain why they are who they are, rather they enter an experiential journey through which pieces of the puzzle emerge organically. I use floor checks and timelines to help protagonists get enough comfort and information to begin to wrap their minds around pieces of their own lives and to experience themselves in a supportive group, sharing what comes up for them through doing the floor check process. Then I use role play to personalize and reenter the more particular inner states/dynamics that shaped who they became.

"As you can infer," said Porges about Helga's work, "I believe the narrative is the greatest barrier to optimal function. Of course, this is where psychodrama comes in. Polyvagal theory provides an efficient lens to understand the human experience. It does not change psychodrama's insightful approach, but it provides a different 'layer' to explain. This layer is both intuitive and has a deep scientific basis. The intuitive aspect is functionally within our DNA" (Porges, personal communication, n.d.). According to Porges, "Polyvagal theory articulates three different branches of the autonomic nervous system that evolved from very primitive vertebrates to mammals ... First, you have a system that is really an ancient one, which is death feigning or immobilization. Then it has a fight or flight system, a mobilization system. Then finally, with mammals, you have what I call a social engagement system, which can detect features of safety and actually communicate them to another. When you trigger feelings of safety, the autonomic nervous system can help health restoration" (Anthony 2019).

When clients get stuck in telling a detached narrative and imagining that it represents trauma resolution, it can act as a defense against entering into the deep states that might allow them to feel and heal. It can be used as the well-known defense of intellectualization. It leaves, as they say on Wall Street, too much "on the table." But in this case, what's left on the table is the untold story that the body might be holding and the deeper layer of truth it knows and can reveal if allowed to have a voice and to enter the therapeutic mileau.

The group in psychodrama provides the necessary role players to encounter the relational network in concrete form, to re-embody role relationships by taking on both sides of the internalized role dynamic, that is, taking on both the role of self and the role of a significant person or people from our lives, or the roles of the self and any part of the self. Then the group can be used as co-investigators, role players, supporters, and witnesses. We reinhabit and process the feeling states that might be driving behavior. And when the role play ends, we can step out of it; auxiliary egos can "de-role" from the characters they portrayed, and the protagonist steps off the stage, symbolically leaving the scenes of the past in the past where they belong.

When I was in my twenties, one of my jobs in the therapy program I worked in was to hook people up to a biofeedback machine and take them through soothing guided imageries for deep relaxation. I had a reoccurring experience, one I observed so often that I began to take note. When

I was hooking patients up, putting conducting gel on them and attaching electrodes to various points in their body, they'd often complain, squint, wince, and make comments. I often wondered if I irritated them or if I should be doing something differently. But then I would lead them through a thirty-minute deep yogic relaxation, and invariably, they'd open their eyes and smile warmly at me, as if I were a close friend. They'd complement me: "You're pretty; your voice is so nice; I like your blouse; this room is painted a nice color, I didn't notice it before." Eventually, I understood that they saw me not *as I was* but *as they felt*. They created meaning, as Dr. Porges describes, based on their physiological state.

The Body Tells Its Story

When we connect with deep memory, there is a body state that is triggered, too, as our limbic world becomes activated. It's why the body needs to be a part of therapy: we need to hear from it, to understand what it knows that we may have "forgotten." It's these inner states that we need to allow to rise into consciousness so that we can finally experience what we're carrying on the inside, which may be shaping how we react to people in our lives, how we read situations, and how we see the world. If we can sit through our triggered states as they make their way slowly into consciousness, our defenses loosen and what lies beneath begins to reveal itself. Inviting the protagonist to let the unconscious pain held in parts of the body have an actual voice, shape, and color, Levine (2010), can give the protagonist a felt sense of the "stories" or inner meanings they have lived by that heretofore have felt foggy and indistinct. As these feelings come forward, the thinking that was frozen in place starts to come forward, too. The body moves and the mind and heart follow. A protagonist may evidence body shakes and shivers, trembling legs, or all sorts of somatic reactions as the role play progresses—their heart may race, their throat may go dry, their head may pound. Their body is remembering and releasing trauma as the feelings it is holding wake up. The meaning they have made and lived by shifts from the bottom up as the episodes and imagery of their lives reveal themselves and find expression through their body/mind.

This can be a confusing and disequilibrating process, so learning to read the body's language of subtle expressions, vocal tones, positions, and gestures is part of therapy, the part that allows the body to say what the mind cannot or will not. "The bodies of traumatized people portray 'snapshots' of their unsuccessful attempts to defend themselves in the face of threat and injury," says Peter Levine, PhD, in *Waking the Tiger: Healing Trauma*. "Trauma is a highly activated incomplete biological response to threat, frozen in time. For example, when we prepare to fight or to flee, muscles throughout our entire body are tensed in specific patterns of high energy readiness. When we are unable to complete the appropriate actions, we fail to discharge the tremendous energy generated by our survival preparations. This energy becomes fixed in specific patterns of neuromuscular readiness. The person then stays in a state of acute and then chronic arousal and dysfunction in the central nervous system. Traumatized people are not suffering from a disease in the normal sense of the word- they have become stuck in an aroused state. It is difficult if not impossible to function normally under these circumstances." Moreno referred to these thwarted states as "act hungers" stored in the body and in need of what he calls "act completion."

The techniques within the drama can help protagonists to connect with these act hungers. Doubles can help the protagonist to find the words that will bring their limbic world toward conscious thought. Identifying that *I want to run, to fight and defend myself, to collapse; I want to talk, to hug, or to be held* can help individuals reconnect with themselves and others. A protagonist may find themselves wanting to collapse in tears, to rage, or to hide. This body/mind **catharsis** of emotion and action is often part of the healing process and can leave a client feeling vulnerable and exposed, as if they have been on a zero-gravity moon walk. The sharing that occurs after the drama, from role players and group members, will help the protagonist to reintegrate themselves into the group and into their own skin. Hearing how others may have identified with them will help them to feel seen, heard, and understood. It is a strange and freeing experience, as the unfelt known becomes real, accepted, and integrated back into the self and the self-in-relation.

It is the unconscious components of the relational dynamic that have been internalized within the self-system that we, as Carl Jung (1970) puts it, "live out as fate." We choose someone to hold that unconscious pain so that we can see it—or maybe because we don't see it. If we work the pain out, we have a choice: Do I want to marry the part of my parent who felt out of control, who was ashamed? Or, because I have never looked at that, will my unconscious seek that out in a blind attempt to have it finally revealed to me through the gravity of an intimacy that will pull it out of hiding and make it real, make it concrete? Of course, this is why relationships are also such powerful healers—because it's these internalized relational dynamics hidden within us that get projected and transferred into new relationships without our awareness. But intimacy also kicks the door open for healing, a door that is wedged shut or stuck but will give under the pressure of our human longing for love and connection.

Using the Role Relationship to Stimulate Memories

In psychodrama we use the role relationship to stimulate the surfacing of emotions to be felt in the here and now. Many therapists make the mistake of placing too much importance on structuring particular events, or overemphasizing the actual words that are being said. But it's what happens inside us that needs attention and certainly the body states that get stimulated. To look at events rather than what occurred in our inner world as a response to them is to miss the "gold" in treatment. It's what comes forward from deep within a protagonist, whether by talking to inner parts or to outer relationships, that provides grist for the mill: here is where the action is, where the body speaks, and limbic, trauma-related memories come to the surface.

Role play and embodiment are at the core of psychodrama. In psychodrama we can meet and talk to any part of ourselves or any other person, real or imagined, on what Moreno called the "psychodramatic stage," a designated area on the group room floor. The protagonist can embody virtually anything within their inner world—for example, depression, shame, the inner child, or the innocent, lost, or found self. They can talk to that part of self and then reverse roles and talk back to themselves as that part, creating an inner sense of space and perspective. Or they can talk to another person from their family or social network of relationships or, for that matter, a pet or a whole institution, represented by a role player. They can have seven mother auxiliaries and one-half of a father or the reverse. They can structure the scene not as it was but as it felt. They can talk to a wall. What I'm trying to say is that in psychodrama, you can have it your way!

The scenes that occur to clients may be **model scenes**, encapsulating and combining many of the relational elements and personal meanings that they struggle with today. The people they need to talk to, particularly if they represent close, long-term relationships, may have played a significant role in their development of a sense of self. Protagonists may opt to talk to parts of themselves. By embodying and locating these inner and outer relationships on the stage in present-day space, they can see, experience, and alter the way in which the role relationships live inside them, providing perspective not only on themselves, but on themselves in relation to those who shaped them. These scenes reveal protagonists' sense of who they are vis à vis others and how the past may have influenced the present. They are small scenes that carry large meaning.

The body, as well as the words, tells the story. If I observe a protagonist holding or tightening a body part, I might ask, "What would your jaw like to say?" or "What would your legs like to do right now?" or say, "I notice a shiver just went through you," giving voice or action to parts of their bodies that hold tension or emotion. In a sense, protagonists walk through time, into the past, to gather up the parts of the self that are there and bring them back into the here and now or forward into the future. We can talk to the sad or happy child we once were, or the happier self we wish to become, and let them be and breathe. We can then reintegrate them into our self today, better seen, felt, and understood. We can revisit the past, experience how it lives or re-lives in the present, and rehearse the future.

Moreno saw the restoration of spontaneity and creativity as being at the core of what psychodrama is able to do for human beings. His vision was that his methods be both a way of healing the mind/body and "spontaneity training" to help people learn to live fuller, deeper, and more satisfying lives. There have been many who have applied Moreno's role play techniques to their own work in various fields, such as Fritz Perls in adopting psychodrama's empty chair.

Moreno also included a then rather heretical idea in which he invited participants to "play God," meaning to talk to God and then reverse roles and talk as God back to themselves. Moreno believed in "cocreation," that is, we cocreate our lives with a "God-force." This philosophy gives psychodrama a spiritual dimension; it is also, it seems to me, compatible with the twelve-step notion of a spiritual transformation being a part of recovery.

The Birth of Group Therapy

"Psychodrama," according to Moreno, "represents the chief turning point away from the treatment of the individual in isolation to the treatment of the individual in groups, from the treatment of the individual by verbal methods to the treatment by action methods"(Moreno 1946, 63). In the United States, group therapy has become increasingly popular, with economic pressures that make it more efficient, along with the growing body of neurobiology research that points to the need for relational, embodied approaches. Psychodrama is the first form of embodied therapy, and Moreno is known to be the father of group psychotherapy.

One of Moreno's early inspirations in developing a role play method, was playing with children in the parks of Vienna. He observed their natural inclination to take on roles as a way of working through their interpersonal conflicts. They took on the roles of authority figures, imagined characters that gave them a sense of empowerment, or they played out roles of the victim and the accuser or bully. They traded or "reversed" roles naturally and spontaneously. He saw that through role play, they were able to creatively resolve complexes that in real life they would likely not have had an opportunity to deal with. They spoke up. They corrected what felt to them like the injustice of their size or the power imbalance they endured, and they played out wished-for roles in which they righted wrongs and fulfilled dreams and fantasies.

Moreno's first attempt at what is now known as group therapy was to gather a group of prostitutes, then considered irredeemable sinners, into groups. Initially the prostitutes shared about their concerns of the day—their children, their pimps and johns. But eventually they began to share deeper layers of themselves, who they were on the inside—not only prostitutes but people. They began to reclaim their integrity from within; they began to feel and heal. In *Psychodrama Volume I* (1946, 49), Moreno gives a rather hilarious account of his first attempt at treating these individuals in a group setting. He describes dragging eight or so couches into one room and inviting those participating to lie down, stare at the ceiling, and freely associate. With only Freud's model to draw from—keep in mind that they were together in the vibrant city of turn-of-the-century Vienna—this was where he understandably began. He soon realized, however, that their fantasies all mingled together, overlapping and becoming somewhat indistinguishable from one another. But he recognized that another dynamic might be at work. So, he made the simple movement that gave birth to an entirely new form of therapy, one that has resonated down through the generations. He abandoned the cumbersome, isolating couches and brought in chairs. Then he invited the ladies to go from a lying position, in which they looked at no one and nothing but the ceiling, to sitting up in chairs and looking at each other. In this simple but profound shift in body, mind, and spirit, *group therapy was born.*

Now another "science" or form of therapy was needed, one that could record and explore the many layers of moment-to-moment connectedness from eye to eye, heart to heart, body to body, person to person, and he called this **sociometry**, a form of therapy that is alive, interpersonal, and entirely in the here and now. While psychodrama "makes the then and there the here and now" through the use of surrogate role players, sociometry is essentially a present-oriented investigation of group dynamics.

The Conundrum: Why I Created Sociometrics

I have found two forces at work for much of my career straddling the addictions and psychodrama fields. On the addictions side, from the beginning of my entering the field in the 1980s, a derivation of psychodrama referred to as experiential therapy was being used very successfully to work with the **family-of-origin** trauma that often drove self-medicating, although there was little awareness that experiential therapy grew out of psychodrama. Doing experiential therapy in an addictions facility helped to facilitate a deep release of pain and anger for clients, so that grief and hence healing could begin. The treatment program itself, often along with the undergird of twelve-step work, gave what was learned and felt from the dramas containment and a continued path toward healing. The problem was that therapists lacked the training to do it well; there was little understanding of the method and theory behind what they were doing, and doubling and role reversal, so core to psychodrama, were rarely used. But their clinical experience was right on, as their work with addictions and trauma was often daily and frontline.

On the psychodrama side, there was full knowledge of the method, and clinicians were trained in doing it with the full range of techniques at their fingertips. However, clinical experience in the addictions treatment field could be lacking. Psychodramatists felt that only fully trained and certified psychodramatists should work with clients, and they of course made a very important argument; but on the other hand, Moreno wanted to see psychodrama "in the streets"; his vision was to heal "all of humanity." And working with addicts and those traumatized by living with addiction or dysfunction certainly fit this description. Psychodrama in the 1980s, was finding its way naturally to where it was effective and needed, and because the addictions field is willing to try anything that works, there was an openness to using what was at that time a more unusual form of therapy. So experiential therapy was alive and well in the addictions field, while it was constantly competing with forms of talk therapy in the mental health field in general. I personally feel that both are needed; group is much more effective when using experiential therapy like sociometrics and psychodrama. And because so much is stirred up and group rarely has time for enough individual processing, one-to-one is important in tandem with it. The addictions field has played a central role in keeping psychodrama alive in the United States, and it's been a daily testimony as to how effective it is in treating trauma and complex post-traumatic stress disorder (cPTSD).

A takeaway from my PhD work was the adage that "you can't be a true scholar of your method if you can't critique it," so I took a hard look at what was and wasn't working in treating addiction and PTSD using psychodrama. It was the advent of trauma and neurobiology theory in the mid-1980s that brought awareness into the mental health field that talk therapy wasn't all that helpful in treating trauma. The ever-expanding fields of neuropsychology, trauma, and interpersonal neurobiology were opening doors into why embodied forms of therapy like psychodrama and sociometry were so necessary in treating trauma; how to use them safely was another question.

That's why I developed the trauma timeline, feeling floor checks, and experiential letter writing, to make for safe and contained experiential processes that didn't require the kind of training that psychodrama did, and why I went on to adapt the **social atom** and **spectrograms** for targeted and titrated use.

CHAPTER TWO

Sociometrics: Turn on the Social Engagement System

Sociometry without psychodrama is sterile; psychodrama without sociometry is blind.
—J. L. Moreno

Moreno famously and rather surprisingly said, "We get them in the door with psychodrama; we heal them with sociometry." Psychodrama is riveting to watch and cathartic to participate in. But Moreno felt—and I have come on board with this thinking—that the kinds of here-and-now, real time, person-to-person connections that happen in sociometric processes offer a powerful potential for healing relational issues. Sociometry explores the quality of connectedness among individuals through both graphing them on paper and putting them on stage.

Psychodrama is often seen as the whole of Moreno's method, although what he really created was a comprehensive triadic system including psychodrama, sociometry, and group psychotherapy.

Psychodrama is a form of role play. We can cast any person from our past, present, or future, including ourselves, and talk to them directly through surrogates or even an empty chair representing them. We bring the then and there into the here and now.

Sociometry is different. It is here-and-now oriented and deals with real people in real time. It offers experiential techniques like the spectrogram, locogram, and social atom for concretizing and exploring the dynamics within any group.

Sociometrics are different again. They are psychoeducational, experiential processes that bond and engage groups around common issues. They connect group members in low-risk encounters and in small-group breakdowns so that the healing potential within the group is accessed. Commonalities are discovered and issues that can be isolating are normalized. The skills of emotional literacy and regulation are woven into the process. When I use the word *sociometrics* throughout this book, I am referring to the floor checks, timelines, and experiential letter writing that I have created myself and to Moreno's spectrograms, locograms, and social atoms that I have adapted and turned into a step-by-step, targeted process for treating cPTSD and addiction issues, e.g., the family of origin or frozen moment social atoms.

Because I do program development, I wanted to create a process that minimizes risk, makes a therapist's job easier, has consistent outcomes, and maximizes the potential for healing within the group. Sociometrics are these processes.

Start with Sociometrics

Sociometrics are designed to take the guesswork out of using **experiential therapy** to heal relational trauma issues and to restore aliveness and resilience. Treatment centers often feel they need to use psychodrama first. I am suggesting we flip this and use sociometrics first. They are safer, more contained, and don't require the kind of training needed to do psychodrama well.

They are psychoeducational, experiential, manageable processes. And if they are the only experiential work you add to your program, they will be more than sufficient. You do not necessarily need to do psychodrama to offer experiential work. If and when you do add role play to sociometrics, such as a floor check (which I see as my strongest and most multifaceted contribution, the trauma timeline being the next), group members are already warmed up. Even a few sentences to the right person (or part of self) at the right moment can feel very memorable. From the trauma perspective, clients being warmed up and knowing just what they want to say and to whom (including parts of the self) they want to say it, means that their emotions are available and their words are on the tip of their tongue. Knowing what work you are ready to do and being in touch with inner states so that the work flows easily are a very significant part of doing trauma work.

See an example on YouTube: https://youtu.be/fcmstI2gXp8

Criterion questions keep the process moving. They are essentially prompts asked by the therapist that allow participants to make their next choice. They move the process forward. In the **symptom floor check**, for example, the therapist might start the process with, "Mill around and choose a symptom that for some reason is drawing you. Stand near it and say a couple of sentences about why you are standing where you're standing." Group members then take their time in choosing a symptom or manifestation that draws them at that moment. They chitchat a little. There may be waves of slightly uncomfortable laughter or real amusement. There is hustling and bustling as they move about. Then something happens: they drop down inside themselves and really look. They start to tune in to what's being warmed up inside them as they walk past hypervigilance, emotional constriction, somatic issues, difficulty imagining a future, and the like. They aren't asked to describe their trauma, which can be daunting. Rather, they can decide which manifestations fit for them—they are choosing for themselves, rather than being told what they feel. They have the experience of a feeling or symptom getting safely triggered inside them in a controlled environment then becoming aware of what they are feeling.

As group members share a sentence or two about why they are standing where they're standing, they experience and witness their own feelings. They name them, translate them into words, and share them with others. Over and over again, they share what amount to moving little case studies or personal deconstructions of the subject matter as it applies to them. The learning is immediate and relevant, pulled off the dull chalkboard or lifeless PowerPoint and given a shape, face, and sense of realness by the clients themselves. Clients cocreate a psychoeducational healing process with each other, and the more they engage in it, the more engaged they become. They grow curious about their own inner world and the inner worlds of others.

Through the questioning process, group members form ever-evolving dyads and clusters that shift in focus and configuration, providing many of what I like to call "incremental moments of healing." In these sharing circles, it becomes easy to put their fear or anger or anxiety into words because the focus is on the symptom, not on them; all they are being asked to do is say a few words about why they chose the symptom or feeling. They are translating inner states into language, elevating these states to a conscious level where they can be thought about and reflected on, and thus rescuing and resuscitating their disowned parts and giving them a voice. Then they listen as others do the same. They attend to the inner experience of another and learn to listen without imploding, exploding, blaming, or running. Then they let their feelings dissipate, they let them go, and they begin the process again. They make a new choice.

Sociometrics actively teach the skills of emotional literacy, self-regulation and co-regulation while incorporating the education that needs to happen in treatment, for example, in addiction, grief, resilience, post-traumatic growth, and PTSD.

Get On Your Feet!

As I hope you can see by now, I am creating a process that has the elements of resilience-building baked into it. Clients are on their feet, grounded, oriented in the room and in charge of their own movements. All systems—body, mind, and emotions—are engaged in the activity of self-discovery. The limbic system is warmed up through physical walking, and the body is invited to participate in the process. Sociometrics teach participants to employ initiative and creative thinking as they make choices that are right to them. Participants mobilize connections with group members on their own behalf, a quality Wong and Wong (2012) underscore as part of the resilient person's capacity to mobilize the supports available to them to meet the challenges of their lives. People in the group can seek each other out, share their emotions, and listen to others do the same. They can break through defenses, try out new ways of being with themselves and others, come out of isolation, connect, and normalize their feelings. They are not beholden to a therapist to tell them what is going on with them because the process is designed such that they have access to information they need to explore on their own, either from each other or from teaching materials like floor checks. They become meaningful members of the group and agents in each other's healing. The role of the therapist is significantly reduced, and the roles of participants are enhanced. Because floor checks are a communal process in which the full group is constantly choosing and rechoosing and then sharing and listening, the group members assess their own level of risk. As floor checks are generally low risk and comfortable, they tend toward transforming emotionally inhibited or aggressive behaviors into more prosocial, engagement-type behaviors. Group members connect in easy, genuine, and often playful ways.

Sociometrics such as floor checks are designed to feel safe, engaging, supportive, and even game-like. There is easy onboarding and lots of choice; they're a flexible system. Because floor checks feel welcoming and good, and facilitate many like-minded, supportive encounters among group members, they offer reparative interactions for attachment deficits through a process that is relational and skill-building. When clients can see what the rest of their community is doing—when they are resonating face-to-face in a group—they **mirror** and learn new behaviors from watching each other in action, and they practice those behaviors. They try them on for size and get immediate feedback through action. They are, as Dan Siegel says, "inspired to rewire." These new connections give birth to more connections in the brain, which influence more experiences and more behaviors, and so on. The emergent process actually takes on a life of its own and influences itself: it becomes a feedback loop for change. Clients are able to move from body states in which they may feel like bracing or be defensive into more relaxed, well-regulated and co-regulated states that engender prosocial behaviors.

With sociometrics, the work takes on a flow. A flow state occurs when what is being learned is just enough of a challenge to keep clients engaged, but not so much that they get frustrated and withdraw from it. Mihaly Csikszentmihalyi named this state in his research at the University of Chicago and published it in his book *Flow: The Psychology of Optimal Experience* (2008). From the trauma perspective, there is less emotional wear and tear on the client as the flow state itself is strengthening and integrating. Once clients enter this state, if it is allowed to work its magic without unnecessary interruption, they emerge with a greater sense of wholeness, physiological relaxation, and well-being. The state itself is nourishing.

TURNING ON THE SOCIAL ENGAGEMENT SYSTEM

I find that much trauma resolution can occur without mentioning the word *trauma*. Introducing the word *trauma* can lead group members to shut down or become overly self-conscious. There is no need to put them in this situation if you recognize and mine the potential for healing through the experiential, relational group processes of sociometrics. Accessing inner states and turning on the social engagement system are key.

The social engagement system was defined and introduced by Stephen Porges in 1998 in his paper "Love: An Emergent Property of the Mammalian Autonomic Nervous System." It offers a scientific neuroanatomical underpinning that adds a layer of understanding as to the healing effects of engaging with the self to develop and practice self-regulation and with others to develop and practice co-regulation. Sociometrics, particularly floor checks, apply these principles in an experiential process of healing.

The forms of therapy that we create, suggests Dan Siegel, PhD, "need to turn on the social engagement system," and they also need to feel "welcoming and good . . . because once we orient as good or bad, we're already generating bodily responses, heart, breath, and facial expression; we start activating behaviors and emotion" (Siegel 2011).

We need forms of therapy that give us practice in reengaging in new, more comfortable, and satisfying ways. I have designed sociometrics to access inner states and mobilize the resources for healing and connection that exist within the group.

Our social engagement system is the mind/body system that allows us to know, in the blink of an eye, whether we're safe to engage and move forward or we need to pull back and self-protect. It's been evolved over time to help us to stay out of danger, as well as to allow us to seek companionship, cooperation, and support. Porges (2011) describes how the nervous system assesses risk and learns to open up or close down: "To switch effectively from defensive to social engagement strategies, the nervous system must do two things: (1) assess risk, and (2) if the environment looks safe, inhibit the primitive defensive reactions of fight, flee, or freeze. . . . Only in a safe environment is it adaptive and appropriate to simultaneously inhibit defense systems and exhibit positive social engagement behavior" (12–13).

Neuroception: Understanding Our Attachment System

Neuroception, which blunts or optimizes access to the social engagement system, is a word coined by Dr. Stephen Porges to describe the nervous system's ability to read safety or threat in others. We do not develop our skills of self-regulation and co-regulation alone. We need, as Allan Schore describes in his book on affect regulation, an external regulator with whom to absorb and practice our skills of self and co-regulation. Each tiny interaction, says Schore, lays down the neural wiring in a child's body that they use to regulate within themselves and their exchanges with others.

Polyvagal theory describes how the nervous system tunes to others in order to use interactions with, for example, attachment figures, to develop the skills of both self-regulation and relational regulation. When early attachment relationships have felt unsafe and caused us to develop patterns of withdrawing rather than engaging in deep connection, our ability to regulate both within ourselves and with others is impacted.

Siegel talks about the mind/body as a self-organizing system that is constantly engaged in interpreting and regulating the information flow that is coming from the outside, a self-regulatory system that interfaces with its environment. The self, therefore, is in a constant state of construction and reconstruction. Sociometrics become a "society in miniature" for each group member. Sociometrics act as an outside regulatory resource that helps clients to relearn how to absorb the skills of self-regulation and co-regulation, and the group offers the soothing, regulating presence and practice in healing attachment issues. Floor checks, for example, offer participants a constantly evolving set of relational challenges that involve choosing a feeling or issue that speaks to them and then tuning in on themselves. The feelings that emerge get named, translated into words, and communicated to someone else. Others witness, attend, and listen. They filter through what is being shared to see what may or may not apply to them; they open an inward gate toward two-way communication and co-regulation.

An Embodied, Bottom-Up Trauma Treatment

The trauma narrative is much talked about as a part of trauma healing. But if a narrative is a stringing together of events or relational dynamics that happened *to* us and ignores what happened *in* us, it is not complete nor especially useful in terms of healing trauma. Our narrative needs to be bottom-up to give shape and voice to our inward physiological responses that changed the body and nervous system, out of which subsequent thinking, feeling, and behavior grew.

Floor checks are the reverse of "tell me your trauma story." The story tells itself. Rather than pushing the client to come up with a story that has not yet been formulated, floor checks are a kind of walkabout through the potential manifestations of any issue. The story emerges spontaneously and through the body and the mind, in manageable, titrated doses, measured and administered by the clients themselves.

Floor checks and timelines are alive, relational processes wherein clients learn to observe which "symptom, "developmental age," or "words" are triggering something inside them that draws them. They then deconstruct this in terms of the self and the self in relation to others. They can hit the pause button and feel what's going on in their bodies and let it arise into consciousness so the body can tell them how "it" experienced painful moments, so that it has a voice. Instead of trying to jam their turgid, painful and swollen, or barely perceptible feelings and thoughts into words, however narrow or inadequate, the embodied, bottom-up narrative allows them to uncover and experience those feelings bit by bit. Then role plays, in which they can actually revisit and revise some of the relational material from the past, can be added to further focus and personalize healing.

Warmed Up and Focused: Adding Role Plays to Sociometrics

Because sociometrics warm people up to what is going on inside of them, the role play sort of focuses itself. The material being explored triggers feelings, associations, and memories, and there is a felt sense of who someone feels they have something to say to or a part of themselves they would like to embody and talk to. The role play needs only a simple sentence from the therapist to move it into action: "Who do you want to talk to and who can play this person or part of you and what would you like to say to them?" For the therapist, the art lies in identifying those moments wherein a group member is sufficiently warmed up so that deep work flows freely and is well-contained—in other words, when the protagonist knows whom they want to talk to and enough of what they are inspired and compelled to say to make a beginning easy and worth the risk.

Sometimes these moments emerge through the person's body, facial expressions, and vocal tones (too soft, too loud, tense). Are they unusually still, or even frozen? Do they look like they have an almost stunned expression on their face? Are they trying to find words to articulate an inner experience that is hard to express? Is their face showing emotion that clearly wants to come forward? Is there a shiver, body posture, or motion that's already saying something? Or is the pain being blocked or caught in the body, in which case a slow and careful invitation to explore a bit more might allow the protagonist to experience enough safety to dare the next moment? All of this is what the body is trying to tell us.

The Basic Sociometrics Protocol
Floor Checks, Timelines, Experiential Letter Writing, and Targeted Social Atoms

I created sociometrics to act as a stand-alone, experiential program or to allow for inclusion of role play. They make the work that needs to be done during treatment psychoeducational and experiential. Role plays can be added according to the skill level of the clinician, but role play/psychodrama is not necessary, for you to bring experiential work into your program.

The sociometrics that I developed are **floor checks, trauma and resilience timelines, experiential letter writing,** and targeted social atoms such as "family of origin" and "frozen moments." You can see examples of these sociometrics on tiandayton.com/sociometrics.

Floor checks are the core of my approach. Timelines provide context and experiential, bottom-up meaning-making. Social atoms are maps that reveal the relational life of the client, and experiential letter writing is one of the most basic and simple forms of role play.

Floor Checks: Floor checks are the psychoeducational, experiential, and relational processes that form the center of programming. They teach the theoretical basics of all of the issue surrounding the treatment of anything from symptoms of PTSD to qualities of resilience and post-traumatic growth. They help clients to shift their body states organically. For example, if they feel slightly triggered and defensive when identifying with something on the floor cards, they can—through the process of translating those inner states into words, sharing them, and listening to others do the same—become more relaxed, self-regulated, and co-regulated in their interactions. Floor checks can be adapted to any subject matter or population, as you'll see in Chapter 13.

Timelines: Timelines supply the when and where of relational dynamics and moments or periods in time when things occurred. Timelines can be used in two ways: as paper and pen activities, or as **concretized**, embodied processes.

The trauma timeline creates context; it gives clients the opportunity to understand their cPTSD from a developmental perspective and to explore how relational trauma may have been reenacted and recreated throughout their lives.

The resilience timeline helps clients to identify their strengths, times when good choices changed the tide of their lives, and people who supported them along the way. The timeline can act as a **warm-up** to talking with or writing a letter to the self at any moment throughout development or a letter to others thanking them for their love and help.

Experiential Letter Writing is a contained role play that extends the commonly used intervention of letter writing, a powerful intervention in and of itself. Making it experiential creates a moment in therapy that can be surprisingly powerful. It is an easy process to execute and satisfying to do. People often remember their "letters" for years. They are moving and significant.

Targeted Social Atoms: Targeted social atoms diagram the relational network at any point in time, or as a sort of family or relational map. The social atom begins as a paper-and-pencil exercise, locating the self on a piece of paper and then diagramming the relationships present at any given moment in time. If all you add to your program are targeted social atoms done on paper as maps and then shared, that process is in and of itself a significant intervention.

The social atom can also be used as a map from which to embody a scene, moment in time, or model scene. This experiential process uses floor space—the "stage"—to reveal the proxemics within the group. For example, in embodying a family, position members to reveal the underlying proxemics: who is close, distant, paired, clustered, and so forth. Moving a scene into a sculpture can also be a powerful intervention. It need not move into a psychodrama/role play to be effective. For example, talking to the trapped self inside the embodied/concretized social atom, then reversing roles and talking as that child to the adult self on the outside of it, and reversing roles again and talking as the adult back to the child's self, can have a profound impact.

I have created targeted social atoms for treatment that focus into particular moments in time that are helpful in healing cPTSD and serve as diagnostic treatment maps. The social atoms that I include in my basic protocol are

- the atom upon entering treatment
- the family of origin atom
- the frozen moment atom

- the future atom upon leaving treatment of desired next steps, including creating a support network

I have broken all of these down into step-by-step processes so that clinicians can work at their level of need and skill.

Over time, clients develop emotional literacy as they elevate the kinds of unconscious pain and anger that drive dysfunction to a conscious level through language. Then it can be shared, heard, and examined in the light of day rather than acted out unconsciously, split off, medicated, or denied. They learn to talk about what they feel. This act of sharing and listening naturally helps to shift the emotional numbness and psychic disconnection and isolation that are so often inherent to trauma; it rebuilds trust in others and bonds group members around common goals of self-exploration and identification.

Role plays can be added. The beauty of adding psychodramatic role plays to sociometrics is that the protagonist has *fully warmed up* to the work *they want to do* and to the person or aspect of the self *they want to talk to* through the floor check or timeline process, so the role plays themselves are focused and often shorter and easier to direct, which reduces possibilities for retraumatization. But again, you do not need to add role play to these sociometric processes to bring an experiential component into your programming. The floor check, timeline, and experiential letter writing processes will do that. Using social atoms as relational maps done on paper and shared is also a complete process.

CHAPTER THREE

Frozen Moments: Psychodrama through a Polyvagal Lens

The body remembers what the mind forgets.
—J. L. Moreno

There can be an emotional and psychic frozenness that leaves a protagonist standing stupefied in front of the drama that they themselves have set up. They long to find words to talk to their father, their spouse, or the child within them, but when they try to dial them up from the inner recesses of their memory, nothing comes. Instead, they stand speechless and motionless before their own inner world, wishing that they were anywhere but here, longing to avoid this moment, this encounter. They feel themselves locked in the same relational silence that they experienced as children. They may experience a psychic and emotional frozenness and a simultaneous physiological urge to bolt. At such a moment, the protagonist may be encountering what scared them and made them feel small and trapped. Now, when standing in a re-creation of a scene or role play, they want to disappear all over again. They feel as little, helpless, and hurt as they did then, and they can have trouble forming intelligent and easily flowing sentences. The protagonist's frozenness can be misinterpreted as resistance, while, in fact, it is often and more accurately a sign of deep engagement.

These junctures, whether they emerge through a psychodrama, a floor check, a social atom, or a timeline, offer opportunities for healing that can be embodied, explored, and unpacked onstage. The role play is already focused and the inner state already accessible, so the work flows naturally.

Shifting From an Events Focus to Understanding the Nervous System

According to Dr. Porges, "Polyvagal theory begins with understanding how the nervous system tunes to others in order to use interactions with for example, attachment figures, to develop the skills of both self-regulation and relational regulation."

We need to help protagonists to shift body states if we want to shift feelings, thoughts, and behavior. The upregulated and defensive body states that we experienced as helpless, trapped kids, for example, get triggered when we're adults. We reenter those upregulated body states, and they drive the kinds of behaviors that make the painful past come alive in the present. This is essentially what reliving is: we're back in the trauma physiology that is still frozen in the nervous system, the state that engendered feelings of panic, anxiety, helplessness, and so on. When we get triggered back into these states, usually through a sensorial cue like loud voices, a smell, a song or sound, a texture or sensation, we reenact the painful past in the present. We layer yesterday's read or interpretations on today's interaction and expect what we got; we see what we saw. We assign motive and meaning to the other person in the present that may have to do with our childhood interactions from the past, where we may have felt out powered, humiliated or unseen. Then we feel and act like a small, voiceless and hurt little kid all over again, but we stand there in the body and with the vocal projection and vocabulary of an adult.

Neuroception: Looking through a Polyvagal Lens

All too often we look to large events to explain our feelings of being wounded or traumatized: "Were you physically abused as a child? Was there sexual abuse? Did someone you loved get killed?" But overt abuse is not the only way that a child can be traumatized. A parent who turns away, who ignores the child's tender attempts to connect or wears a scowl, who begrudgingly reaches for their child's hand and drags them across a street, or who humiliates their small efforts to take care of themselves can leave a legacy of hurt behind them. The barely perceptible experience of watching those from whom we long for love the most dismiss us or treat us as if we have no feelings to hurt is also a part of relational trauma that alters the way we live in our own bodies. For small, developing children, this refusal of empathic, reciprocal connection can make them feel that their needs are somehow incomprehensible. It can interfere with their ability to attend, settle down, or live comfortably in their own skin. It is like an invisible wound that gets called everything but what it actually is: the living, breathing, body/mind manifestation of attachment pain. A focus on events can cause a client to feel that their "problems" aren't worthy of much attention or that they aren't even real, which of course is a repetition of how they felt in the past. So they can find themselves in therapy, feeling invisible all over again. The shift of focus is crucial in understanding what we're really treating—not an event but a person, not a circumstance but our inner response to it.

So, relational trauma can occur at very subtle levels of engagement or a lack thereof, as well as in its more obvious forms of living with abuse, neglect, illness, or addiction. The failure to comfortably engage and create a sense of feeling connected, wanted, and cared about, or to communicate needs and desires to those people we depend upon for our very survival, can cause us to feel anxious or even alone and disconnected from those we wish to feel connected to. It can create a deep disconnection both with the self and the other. If there is a cry of the child who has been traumatized in their intimate relationships, it surely is, "Why don't you see me? Why don't you love me as I love you, need me as I need you, hold me as I long to be held by you? You are my mother, my father, my any and all. If you don't see me, then who can?" All of this becomes a part of the meaning that the small child has made out of a disconnection that they take with them when they try to connect. When they seek out deep attachment as adults, this inner experience of childhood attachment comes along with them.

Neuroception is the system that has evolved over time to enable humans and mammals to establish the mutually nourishing bonds that we need to survive and thrive. It is also our personal security system, designed to assess in the blink of an eye whether or not the situations that we're encountering are safe or in some way threatening. If the signals that we are picking up from others are cold, dismissive, or threatening, that system sets off an inner alarm that is followed by a cascade of mind/body responses honed by eons of evolution to keep us from being harmed (Porges 2004). And it sets off equivalent alerts whether we're facing the proverbial saber-toothed tiger or a saber-toothed parent, older sibling, school bully, or spouse. Our primary attachment relationships impact the way in which we experience ourselves and ourselves in intimate connection. They shape our neurological system and our ability to both self-regulate and regulate in the presence of others.

Our neuroception is what we use to settle into intimacy with another human being when we find them safe and nourishing. Or it's what signals us to "remove" ourselves through dissociation or withdrawal in order to maintain our sense of self, without fragmenting on the inside, when we feel threatened. "In pain-engendering exchanges, people are not able to use their interactions to regulate their physiological states in relationship. . . . They are not getting enough back from the other person that can help them to remain calm and regulated, quite the opposite. The other person's behavior is making them go into a scared, braced-for-danger state. Their physiology is being up regulated into a fight/flight mode" (Porges, personal communication, n.d.).

When the child's attempts to bring love toward them are not met with reciprocal caring, concern, and tenderness, they tend to wonder what is wrong with them: "Why can other children be loved and I cannot?" They try to explain this rejecting behavior to themselves and often come to the conclusion that they must be somehow at fault. And if the parent or caregiver is lost in their own dysfunction, they may well be telling the child in all sorts of ways—through their disinterest and lack of genuine desire to connect, through their eye rolling, dismissiveness, or outright abuse—that the child is right, that they are in some way lacking. Or, if the parent is too dysregulated or anxious, the child will stay on guard because what they're getting from them is too rapid an oscillation between states for them to incorporate it as their own sense of successful self-regulation. The parent is making the child feel dysregulated rather than soothed by their presence.

Small children can't successfully feel intact and safe when their nervous system is being overactivated during a painful interaction with a parent. They cannot fight; they would risk being mortally wounded. They cannot flee; where would they go in their footie pajamas, holding a sippy cup and teddy bear? So they do what they can do: they freeze, they dissociate, and they remain present on the outside but gone on the inside. When we cannot act on our own behalf to feel safe and secure, as is the case when we are small and dependent children who are at the short end of a power dynamic, we go into defensive strategies such as dissociation and withdrawal. We move toward a freeze state, and our nervous system stores these immobilizing, collapsing, numbing responses in our body/mind. "The point that we have to understand," says Porges, "is that when a person has a reaction or response to trauma, the body interprets the traumatic event as a life threat. There's a massive retuning of how the nervous system works, how it regulates underlying physiological systems that impact social behavior, psychological experiences, and also physical outcomes."

Whether we're babies being cuddled close or kids standing in the living room facing a raging parent several feet taller than we are, we've been prepared by eons of evolution to assess risk. If we find an interaction safe, we snuggle in, we reach out and touch, we relax and smile. If we feel threatened, we stand alert and adrenalized, ready to flee for safety or stand and fight. But if we can do neither, if escape seems impossible because we are children growing up trapped by our own size and dependency within pain-engendering families, then something inside us freezes. Just getting through, just surviving the experience, becomes our paramount concern.

When a child is not able to fight or flee from what they are perceiving as a danger or threat, it incites a panic response that causes them to go numb or freeze. They are no longer present in the situation internally because the situation is causing them too much pain and they lose faith in their innate sense of fine-tuning, in their neuroception that allows them to pick up on the signals from others and accurately read them so they know how to fit in.

The result of such an unsafe attachment relationship with caregivers is that the child's neuroception becomes faulty—they can no longer rely on it to assess the situations that they enter in order to determine whether it is safe to engage or they need to self-protect. Their primary attachment bonds may have somehow introduced too much fear, so they brace for danger even when none is there. Or they may not pick up on signals that they actually do need to protect themselves; they may get themselves into situations or relationships that are unsafe. The child or adult with faulty neuroception finds themselves in a sad bind because they cannot accurately read the signals coming toward them. They often misread them according to the meaning they made in their early attachment relationships. They often draw the very behavior toward them from others that matches their previous interpretations of events and relational dynamics, their set ideas about relationships, and they can continue to do this throughout their life.

The dependency and vulnerability that are so much a part of intimacy can trigger a person who has been traumatized in their primary attachment relationships into the defensive behaviors that they relied on as children to stay safe and to feel whole rather than splintered. In other words, when the child, adolescent, or adult who has these frozen moments stored in their nervous system gets triggered or overwhelmed in connecting with others, or attempts intimate connection with others, they may freeze, withdraw, or shut down all over again and become unavailable for close connection. Or they may find it difficult to self-regulate in other situations when a comfortable connection is called for; they want to withdraw.

"Faulty neuroception," Porges states, "might lie at the root of several psychiatric disorders, including autism, schizophrenia, anxiety disorders, depression, and Reactive Attachment Disorder" (Porges 2004, 19).

We need to somehow remobilize that system and enter these inner spaces so that we can begin to revive, process, and heal them. How we heal these inner states, then, becomes a road map for the kind of trauma resolution I do and indicates why I find this polyvagal lens so useful. Applying polyvagal theory makes clear how both sociometrics and psychodrama are healing for the nervous and social engagement systems.

Frozen Moments: Psychodrama through a Polyvagal Lens

When you experience what Porges describes as a parasympathetic breakdown, your nervous system retunes itself so that you can feel safe rather than splintered in connection with another, and that retuning often consists of retreating into the defenses of shutting down, dissociating, or withdrawing from deep connection. What follows when we make this kind of profound adjustment is that we disconnect from many of our real feelings. We stop tuning in to ourselves because no one has stayed with us or remained close when we felt scared or hurt or shut down. The very people to whom we long to remain close were the ones telling us to stop feeling, to shut down. This is the beginning of disconnection both within the self and with others and for dysregulation in the nervous system.

"The detection of a person as safe or dangerous," writes Stephen Porges in *The Polyvagal Theory: Neurophysiological Foundations of Emotions, Attachment, Communication, and Self-Regulation* (2011), "triggers neurobiologically determined pro-social or defensive behaviors. Even though we may not always be aware of danger on a cognitive level, on a neurophysiological level, our body has already started a sequence of neural processes that would facilitate adaptive defense behaviors such as fight, flight, or freeze." When we feel unsafe in the presence of another human being, whether because they are refusing empathic, attuned care or are actively hurting us, our nervous system can go into what Porges describes as a "braced for danger state." Over time we can develop the habit of withdrawing, dissociating, or shutting down, which can lead to what is at the core of the effect of trauma: a loss of connection with the self, which, of course, morphs into an inability to connect with others in a fully authentic way. Until we are able to alter the way that the nervous system responds, we are skating on the surface in terms of healing relational trauma.

Once the nervous system freezes, it begins its meaning-making process from this disconnected place, and it attempts, as Porges describes, to make sense of why it is feeling the way it is feeling.

As someone who uses psychodrama, I have worked for many years with the meaning-making of the child mind. Adding the idea of a parasympathetic breakdown to this gives psychodramatic trauma work a grounding in the nervous system. I have long "let the body have a voice," but through polyvagal eyes that break down with the self that the nervous system holds on to, is easier to see. Dr. Gabor Maté talks about trauma being a loss of connection with the self, and polyvagal theory gives this idea a neurophysiological basis.

Creating Lasting Change

Identifying a frozen moment or a moment/dynamic that caused a client to withdraw connection—when there was a parasympathetic breakdown and they recalibrated their nervous system because their neroception told them they weren't safe—focuses the work that needs to be done. It lets both the protagonist and **director** form an alliance, revisit those interactions and work through pain and feelings of helplessness toward a ventral vagal state or a coregulated state in which they feel grounded, open, curious, and empathetic. The protagonist can move from shut down toward a more alive and spontaneous state.

Small children are egocentric; they tend to make everything about themselves. So the question they ask themselves, more unconsciously than consciously, often is *What am I doing wrong that is making the person I love so mad at me or so disinterested in me?* In other words, they tend to set the foundation for a reactive, negative self-image. But they are also creating meaning: *Why do I feel so uncomfortable in my body when I am around other people, or loud sounds, or arguing? Why do I want to get away because my body is signaling me, through nervousness, queasiness, tightness, or an urge to hide or get away, that all is not well here?* Or, in more scientific terms, *Why am I so dysregulated?* Once this meaning-making is firmly in place in the child's mind, it can act as a baseline of learning that we take into other relationships, that is, we read or misread what is coming toward us while in connection with others through this unconscious lens.

Accessing the roles from which these inner states grew—the status nascendi—and adding into that the introjected roles that became a part of us because those attachment relationships became internalized as parts of ourselves, brings them into conscious awareness so that we can begin to heal. The sense we made out of the early relational dynamics with our attachment figures begins to change; the meaning shifts.

Working with the Trauma Transference

Porges talks about how as adults we "misread" what is coming toward us from, say, a close person in our lives because we're reading the interaction essentially through the eyes of a child in which a breakdown occurred. We layer the meaning we made originally onto the relationship today, I have referred to this as our "trauma read" or a "trauma transference" (Dayton 2000).

Porges describes "faulty neuroception," or when a person can no longer rely on their neuroception to keep them safe. This happens often to kids living in chaotic families where they are told that their feelings are wrong, irrelevant, or when reality is denied or there is gaslighting going on that makes a child doubt their own perceptions. Through a polyvagal lens, we're witnessing and validating their original perceptions so that they can finally see what they saw, make sense of their safety responses, and move toward greater awareness of how they came to conclusions about relationships. Then they can begin to shift their thoughts, feelings, and behaviors that grew out of those early conclusions, and move toward a new felt sense of co-regulation, greater autonomy and aliveness, and more prosocial attributes.

Shifting the Meaning-Making Process Experientially

The use of doubling as a grounding, witnessing presence, helps the protagonist come to terms with what they carry inside. Role reversal empowers them to literally stand in both sides of the relational dynamic that hurt them and loosen the tight band that holds these dynamics in place inside of them. Body states can shift from feeling anxious and scared in connecting then processing those feelings toward greater inner and relational comfort and a better sense of co-regulation. Scenes can be broken into roles as the protagonist needs. Perhaps they long to talk to the parent or peer wherein a breakdown occurred, or to a part of themselves that shut down or went into hiding. Maybe they want to reconnect with the freer self that their defenses kept safe and bring it into a state of co-regulation. The possibilities are many, but they need to be focused on the goal of working through these moments of disconnection toward more comfortable states of co-regulation, both with the self and the self in relation to others.

As I have said previously, both the beauty of and problem with psychodrama is that it is so open-ended. It's what I love about it, but for trauma work and treatment centers, it is *too* open-ended. That's why I developed floor checks, the trauma timeline, experiential letter writing, and targeted use of the social atom, the frozen moment being one of them.

Sociometrics fundamentally lead to greater co-regulation or a ventral vagal state through the process itself, which is meant to feel safe, welcoming, and full of free choice. The tuning in on the self and moving through ever-evolving dyads and clusters and sharing and listening to meaningful, personal material is relaxing, enlivening, and encourages openness. Being on one's feet and navigating through a choice-making process is grounding. Choosing is empowering. The whole process is animating and relational while also low risk. As with play, there is easy onboarding and constant interaction. Sociometrics offer, moment after moment, opportunities for recalibration and co-regulation.

I see healing from relational trauma as accessing these inner states through both psychodrama and sociometrics. By moving around the room during a floor check, for example—making choices, feeling, sharing, and listening—we can experience connecting to ourselves and others in more attuned and authentic ways. Or we can use role play to embody the various roles involved in interactions with self and others, so that the self or selves that have been frozen beneath them come back to life.

I see my work within the polyvagal frame as working from the point of dissociation/shutdown, or the parasympathetic breakdown. In seeing psychodrama through a polyvagal lens, we are using embodiment of roles to bring that physiological experience in role relationship from where the breakdown set in to life. And we're using the techniques of doubling and role reversal to deepen contact with the self and to experience both sides of the role relationship.

A polyvagal perspective when using psychodrama in resolving relational trauma functions like a laser that lights up the particular mind/body work we are already doing. It shortcuts and focuses the work I do with relational trauma repair (RTR) and dovetails perfectly with psychodrama. I have referred to this as "laparoscopic role work," but seeing it through the polyvagal lens gives that work a scientific basis that makes both the negative impact clearer and the path to healing more precise. I can then use role play to recreate the role relationship in which this parasympathetic breakdown occurred, allowing the original interpretation of events to emerge.

As the protagonist encounters both the people they longed to be close to and the defensive strategies they used to stay safe, I can follow the protagonist into the labyrinth of their mind/body and help them to enrole some of those stronger defenses as they emerge throughout the drama so that the protagonist can talk *to* them rather than *about* them. This subtle but highly significant shift from talking *to* rather than *about* is what bypasses the lack of words that directly results from the shutting down of the thinking mind during high-stress states. Role play allows us to access more directly the limbic world of the mind/body within which the sense memories and emotions swirl around.

Completing the Ventral Response

Porges speaks of using therapy to "complete the **ventral response**," similar to Moreno's notion of "**act completion.**" Both allow the body to finish a defensive action that they didn't have a chance to complete in real life so they can move out of a self-protective state or an **adaptive survival response** (Dana & Porges, 2018; Porges, 1969), and they can move from an unsuccessful attempt at co-regulation toward a more adaptive and successful co-regulating state. In the process

I have been describing, we're completing the ventral response through the use of embodied role play. And we're shifting the meaning we've made from being top-down to a bottom-up. We are allowing the old meaning and body responses that arise from it to become a felt experience, and feelings that are attached to it can be experienced rather than shut down. If this happens in an uninterrupted and safe manner, the protagonist will witness their own self in action and see how they became who they became. Additionally, we can enrole new re-formed auxiliaries to represent a version of anyone or a part of the self we want to experience as different; we can offer experience of, and practice in, a "re-formed" role relationship with the self or another. We can reshape the full scene—incorporating the use of space to reflect distance, closeness, and proxemics—to experience the scene or dynamic as we wish it had been, satisfying an inner yearning for what we have longed for beneath our frozenness. We see, as Marcel Proust put it, "the same landscape, through new eyes."

Throughout this process, a new, more experiential, and body-informed meaning begins to naturally form because the protagonist is now seeing their own experience as a child through their more mature eyes of today. As they reinhabit the body they lived in at the time of the painful dynamic, they may also begin to relive their trauma. But reliving can be hard to identify, and although the feelings that are emanating from the protagonist can be intense, they may be simultaneously withheld and hard to see or access. Staying with what the protagonist is warmed up to and following their lead into the drama is helps to make the work smoother, because it's what the protagonist is saying they are ready to look at, and it also guards against retraumatization. If we make our goals simple and recognize that a moment of genuine engagement is worth more to the protagonist than a forced catharsis, it's safer and often sets a better groundwork for deeper work over time.

I like to use floor checks, trauma timelines, and social atoms to slowly and gradually focus the work that someone may wish to explore. These can be full work in and of themselves, or they can help group members to focus role plays to take a deeper look at what's coming up for them. I don't use contracts of any sort because in my experience that work is not reached through cognition but rather through a warm-up process that may trigger more unconscious roles and desires to explore that arise spontaneously. In other words, the "work" comes forward spontaneously and should not be forced, planned ahead, or in any way prescribed.

Helga: Unpacking Frozenness

Helga, a therapist herself, was part of the demonstration group for an International Conference on Addiction, Trauma, Recovery, and Associated Behavioural-Mental-Emotional Disorders (iCAAD). Because she understands this work, she wanted to address something inside her that our process of group work on zoom was triggering. "I feel both activated and shut down simultaneously. . . .

I have heard a lot of ACAs talk about this experience," she shared. We bookmarked this moment and met later in a one-on-one session so that Helga could explore this in more depth. You can see the full work including commentary by Dr. Porges here: tiandayton.com/socio-metrics.

The Warm-Up

We started out by recalling the "place" she described and how it affected her. "I developed a sort of 'poker body,' I'd call it," said Helga. The descriptor says it all: a face and body that give nothing away. This is just one of those psychodramatic gifts that I have learned to love and to follow, where the protagonist is leading us into their unique and descriptive meaning-making and creativity. Of course, I imagined that in her early environment she had reasoned that letting those around her see hurt or vulnerability, or what she imagined to be weakness, could get her into trouble of some sort. By enroling her "poker body," we could use this highly clever imagery as a kind of shorthand. As Helga became more warmed up to her own body/mind story, she was interested in unpacking this part of herself. She wanted to talk to the parts of herself that were "in her way today"—the defenses that keep her feeling stuck, along with the roles (read: people) with whom they had gotten set up to begin with. So we enroled her poker body, and she talked directly to it, then reversed roles and talked as her poker body back to herself. When Helga asked her poker body what it was doing, she could reply from the role. The spontaneity of creating this image to work with and enroling it, and then being able to talk with it and as it, became a gateway to the unconscious "job" or purpose of this defensive role. Her poker body replied, "What do you mean, what am I doing here? I'm doing my job, I'm keeping us safe."

As simple as it sounds, by enroling that part of herself, separating it, and placing it in an empty chair, Helga was able to gain some space and distance from her own frozenness so that she could begin to see what was underneath it. Now as an adult, no longer the disempowered child, Helga could talk to the part of herself that had felt vulnerable and at risk of being hurt. She could talk to and as the child she was, who "braced for danger" in her early relationships. Once she saw this part of herself, she could begin to comprehend the meaning that she had made of that role relationship, to feel directly why she had felt a need to withdraw from authentic connection. This awareness first evidenced itself in her body, in her simultaneous physiological experience of feeling "both activated and shut down."

Throughout her drama, I simply followed her lead and enroled the parts of herself that she used as protection, and then other, more vulnerable parts that lay beneath the protective defenses such as her creative, innocent child self. We also enroled her parents when she felt a need to talk with them.

Doubling through the Witness Position

A final piece slid into place for me through Dr. Porges's comments on Helga's psychodrama. He was talking about the power of witnessing, which is of course a part of the psychodrama process: the protagonist gets to witness themselves in action and have **action insights**. And the group members witness the drama, which allows them to have an internal shift through witnessing another's drama and allows the protagonist to feel held and witnessed by the group. I occasionally ask them if they think it would be a good idea to enrole someone as the witness, and I routinely ask them to choose someone to represent themselves in trauma work so they can stand outside the drama and the protagonist can reverse in and out of the scene. Porges replied that there was no need, as the double was already acting as a witness. My mind spun around, because he said in a sentence what I try to get across in paragraphs. In working with frozen moments, the double has to feel like a soothing inner presence, a joining, an inner witness, because if we get too far ahead of the protagonist through the double position, they can feel unseen and misperceived all over again, and they will slip back into their defensive shell. No one will necessarily even see it happening, including them. Then we recreate exactly what the protagonist got when traumatized and reinforce their feeling that intimacy or connection is just not for them.

Seeing the double as a witness is not strictly classical, although I think it's very consistent with Zerka Moreno's, J. L. Moreno's wife and cocreator, direction that the job of the double is to bring the protagonist to the threshold of their own experience.

But in this polyvagal approach to trauma work, and indeed in the way that I have done trauma work for years now, you can miss the mark if doubling doesn't feel witnessing and joining to the protagonist. Someone who has pulled away, dissociated, or shut down in deep relational connection, and who feels a bit panicky when they reach out, has clearly felt invisible to themselves and unseen by others. An attuned, witnessing double can be a corrective and inwardly soothing experience in and of itself. It can teach someone what it is like to feel seen and heard. If doubling makes them feel misperceived or distanced from themselves all over again, it won't be helpful when they're in this delicate state of revealing and reliving.

CHAPTER FOUR

Psychodrama Basics: The Fundamentals of Role Play

The stage is enough.
—J. L. Moreno

O ne of the frequent mistakes I see with inexperienced directors is that they feel that they have to do too much, that it is up to them to get the client to say and do things, that it is they, the director, who generates the healing. But the experienced director understands the importance of warm-up and the power of embodiment. Once a role is cast, concretized, and put on stage, the role relationship itself acts as a stimulus for what will come next. Even if what comes next is silence, it will resonate for the protagonist and tell us something about how the protagonist is experiencing themselves in the role relationship. Once the role relationship is set up, the director can use the techniques available to them in the method to assist the protagonist in clarifying their own moment. In this way, psychodrama accesses the deep social engagement system, allows it to be a part of the role-playing process, and offers reparative experiences so that the protagonist can feel safe and in charge of a shift. They can try something new.

As Moreno famously said, "The stage is enough." "Why a stage?" he asks in *Psychodrama Volume I*:

It provides the patient with a living space which is multi-dimensional and flexible to the maximum. The living space of reality is often narrow and restraining, he [the client] may easily lose his equilibrium. On the stage he may find it again due to its methodology of freedom—freedom from unbearable stress and freedom for experience and expression. The stage space is an extension of life beyond the reality tests of life itself. Reality and fantasy are not in conflict, but both are functions within a wider sphere—the psychodramatic world of objects, persons and events. In its logic the ghost of Hamlet's father is just as real and permitted to exist as

Hamlet himself. Delusions and hallucinations are given flesh—embodiment on the stage—and an equality of status with normal sensory perceptions.

The protagonist, as you see from Moreno's words, is allowed a free hand to spontaneously and creatively bring the parts of himself or others from his network of relationships onto the stage. They can embody anything from a beloved nanny, a loathed part of self, or even things, such as the wallpaper they stared at as they fell asleep each night. Anything and anyone can be brought to the psychodramatic stage and made real through role players from the group, or what psychodrama refers to as "auxiliary egos." We can embody our favorite pet, the spirit of our home, or fantastical imagery, and deal with our inner world transferred onto the stage in concrete form. And we can enrole God, our Higher Power, our witnessing self, or any guide, if we wish.

If we are bringing a person from our network of relationships onto the stage, we can exercise a kind of freedom in dealing with them that normal life constrains. We can say what we couldn't say in real life. Then we can reverse roles—by physically changing places with the other person or part of self and temporarily becoming them, seeing as they see, feeling as they feel—and talk back to ourselves. We can momentarily see ourselves through their eyes and gain a new perspective.

If a director understands that they have the freedom to enrole anything or anyone, they will be opening the limitless world of possibilities that psychodrama can offer for the protagonist, where anything can happen, anything can come to life. A good director understands how to use the basic techniques of psychodrama to maximize their inherent power to heal, without overusing them in such a way as to get in the way of the protagonist's own process.

For the group members or "**audience**," as their feelings while witnessing or participating in the scene emerge, the process slows down like a movie in slow motion. They feel themselves identifying with what goes on in the drama, or noticing what doesn't apply to them. They can feel if they want to shut down, turn away, run out of the room, or jump in and rescue. Sometimes it's easier to see aspects of themselves through others. They can take what fits for them and integrate new awareness. The process becomes something that everyone can learn and grow from.

We do not prescript in psychodrama; we do not tell the protagonist where to go, whom to talk to, or what to say. We follow the lead of the protagonist and allow the drama to unfold. In trauma work this is a main safeguard against retraumatization because we aren't asking the protagonist to go where they are not ready and warmed up to go; we are trusting their process to bring forward that which they are ready to experience and reexperience.

The Five Main Elements of a Psychodrama

In psychodrama there are five main elements of the drama itself. We have the stages of the process and the techniques that can be used to move the drama forward. Understanding all of these is what gives psychodrama its structure and safety.

The five main elements of a psychodrama are the *stage,* the *protagonist*, the *director* (therapist), the *auxiliary ego or egos*, and the *audience* (the group). Here we take a closer look at each of these elements. (I have excerpted some of the following from my book *The Living Stage*, which goes into all of these categories more fully.)

1. The Stage

The stage is any space that has been designated as a working space. To give someone the stage is to give them the opportunity to meet themselves, to take a journey inward, with the support of the director, **auxiliary egos**, and audience. It is to provide a place or a platform where their story can be told, shown, and witnessed by others.

As we'll discuss in Chapter 5 on directing, space is a dynamic part of the psychodrama process, so how and where role players are located on the stage is part of the work.

2. The Protagonist

The protagonist is the person whose story is unfolding on stage. Identification with the protagonist is one of the ways that healing takes place through witnessing, which is healing for both the protagonist and group members. It is the protagonist who makes all choices as to who will play which role in their drama. This choosing process is part of their warm-up to the material being explored. It may take time. The protagonist may even, after making a choice, wish to change it for someone who feels closer to the role, and this can occur at any point throughout the process. They may choose many characters to represent one person—a man can play a woman and a woman can play a man. Virtually anything can be brought to life by the protagonist on stage.

Another part of the protagonist's warm-up is **scene setting**, either through the use of props or by describing the scene to the therapist and group. The protagonist may wish to reverse roles and say a few words as each person in the drama as they choose the auxiliaries, in order to provide a moment of role training. They can choose them and reverse roles at that point in order to role-train them, or simply tell them where and how they are placed in the scene. Some directors like to give lines to role players; I do not. I feel it's too prescriptive and can even overwhelm the protagonist.

Protagonists work alongside the director in identifying and warming up to their own scene or story and concretizing it on the stage. Their willingness to fully engage in their own drama with the auxiliaries, and to move with the action and the director, will influence where and how deep the work will go for all participants. Protagonists are responsible for staying true to their own story and engaging in the action as honestly as possible. They have been given the stage, and they owe it to themselves and the group to be present.

3. The Director/Therapist

The role of director is to aid the protagonist in actualizing their story so that it can be reconstructed, shared, and examined in concrete form. The protagonist is allowed to lead the way in choosing what material to explore with the director, empowering the protagonist to take coownership of their own process. This allows the protagonist to be in charge of the material to be explored without force or pressure and creates a therapeutic alliance that can securely revisit traumatic material. The job of the director is to follow the lead of the protagonist in the production of the protagonist's surplus reality, always allowing them to define that reality as they see it and being willing to go where they feel internally led. The particular associative process that represents the unique internal journey of the protagonist, along with the sense and meaning they have made of the events of their life, is what will most likely yield the most useful insights and "aha" moments for the protagonist.

4. The Auxiliary Ego

The role of the auxiliary ego is to represent the people in the protagonist's life or aspects of the protagonist's inner world as accurately as possible, using information shared by the protagonist as well as their own experience of what thinking, feeling, and behaviors appear to be a part of the role portrayed. This allows the protagonist to view their own reality as it is stored within them, whether it be distorted, illusionary, or grounded in reality, and to identify the manner in which they experienced their own relationships and the meaning they made out of the quality and nature of those connections.

In psychodrama we explore the protagonist's subjective reality and offer the opportunity to deal with the real rather than the unreal. Reality is brought to life through the use of auxiliary egos or improvisational actors chosen by the protagonist to represent particular people in their life. According to Zerka Moreno, these auxiliaries have five functions: 1) to represent the role required by the protagonist, 2) to approximate the protagonist's perception of the person being portrayed, 3) to find out what is really going on within the interaction, 4) to reverse roles and understand the inner world of the protagonist, and 5) to provide contact with real people rather than imagined people, thereby enabling the protagonist to begin making a connection that is real.

Auxiliary ego work is also a part of spontaneity training. In a split second, auxiliaries are asked to come up with an adequate response to the situation as dictated by the protagonist, to put their own needs aside so they can work in service of the needs of the protagonist, and to simultaneously draw on their own histories, learning, and creativity in order to best approximate the role as it was originally experienced by the protagonist.

Roles that lie dormant within the self-system of the auxiliary may reemerge in the psychodramatic moment, to be played out through the auxiliary role. As long as it is tailored to the needs of the protagonist and the auxiliary does not get lost in their own interpretation, this process is healing for all involved. The auxiliary who had a critical father, for example, stands for a moment in the shoes of the protagonist's critical father, both experiencing the inner workings of the role and gaining insight as to the motivations, needs, and drives that might be a part of that role.

Re-formed auxiliary ego (a more ideal version)

Once the protagonist psychodramatically works through their complexes, wishes, **act hungers**, **open tensions**, and desires, offering a more ideal experience in the form of a re-formed auxiliary ego can sometimes be useful. The auxiliary ego can be given back to the protagonist in a re-formed sense; that is, as they "wish it had been." Here, too, the protagonist chooses a new person to template a new experience. This can also happen spontaneously with the role player they are already working with; this person can transform during the role play, and if that is satisfactory, then that's good too—as long as the role player is true to what they are getting from the protagonist and not introducing their own ideas of a "nicer" person.

The protagonist may also reverse roles during the drama, giving themselves the experience they longed for and internalizing that experience into their self-system.

Paradoxically, finally receiving what has long been wished for can be painful; it can bring up tears or discomfort to finally get what you've longed for. The re-formed auxiliary ego is a useful model for the protagonist to take into life so that they can begin to know what it feels like to have what they want, and to learn to accept it in small doses within a safe structure. It may also be useful for the protagonist to interact with the re-formed auxiliary as a form of role training. "The hypothesis here," explains Moreno, "is that what certain patients need, more than anything else, is to enter into contact with people who apparently have a profound and warm feeling for him. . . . The all-out involvement of the auxiliary ego is indicated for the patient who has been frustrated by the absence of such maternal, paternal, or other constructive and socializing figures in his lifetime."

5. The Audience (the Group)

The role of the group is to play auxiliary roles and act as witnesses to the protagonist's life drama, as well as to create a safe container for personal exploration.

Deep healing work can take place within the audience role. Through the process of identification, those watching an enactment can experience feelings as powerful as those of the protagonist. Good group members learn to use those portions of the enactment with which they identify to concretize their own internal dramas so that related feelings can become conscious and available to them. Sometimes the heat of the psychodramatic stage is too much for a protagonist, while the audience role offers full access to the material being explored from a "safe distance." The opportunity for profound healing exists through this identification. Group members may feel themselves alternately pulled, repelled, moved, or shut down as the scenes unravel before them in the psychodramatic moment. They can cultivate the ability to deconstruct the scene *as it relates to them.* Because a scene is occurring in a safe clinical situation, the audience members can afford the luxury, so to speak, of observing their own reactions to it. For instance, why do they identify so strongly here, shut down there, feel their stomachs tighten and their heart race here, wish to cry at still another point, or feel liberated at some other juncture?

It is important that audience members have plenty of time to share what has emerged for them during the enactment in order to deconstruct the scene as it relates to their own lives through the sharing portion of the psychodrama, e.g., warm-up action and sharing.

The Stages of Psychodrama: Warm-Up, Action, Sharing
Warm-Up

The warm-up describes both the internal and external processes that the protagonist and the group go through to ready themselves for actual role play. The protagonist's warm-up may have begun anywhere—in the beginning of group, in a previous group, on the way to therapy, in the hallway while encountering various group members, or in the privacy of their own imagination. The warm-up allows the work to focus and flow smoothly. Sociometrics can be used as complete processes, as warm-ups to small role plays, or as warm-ups to a classical drama on the stage. "What work is the group warmed up to?" "Who is warmed up to work?" "What was your warm-up in coming here this evening?" Such questions open the avenues into psychodramatic work. People vary in how quickly and in the ways in which they warm up. Clients can be helped to understand how they warm up to any of their activities in daily life, whether cooking dinner, reading a book, playing golf, or going to work. Becoming aware of your own personal warm-up allows for a fuller engagement in the activity you are about to enter.

On a scale of one to ten, the degree to which a protagonist is sufficiently warmed up is somewhere between four and seven. The protagonist who is not sufficiently warmed up may drag the work out by not engaging on an emotional level, while the protagonist who is too warmed up may jump into the work so vigorously that they almost avoid deep connection with themselves.

Enactment/Action/Drama

The action or enactment phase is one of embodiment. Concretizing or embodying and then role playing allow the protagonist to encounter and explore their inner and outer worlds through action, to externalize an act hunger, to concretize open tensions. This hunger for action that humans feel is at the core of psychodrama. Allowing action to be lived out on a psychodramatic clinical stage, where the protagonist's truth can be honored before it is tinkered with and where their deep need to physicalize their emotional and psychological world can be met before they are asked to reflect upon it, recognizes this need.

Psychodrama's magic exists in these opportunities to stretch the boundaries of everyday life and to explore not only reality, but surplus reality. Experiencing the self in all of its complexity; giving voice to the rumblings, wishes, and concerns of the inner person; answering questions in a way that reveals what is living inside the protagonist; and standing in the shoes of another and experiencing them and staring back at the self through their eyes make this method unique among all others. This is where the psychodramatic stage becomes a path into another world, where it allows a protagonist to time-travel into and out of the narrow dimensions of their everyday life. It is a moment carved out of time that allows one to live on several layers at once, and to pull those layers toward a broader integration of the self.

The protagonist can choose their needed auxiliary egos in a couple of ways. One is that the director may simply ask them to look around the room and find someone who can play "so-and-so," and can then proceed with the drama by simply saying what they need to say to those they have chosen, adding role reversal, and so forth. Or the director can ask the protagonist to "reverse roles with Mom, brother, or partner." Show us how they're standing and what they're saying in order to role-train the group and potential auxiliaries.

Sharing

The importance of the sharing phase should not be underestimated. This is when the group has the opportunity to continue its healing by genuinely sharing how its members experienced the drama from their own chairs, from their own lives and those who played roles can de-role and share. They can do this by saying, "I'm Cathy, not your mother, but playing your mother I felt . . ." and they can share their experiences of that role and also what playing the role brought up for them from their own lives. After they have shared from playing the role, they can share anything that may have come up for them from their own lives, although some role players are so into the role that nothing really does come up from their own lives at that point. Some role players also like to "brush off the role" physically so that they can concretize letting it go. De-roling should always be a part of the sharing process so that transferences from someone playing a role don't carry over in the mind of the protagonist, and so that there is not a "role hangover" for an auxiliary who may have played a difficult role.

The sharing phase also allows the protagonist to reintegrate themselves into the group. During an enactment, protagonists often feel "out on a limb," as if they are saying and showing things that no one else can understand. The discovery that group members were themselves riveted to the action, watching their own lives flash across their minds, can be very healing for the protagonist.

Sharing, in the psychodramatic form, is *not* feedback. It is sharing what emerged in the witness role from one's own self and life. It is identification. In fact, feedback should not be part of the sharing phase, as it is too mirroring. It deprives the protagonist of the warmth of the group members' identification and it allows group members to stay in their hands rather than identify through their minds and hearts. This opportunity to share from such a deep place gives the group member their own chance to heal what came up for them; it's part of how psychodrama can be healing for everyone in the group. An additional benefit to being an audience member is learning to sit through intense emotion rather than acting it out, dissociating from it, or shutting it down. Developing this skill—modulating emotion—is part of emotional literacy and regulation.

Techniques within the Drama

Two of the most useful techniques of role play are doubling and role reversal. The double connects protagonists with their inner world, and role reversal connects them with the inner world of another. It's experiential empathy training. It also allows the protagonist to view themselves through the eyes of someone else.

Doubling for a Role

The purpose of the double is to speak the inner world of the role being played, to give voice to what might be going unspoken or even unfelt, and to make the less-than-conscious conscious. The voice of the double represents an inner voice; it is the thought balloon in a cartoon that reveals what is going on inside a character's mind and heart that is not being said out loud. So much of what goes on within us goes unspoken, and we are often not aware of it.

Doubling trains a person to sink down into themselves and identify what they might be feeling that is not fully part of their conscious awareness. Doubling brings us to the threshold of our own awareness and brings what's in the background into the foreground.

In terms of trauma resolution, it can reawaken an inner world that may feel numb or out of reach and then connect the less-conscious limbic world with the conscious, thinking mind. Doubling is stage one in Moreno's theory of personality development; the stage of the double is part of the infant-mother costate (Dayton 2005), that state in which the mother intuitively tunes in to and understands the child's inner world.

How Doubling Is Done

When I talk about doubling, know that I am describing a technique that is part of a basic role play but that can become portable. Once group members understand how to double, they may want to double at any moment that the group is together—during a floor check, a timeline, experiential letter writing, sculpture, drama, or even in group process. Developing the ability to double for the self trains an ability to become one's own internal witness. Developing an ability to double for another person trains empathy. These are skills that can help in healing enmeshment and codependency as we consciously separate the self from the other and explore them as different entities. We sense our way into both our own role and the role of another person so that ways in which we've become enmeshed become clearer and we can begin to separate what feels like "us" from what feels like "another." Identities in intimate connection will certainly have overlapping points, but this kind of doubling can create some separation and choice around how and where those manifest.

By the Therapist

A therapist can stand behind a protagonist or group member and double for them by saying what they imagine is going on within the person they are doubling for. I always like to check out whether I am getting it right by saying something like "Does that feel right? If not, correct it or ignore it . . . or find your own words." Giving the protagonist the right of refusal, so to speak, allows me, as the therapist, to feel freer to double and allows group members more freedom as well. It can be as useful for protagonists to reject and correct what a double is saying as to identify with it. In both cases, it helps to make unconscious feelings conscious. The only caveat to this is that when a protagonist is in their trauma vortex or **psychodramatic trance** state, I am very careful as to when or if I double at all. This is such a delicate state that I prefer to err on the side of not doubling so as not to risk pulling the protagonist out of their very tenuous moment of reliving. For example, saying "Correct that if it's wrong" to someone who is in the midst of reliving will force them to leave that trance-like, limbic state and be in their thinking mind to answer the question. Once a state of reliving is engaged, the client is healing themselves. One way to double in these cases is to simply repeat words that the protagonist is already saying if you feel they would benefit from witnessing.

By Group Members

Group members can be invited to double for a protagonist whenever they feel they have something useful to say. This is a great way to keep group members engaged with the drama and to allow them points of participation. In my own groups, I invite group members to jump up and double whenever they feel warmed up to do so. All I ask is that they do so quickly so as not to miss the moment when their doubling statement fits into what's going on, and to sit down equally quickly. One or two sentences usually is enough to help the protagonist focus on their own inner experience without overwhelming them with another point of view or leading them from behind in directions that are not really theirs.

As I said above, group members can also be free to double at any time that the group is in process. It's up to the therapist whether or not they wish to have group members ask permission to double. My preference is to have as much spontaneity and freedom around doubling as possible.

By the Protagonist

The instruction to the protagonist here is "Take a step back and double for yourself, for what's going on inside of you that is not getting said." The protagonist can also double in this manner for any role they are playing; for example, if the protagonist reverses roles into their mother, they can double for their mother in order to let a deeper layer come onto the stage. An auxiliary ego can also be invited to double for the role they are playing in this same manner if it seems like it would let the drama expand.

Tips on Doubling

- Be immediate. Often, group members think of something to double and wait to actually stand up and double. They miss the moment, and then the doubling feels like a badly dubbed movie. It's out of sync with the immediacy and spontaneity of the moment, and by the time it happens the protagonist is forced to backtrack rather than move forward with the trajectory of the drama.
- Tune in as much as possible to what you imagine to be the inner world of the protagonist. Put their inner life into words. Do not elaborate on what they are already saying, but bring forward what is still unclear for them or what they are not able to put into words. Even doubling for the body can be useful in making the unconscious conscious: "My gut is dancing," "My throat is dry and my words are caught in it," or "My legs are shaking," can put words to the feelings that are being experienced and expressed by the body.
- Ask the protagonist, "Does that feel right? If not, correct it. Don't wear it if it doesn't feel right!" In this way, you need not fear doubling imperfectly. Sometimes getting it "wrong" can even help a protagonist to clarify their feelings.
- Doublers should not double for role players, only for the protagonist or the protagonist in role reversal.

- Stay within the framework of the protagonist; don't make things up or push them too far beyond where they are at the moment.
- Seek to have a broader awareness. It is ideal if one, especially the director, is able to double for both roles—the role of the protagonist and that of the protagonist in role reversal. Relational dynamics have two sides, and both sides are stored within us. Both sides are part of a reenactment dynamic. Both sides, therefore, need to be made conscious so that the protagonist can reflect on the full dynamic that they carry internally.
- Double the resistance. If a protagonist appears to be blocked, the director or group members can double for where they are (e.g., "I just don't want to talk to you" or "I don't trust this; it feels bogus" or "I can't speak" are some possible examples of this).

Frequent Mistakes while Doubling
- Doublers do too much of their own psychodrama while in the role of the double. It is natural for identification to take place, and it is part of attunement, but it becomes diagnostic when someone can do more of their own work in the role of the double than they can in their own role. If this keeps happening, I look for codependency or identity fusion.
- Doublers outpower the emotional level of the protagonist (e.g., in frustration at wanting the protagonist to release anger, the doubler shouts or even rages while standing behind the protagonist). Again, some of this can be natural, while too much can shut down the protagonist.
- Doublers become physically too close to or too attached to the protagonist. I prefer no touching, just standing behind the protagonist and doubling. Not all protagonists wish to be touched.
- Doublers baby-step their way into the drama while waiting for the "right moment" to double. Not only does the moment generally pass by, but it is distracting for all concerned to have someone extra on stage.
- Doublers are in their heads. They give advice from behind or try to steer the drama through the role of the double. They get too cognitive, forcing the protagonist away from the limbic world that is coming alive for them and toward their head. It takes the protagonist out of the here and now, as they have to think about what is being said rather than having it feel like doubling or witnessing.

Role Reversal

Role reversal is one of the most important contributions of psychodrama to the mental health field or, for that matter, to any discipline, as it can be brought into a variety of settings, such as business ("Role reverse with a frustrated customer") or social issues ("Role reverse with this person from another race, neighborhood, socioeconomic situation, or gender"). It can be used in anger management workshops so that an angry person can reverse roles with the recipient of their anger and see how it feels to be on the other side of it, and in family or couples therapy so that family members can learn to empathize with one another's roles. There are no limits.

My trainer and mentor Zerka Moreno referred to role reversal as the *sine qua non* of psychodrama, or that without which you are not seeing true psychodrama. I would add that good, attuned doubling that elucidates the experience of the inner world of the protagonist is equally at the core.

The double lets us see more deeply into the self, and role reversal lets us see the self in relation to another. It provides a fuller context. When we don't use role reversal, we over-empower the role of self and do not get any sense of the other—in fact, the other, more often than not, is objectified when we leave role reversal out. We lose the empathy training and the insight that role reversal teaches. And if we leave doubling out, we leave out the stage of joining our protagonist at deeper levels and helping them to make their inner world more explicit.

I see the double as helpful in making what is swimming around in the limbic world clearer by helping to find words to express it, by moving it from body memories into language so that it becomes elevated to a conscious level. This is why it is so important that we not put words in the protagonist's mouth. All of this is part of making the dynamics of the attachment relationships, and indeed any and all relationships, more explicit.

There is a freedom and spontaneity that is an inevitable by-product of momentarily leaving the self and exploring the world from a different point of view. We can become trapped in our own point of view, guarding the boundaries of the self too rigidly and seeing the world only through one narrow lens. Role reversal allows the protagonist to actually stand in the place of the other person and feel and respond as that person might. It allows us, for a moment, to leave the confines of our own experience and see the world as another person might see it, to feel as they might feel, to stand temporarily in their shoes and live for one brief moment within their skin. Possessing the ability to think and feel through the mind and heart of another person is a rare talent, and those who can do it have something special to bring to their relational world.

Additionally, as we spontaneously move back and forth between our chair of self and the chair of another, we have the odd sensation of taking ownership of our own point of view in a whole new way. We see our point of view while at the same time developing the ability to hold the point of view of another. This is empathy. And this empathy has the effect of strengthening the self and the self-in-relation. It also allows us to have a more flexible ego structure.

Moving Past Projections

Many people make the mistake of reversing roles with their ideas and projections of a person. But a true role reversal requires us to temporarily leave our own role behind and inhabit the role of another. One of the dangers in psychodrama is that we strengthen the protagonist's projections rather than reduce them. Part of the work we do in a drama is to cast roles and say what needs to be said, but this is not all of the work. If role reversal is used incorrectly, if the protagonist in role reversal gives us only a parody of the role they have reversed into—a cartoonish version—and if they are using role reversal not to reveal the character of another person but to "tell on them," they are not really reversing roles. In this case, they are likely to strengthen their own projections because they are playing both sides of them—that is, they are playing out the projections from their role onto the other person and, in role reversal, they are still playing out their skewed version of that person. As much as possible, protagonists need to shake off their own role and simply stand in the role of the other person, responding as them, feeling what they might feel, even doubling for them by taking a step back and doubling for what is going on in deeper levels of the person they are playing.

To gain empathy, we need to move past our own projections and feel our way into the inner world of another human being. Some find it hard to do this, and if that is the case, it may mean that they are not fully ready to make such a bold move, that their own sense of self doesn't feel well enough consolidated to leave it. If this is the case, there are several options. One option is to not push it if it seems contraindicated, but to simply allow the person to spend more time in their own role, doubling for themselves and being doubled by others so that they can strengthen their connection with themselves. Another option is to invite the person having trouble role-reversing to stand behind the chair of the person they are reversing roles with and double for them, to attempt to feel their way into the world of that role. Still another and often effective way can be to **interview** the protagonist once they have reversed roles. The more someone is called upon to answer questions "from" and "as" the role of another, the more aware of the interior life of the other they can become.

When to Use Role Reversal: Some Tips

1. Reverse roles when the protagonist asks a direct question of a role player (e.g., "Why don't you pay attention to me?"). The protagonist is the one with the answer (or nonanswer) to the question or the pertinent information about the scene or role being portrayed. We don't want the role player to be in a position of having to make up responses that are inaccurate, and thus lead protagonists in directions that are not useful or helpful.

2. Reverse roles in an attuned manner. Too much role reversal becomes distracting and can keep a protagonist from going deeply into either role, while too little can be unenlivening. Reverse when and where it moves the scene forward or deepens the dyadic communication.

3. Interview the protagonist in the role of another. By answering questions posed by the therapist/director as another person, protagonists have to feel their way into the inner world of that other person and come up with a spontaneous response that feels organic.

4. Role reversal should be a part of any role play whether adding role play to sociometrics, sculpturing, timelines, experiential letter writing, and of course in a psychodrama.

Frequent Mistakes while Using Role Reversal

1. Always use the term "reverse roles" when reversing roles. Avoid terms like "switch places," "change chairs," and so on. When you are using action techniques, you are putting people into a very vulnerable position; they often feel exposed. Use few instructions and keep them simple and consistent. They are learning a new language, so teach it correctly.

2. Stay away from expressions like "Now I want you to . . ." Keep the "I" out of it. This is not about what you want someone to do; it is about creating a safe space in which the protagonist can discover themselves experientially.

The Role Reversal Interview

This is one of my favorite techniques that I learned from Zerka Moreno. Begin by asking the protagonist to reverse roles, and when the moment feels right, ask the questions that they can respond to as the other person or from the role of the other person. Zerka would often begin with something like "Why do you think so-and-so brought you here today?" and the protagonist would answer as that person. I may stretch this out and do this form of questioning for a longer time if I feel it might benefit the protagonist. It can be very satisfying for the protagonist to act out what they have modeled. They can become their drunk parent, their abusive caregiver, or their loving grandmother. The protagonist can "show and tell," and the director can get to know how they experienced people in their lives. Another benefit is that as the protagonist answers questions coming from the director or even from a group member, aspects of that person come forward that may not have come forward otherwise.

Soliloquy/Walk and Talk

The **soliloquy** is a wonderful way to help people who feel stuck at a certain point to step out of the drama and gain some perspective. The soliloquy is essentially a monologue done by the protagonist that reveals what's going on inside them. Think of Hamlet: they are both letting the group know and letting what is underneath come forward. Often the director walks beside the protagonist, and we call it a **walk and talk**. The director and group members can double if they wish to. I sometimes use soliloquies in floor checks: if a group member is identifying with several floor cards, I invite them to cut a path among them and soliloquize about their inner world as they pass the cards they identify with.

Core Concepts

Spontaneity and Creativity: Spontaneity and creativity are two core principles of psychodrama. Spontaneity is defined here as an "adequate" response to a situation: neither too much nor too little, but right and attuned to what is needed. Moreno refers pejoratively to the "spontaneity of the idiot" as something that is too much, that is unattuned and not truly spontaneous. Spontaneity is enhanced by simply doing psychodrama and learning to think on our feet in order to feel our way into our selves, others, and situations. In fact, psychodrama is also referred to as spontaneity training. Spontaneity is, of course, a quality that makes life a more dynamic and personally alive experience.

Creativity is the other core concept of psychodrama. Doing psychodrama over and over again calls us to come up with novel solutions to both old and new situations. It trains us to see something from all sides and even to pop out of situations entirely and see them from the outside. It creates new perspectives and, because it trains us in spontaneity, we become more creative in meeting the moment with adequacy and enthusiasm.

According to Moreno (2019):

> In the spontaneous-creative enactment, emotions, thoughts, processes, sentences, pauses, gestures, movements, etc., seem first to break formlessly and in anarchistic fashion into an ordered environment and settled consciousness. But in the course of their development, it becomes clear that they belong together like the tones of a melody; that they are in relation similar to the cells of a new organism. The disorder is only an outer appearance; inwardly there is a consistent driving force, a plastic ability, the urge to assume a definite form; the stratagem of the creative principle which allies itself with the cunning of reason in order to realize an imperative intention. . . . Therefore, [the protagonist] is not merely following a pattern: he can alter the world creatively.
>
> Protagonists become different on the inside, which allows them to be different on the outside.

Role: Role is, of course, central to all psychodrama. Psychodrama is a role-based method, and role is the vehicle through which we concretize inner parts and outer relationships. Moreno felt that the self emerges from the roles we play, that the role is the concrete form of expression of the inner self, so that when we explore the role, we reach into the self and actualize it on stage in all of its dimensions. We think, feel, and behave according to the role we are playing, for example, if we are a daughter, we think, feel, and behave like a daughter. If we are a police officer, we think, feel, and behave like a police officer. If we are a father, we think, feel, and behave like a father. As we explore the role onstage, we explore its full development from birth, or even in utero, onward. So, role work is inherently developmental, as well as an ideal vehicle for attachment work. In fact, Moreno's role theory includes the development of the self, beginning with a costate with the mother/attachment figure, so psychodrama has always been attachment therapy.

We have intrapersonal roles that represent inner parts of the self. We have external roles that represent those in our relational world.

Warm-Up: The concept of warm-up is everywhere in psychodrama. The therapist works to "warm the group up" using devices such as floor checks, spectrograms, and locograms before launching into psychodramatic work. But the concept quickly becomes portable in the minds of all. We speak when we're warmed up; we pay attention to other people's warm-up and talk to them when we see that they, too, are warmed up—for example, to a topic. We take the idea into life and learn how to warm ourselves up to do a particular task, for example. Is coffee our warm-up to the morning? Is exercise a good warm-up to the day? Do we need to warm up to cooking or cleaning, or are those warm-ups in themselves? What's our warm-up to writing, to working, to preparing the kids to go to school? I often tell clients as well as my own children to "go where it's warm"—where you feel warmed up to a subject or ready to work in a particular way. By paying attention to our own way of warming up, we enter any situation with less resistance and more willingness and openness.

Warm-ups can happen in a variety of ways. Along these lines, I recall one evening in group when we were about ten minutes into a more traditional warm-up, and there was a resounding knock at the door. Everyone jumped. It came again, louder and more determined. People started to shift in their chairs. I noticed the looks on everyone's faces—they were in group, their safe space, beginning to relax, and then *boom!* The silence was broken, their reverie interrupted. When I went to the door, it was a delivery from a Chinese restaurant that went to the wrong room. As I went back to my chair I saw sighs of relief, smiles, and some near-frozenness. We'd lost our warm-up anyway, so I asked, "Where did you go on the inside when you heard that knock?" You couldn't have planned what came forward.

In spite of all of our carefully laid plans, life itself seems to be the most reliable trigger, and inherent in that is the potential for healing. So, whatever we teach clients in therapy, we want to become portable so that they can learn to use the triggers that will happen in their own lives, to understand themselves better, using them as grist for the mill of self-discovery.

Catharsis: Catharsis in psychodrama, much like the Aristotelian definition of the word, represents the release of deeply held emotion on stage so that the need to release it in life becomes reduced. In psychodrama we make a distinction between a "**catharsis of abreaction**," an expulsion of emotions against something—say, a release of rage—and a "**catharsis of integration**," in which there is a shift in perception. Catharsis itself is not a singular goal of psychodrama; it needs to eventually become a catharsis of integration so that new understanding, new meaning, can lead to a shift in perception that becomes permanent.

One of my concerns in doing prescribed, experiential work in which catharsis is seen as the goal of the work is that we "train blame"—we see expulsion of emotion as communicating our feelings, and we take that thought into our relationships. This is why I love role reversal: it offers an experience of standing in the shoes of another person and seeing the dynamic through their eyes rather than exclusively through our own. And of course, doubling for ourselves or, when we're in role reversal, doubling for the role of the other allows us to drop even further down into both inner worlds, which is part of empathy and intimacy.

Surplus Reality: Surplus reality is all that we carry within us in our psyche. Zerka and J. L. Moreno observed that those with serious mental health issues tend to carry more in their surplus reality than others; they live in their imaginings. We all carry much in our minds that is real and vital to us. We live very much in our minds much of the time. Having a stage on which we can place our imaginings and embody them, and on which we can create some air, space, and light, can help us to right-size our inner world. We can encounter and experience what lives in an imagined state in concrete form and gain perspective and insight. We can play out our **act hungers** and **open tensions** on stage and, as Aristotle said, "purge the violence" within us so that we can grow from it rather than play it out in destructive ways.

Act Hunger: The body may have a hunger for action that can be allowed to move into real action through the psychodrama. The action may be to shout, run, or move frozen feelings into words or actions that have been withheld or that constitute a thwarted intention from the past. Embodiment allows these urges to be moved through on the stage. In psychodrama we'd say that these act hungers move toward act completion through embodiment and action.

Open Tension: An open tension might be translated into a mind/body version of unfinished business, or an issue that is left unresolved.

Action Insight: An **action insight** is simply an insight or "aha" moment that comes to a protagonist or group member through the embodied, experiential process. Psychodrama remember allows for the protagonist to physically, mentally, and emotionally embody and experience their inner and/or outer relational network first. Then feelings grow out of this direct experience. The thinking mind then comes on board and translates feelings into words. Then reflection and meaning making grow out of the embodied, experiential process. It's a bottom-up, experiential form of therapy.

Psychodramatic Trance State: The psychodramatic trance state is one that the protagonist may enter while doing deep work. The protagonist is semiconscious and loses an awareness of their surroundings; however, they are engaged with their object as represented by an empty chair or role player. In a psychodramatic trance state, the "as if" falls away and becomes the "as."

CHAPTER FIVE

Tips When Directing Trauma and Other Dramas

Trauma victims cannot recover until they become familiar with and befriend the sensations in their bodies. Being frightened means that you live in a body that is always on guard. Angry people live in angry bodies. The bodies of child-abuse victims are tense and defensive until they find a way to relax and feel safe. In order to change, people need to become aware of their sensations and the way that their bodies interact with the world around them. Physical self-awareness is the first step in releasing the tyranny of the past.
—Bessel A. van der Kolk, *The Body Keeps the Score: Brain, Mind, and Body in the Healing of Trauma*

Embodying a role-relational dynamic on stage becomes a "royal road" to the unconscious nature of our attachment dynamics. It provides an actual experience of reconnecting and reworking our relationship with the self and the self in relation to others. It reveals who and how we were while living in relationship with others and the meaning we made out of the quality of connection that we have been carrying around in our bodies and minds throughout our lives. Accessing these hidden places within ourselves is the work of trauma healing. These moments are hard to achieve, and they are precious.

Even someone saying, "I want to talk to my father, to the part of me that shut down while I was in his presence" is diagnostic; it shows us where to go. Recognizing these moments as a part of a *sotto voce* narrative of attachment allows the director to work with them psychodramatically so that the narrative is bottom-up rather than top-down. Keeping it simple and noninterpretive is key during the process to give the protagonist time to witness themselves in action, to become their own internal observer and connect with what Zerka Moreno called their own "autonomous healing center." Psychodrama is naturally trauma sensitive in this way: we don't ask the protagonist to come up with a description of their inner state until they have had a chance to embody their experience.

If we ask clients to talk first, we're asking them to do what they cannot do. Remember, the thinking mind is often offline during terrifying or highly stressful moments, so we don't make intellectual sense of traumatic moments as we experience them. We shut them down, we fight or flee, we dissociate, which is why when we get triggered—we become mindless, immature, and welded to interpretations from the past. "What is required is a backward movement into the brain itself. . . . We find that by entering the paleo-mammalian brain in reverse via proprioception, that is, by using our very skin, muscles, and natural abilities to locate ourselves in space, we have a fuller realization of self" (MacLean 1968). Role play allows the protagonist to feel and sense their way toward this "fuller realization of self."

Embodying the pain in a role relationship with the self or others allows the protagonist to see themselves in action, to begin their own interpreting, to become their own therapeutic ally and friend. The beauty of adding role plays to sociometrics is that the protagonist often gets to these inner relational spaces, through the structured activity that warms them up and allows them to discover and uncover what lies beneath.

Scene Setting: Gateways to the Unconscious and Creating Context for the Protagonist

We can enter the details of a memory through many doors: a song, a smell, or the atmosphere of a place. How we allow the protagonist to arrange role players and objects on the stage can act as a primer for the fuller memory to come forward. It is amazing to watch as a protagonist moves chairs or benches onto the stage, and suddenly their inner world is available to them. They may say, "Oh, this isn't in the right place," and although the move to correct the spacing may seem imperceptible to the group, the effect it has on the protagonist can unlock some invisible door in their unconscious, allowing a flood of memories to come forward.

When we're frightened, our hippocampal and amygdalic memory records the sensory and emotional aspects of that experience *and the context surrounding it*, but not our reasoned thoughts about it. The who, what, where, and why can feel foggy. Scene setting can be a part of what allows memories to come alive. Re-creating aspects of an environment can be an invaluable warm-up that places the protagonist inside their own memory.

Allowing the child mind within the protagonist a full range of expression can open a portal into unconscious memory that looks much like a dream state. Animals can play very protective roles in a child's world and can be important auxiliary egos in dramas. A client may even want to cast a role player as the wall of a particular room (think: "if the walls could talk") and then reverse roles and "talk as the wall." A protagonist may choose a nonhuman auxiliary and talk *to* and *as* a cherished stuffed animal, a baseball mitt, a tree, or a dollhouse. Entering their memory through these less-human portals can have the effect of freeing their associations from the confines of interpersonal roles, allowing the flavor of the atmosphere that they grew up in to emerge. It lets them slip into the creative and imagistic child mind, where everything feels real. The director should let the protagonist get it exactly right for themselves without interference. All of that said, you can also simply move into a role play without scene setting, if that's the protagonist's preference, if time is an issue, or if the role play is emerging from a sociometric.

Observing the Body

Often, as painful memories emerge, the body will react before the client is even aware of what they are feeling. As the protagonist brings a person, part of themselves, or characters from their own life forward to talk to, they reexperience the body state they lived in at that time. "Trauma is not the story of something that happened back then. It's the current imprint of that pain, horror, and fear living inside people," said Bessel van der Kolk in a *Psychotherapy Networker* interview.

When protagonists are reexperiencing intense affect, you can see the effect on their bodies, which may hold tension in the throat, jaw, chest, arms, hands, feet, or other body parts. A protagonist may report their throat going dry or their heart or head pounding, or their limbs may shiver and shake, as Peter Levine describes in his book *Waking the Tiger* (1997). It is up to the therapist to read these signals and use them as information in helping the client recognize the signals they're getting, to stand by and witness as they let their body shiver and shake off the trauma that's coming up for release and healing. As you see their body reacting, you can say something like, "I notice there was a shiver that just went through you," or "I notice that you're collapsing inwardly." You may invite them to give parts of their body a voice through questions or prompts such as these: "If your throat had a voice, what would it say?" "Put your hand on your chest and let that part of you speak." "What do your legs want to do?" When asked, "If this part of you had a voice, what would it say?" the thinking mind can then find the words to describe its own inner experience. Words that we have longed to say come flooding out of our mouths, and along with them, frozenness emerges in the body. A tight throat or chest, legs that shake, a downward stare, a shiver are all telling us how the protagonist experienced themselves while in connection with their attachment figures. The body state, with attached feelings that have given way to interpretations and meaning that the protagonist has made out of the events that shaped them and that they have subsequently lived by, emerges organically, stimulated by the role relationship. And the words flow from that inner state.

The body, after all, can't lie. When it freezes up or sucks in breath or begins to shake or collapse into itself, when the arms and head go down, it is calling out, "See me, look here, find out why I am doing this to preserve myself in this moment." It is the body, as well as the words, that tells us the unconscious part of the role relationship a protagonist experienced, that forms the basis of their intimacy experience. Learning to use the body as a "royal road to the unconscious" allows more of the relational history of the protagonist to come forward. So if I say, "Who could play the part of you that freezes up, and what would you like to say to this part?" the body/mind is called upon to speak and act, in the role relationship that is part of the protagonist's relational or inner world. The next question can be, "Where did this start for you?" and the protagonist can then talk to their primary attachment figures or others where they may have had breakdowns in connection and intimacy.

Occasionally, I use the role relationship to redress a power imbalance by saying something like, "Can you stand up and say that?" or "Shall we shrink your father and you can tower above him for a change?" Changing the proxemics of the outside, helps to change them on the inside. Remember that when you are working with interpersonal neurobiology, you are working with the dyadic or family relational dynamic and the neural imprint as it lives within the client. We carry in our psyches not only how we felt at the time something took place but how we saw the world, perhaps through the eyes of a small child confronted with a large and looming parent. By changing those size relationships on stage, we create a new sense impression to balance out the old one. We not only find our voice, but we change our relative relationship vis-à-vis another person. All of this can become part of a new experiential attachment narrative, one that is bottom-up rather than top-down, based on interpreting body states and proxemics that are informing the story. Rather than a fixed story or interpretation that keeps engendering body states that drive reenactments and projections, it is an ever-evolving reinterpretation and new understanding of relational dynamics, and the healing is an ever-evolving shifting of body states that have the power to engender new, more regulated behavior.

Through psychodrama we can shift body states from hyperarousal to calmer and more regulated within and co-regulated in relationship. Moreno's role training becomes an important part of the new co-regulation, as it allows protagonists practice in trying on new behaviors. Floor checks are also processes in which group members are constantly trying on healthier relational behaviors.

Use Space as a Part of the Therapy

On the psychodrama stage, distance and closeness can be strategically used as part of the therapeutic process. Space can be used to create distance and closeness, and the proxemics of the family can be revealed through how they are placed on stage in relationship to each other.

If there was a significant size or power differential or distance between family members, then the protagonist can put auxiliary egos in the relative size and distance from each other that feels right. A family's covert or overt alliances or trauma bonds can be made explicit on stage, for example, through placing auxiliaries who have covert alliances near each other, and the distance that that creates among other family members can be structured as well. Alienation, factions, overlaps, or over-closeness can all be embodied on stage.

Once this stage of exploration is moved through, we can *redo* the placement: we can make it as we might have preferred it to be and feel what it could have been like had things been as we wished. This process of seeing things as we wished they had been can bring up feelings around what never happened. But in grieving what was lost and experiencing having what we always wanted, we can template something new.

Here again you can see the power of simple concretization or embodiment. Clinicians needn't get elaborate and think that they need to add all sorts of bells and whistles to the process, because embodiment itself is so illuminating and informative. Knowing how and when to use techniques like doubling, role reversal, soliloquy, and role reversal interview keeps the process contained and fluid.

"In response to threat and injury," writes Peter A. Levine, PhD, "animals, including humans, execute biologically based, non-conscious action patterns that prepare them to meet the threat and defend themselves. The very structure of trauma, including activation, dissociation and freezing are based on the evolution of survival behaviors. When threatened or injured, all animals draw from a 'library' of possible responses. We orient, dodge, duck, stiffen, brace, retract, fight, flee, freeze, collapse, etc. All of these coordinated responses are somatically based—they are things that the body does to protect and defend itself. It is when these orienting and defending responses are overwhelmed that we see trauma."

Hit the Pause Button

Too much interference at sensitive moments of reliving can not only take healing off track, it can also squander the protagonist's hard-won readiness to do deep work. It can derail or curtail what has taken such careful and thoughtful preparatory effort on the therapist's part to set the groundwork. We need to let the moment pulse with tender, often barely perceptible recognition on the stage, to observe the stored or blocked energy that is locked within the self-system, as it begins to move. If at this point we force anything, we run the risk of shutting the protagonist down, and they may, almost imperceptibly, slide right back into their early defenses.

When a protagonist enters this inner space of reliving, they need time and space. Or, even more accurately, time and space disappear, and they need to simply hit the pause button and be in the moment. This is a highly sensitive state for the protagonist, and it requires, in my opinion, a kind of "stop the clock, we're finally here" style of directing. If a director imposes a preconceived agenda or engages in overdirection or overquestioning, it can feel to the protagonist as if the director is crashing in on a deeply held personal experience and trying to get it to go somewhere that, in fact, interrupts the authentic reliving process. Remember, the protagonist may be barely making contact with their inner world, or they may be filled with an mysterious sense of revisiting their own life safely, seeing themselves almost as if in a dream, witnessing what made them *them*. The process can too easily get away from the protagonist who is in the midst of reliving if the director has agendas or group members become triggered themselves and act out their own issues and transferences through auxiliary or doubling roles.

The protagonist needs to find their own consciousness and coregulation around these moments so that in the future when they get triggered, they will have developed the skills to deal with it: they will have an internalized template of slowing their reaction down, breathing, and becoming mindful of what's going on within them so that they can increase tolerance of their own intense internal states. I have learned to trust the healing power of witnessing and holding this moment. I have also learned to trust that the group can hold it, and that they are seeing what I am seeing, or something close enough, or they are at least willing to grant space for it.

When clinicians can recognize these moments of reliving or deep engagement, protagonists can begin to reknit the fragments of their personal experience back together into a more coherent whole and then emerge with a greater sense of self. According to van der Kolk, "If clinicians can help people not become so aroused that they shut down physiologically, they'll be able to process the trauma themselves." Porges, in commenting on Helga's work, observed that in doing this work through role play, the protagonist was learning to "apply their own vagal brake," noting that these role plays could become opportunities for learning new ways of co-regulating, both intra- and interpersonally.

Refrain from Unnecessary Interpreting: The Danger of Too Much Talking

Being asked to come up with a narrative before we feel it, before we *know* it, runs the risk of that narrative becoming an intellectualization that the protagonist can use to create distance from their inner experience. It can make us want to look for quick solutions to the kind of unconscious pain that surrounds trauma or use words to shut it down rather than feel it. Eventually being able to talk about our trauma or pain without acting out or shutting down is a sign of healing. But if talking is used as a way to distance every time we feel too vulnerable, then it becomes a defense, the defense of intellectualization.

The Experience of the Group

Contrary to what many might think, trauma-related material does not necessarily come pouring forth in treatment; it is slow and painstaking work. When a protagonist is reliving or doing deep trauma healing, it can be triggering for all concerned. At times group members pick up on intense emotion but see little outward expression of it. A conundrum for the therapist and group is that although this state is often subtle, it can have an emotional suction that pulls others toward it, which can feel disequilibrating to those feeling the pull. Therapists and group members alike can pick up on the protagonist's intense mixture of conflicting emotions, and that anxiety can lead them to overquestion the protagonist or try to force premature or facile solutions in an unconscious attempt to control, titrate, or even shut down a process that is evoking emotional angst within themselves.

Protagonists who are confronted with people who hurt them in their past, may revert to defenses such as denial, avoidance, dissociation, or withdrawal. Groups witnessing this can get frustrated. Or protagonists may try to explain their way out of what's coming up for them on the inside, or get angry, or feel tricked into going to a place they suddenly feel they don't want to go after all.

I am careful at these tender moments not to give auxiliaries too much latitude. For example, when the protagonist asks a question of the auxiliary, I ask the protagonist to reverse roles and respond. Only the protagonist truly knows the right answer; they have all the information about their own lives. I try not to let role players make things up.

What we're working to heal is the relational dynamic that lives inside the protagonist. I do this by observing what the protagonist says in their own role and in role reversal as they take on the role the other person, and I study their bodies carefully. I look at expressions, body postures, and areas of tension or relief, of empowerment or collapse. Protagonists have introjected important attachment figures from their lives, through role play they can *show* us rather than *tell* us what they experienced.

When Group Members Get Triggered

Because sitting with disequilibrating emotions is so difficult, group members often want to see a big catharsis—they want the uncomfortable feelings to come out. The auxiliaries and group members may take the drama in directions that they imagine will help the protagonist, and/or the director may become overly directive. Group members may have trouble staying within the framework and emotional range of the protagonist if their own "stuff" is getting triggered. They may jump in and double at an intensity of emotion that blows the protagonist's circuits and makes the protagonist feel like they are failing to get to their pain or rage, for example. Or group members might insert pieces of their own personal experiences by doubling or role playing in a way that is an attempt to lead the protagonist to where they want them to go.

If the group members can develop their **window of tolerance** at these challenging moments, it can be very healing for them as well as for the protagonist. It is these triggered states that we need to tolerate so that the protagonist and group members alike can learn to be with them rather than run from them. Teaching group members to use these moments to become more aware of where their own triggers lie makes the protagonist's drama a healing opportunity for everyone in group.

Sometimes a group member is triggered because they identify with a role in the drama; reflecting on this in their own minds and unpacking this during sharing can be illuminating. This is why it's important to leave plenty of time for sharing, it's the place in the process for group members to share what comes up for them when witnessing a protagonist's drama so that they can heal, too.

Gateways of Participation for Group Members: Provide Points of Entry

I like to provide many points of entry so that everyone can feel engaged in a protagonist's drama. As long as group members understand that this is not their drama, but that they are part of bringing the protagonist's drama to life, it works beautifully. If group members forget this, they will need reminding, as protecting the protagonist comes first when we are asking them to enter these vulnerable inner spaces. This can have a side benefit of teaching group members boundaries and attunement, and once they get good at it, it becomes teamwork at its best.

Here are some easy entry points:

Doubling: I allow the group to double as they wish to. I point out things to watch for that can go wrong in "psychodrama basics." But generally, once the group understands how to double well, it's a great way to engage the group in the process, and to help the protagonist to move forward and feel seen and witnessed in their work. Becoming an attuned double teaches group members how to relate to others at a deeper level. It's spontaneity and empathy training: doubling is only done for the protagonist and for the protagonist in role reversal, never for group members playing a role.

Playing auxiliary roles: Of course, playing a role in someone else's drama involves group members. Often people love playing roles. It's important that group members understand that they are there to get it right for the protagonist's drama—not to lead the protagonist but to approximate the role *as the protagonist experienced it* as closely as possible. Playing roles well is a great talent, highly creative, and wonderfully helpful to the protagonist and group members alike. It can also be enlightening for the role player as they try on different identities and learn to respond spontaneously as another person. De-roling is important, so that if group members play difficult roles, they can shed them both to release themselves from the identity and so that the protagonist doesn't keep seeing them as the role they played.

Lots of sharing: Allow group members to share freely and deeply. Sharing is not feedback; it's for the continued healing of the group members. Group members share what came up for them from their own lives while witnessing or playing a role. Sharing lets everyone leave group without carrying unexpressed feelings. When de-roling during the sharing process, invite the role player to first share how they felt while playing the role, then have them brush the role off and say, "I am [their own name], not [the name of the role]." Afterward they can share anything they wish that may have come into play for them from their own lives. Sometimes role players have nothing much come up from their own lives because they were so focused on role playing; that's perfectly normal.

Finishing chair: One protagonist's drama can warm up other group members to their own work. If that is the case, I sometimes put a chair out and let that group member do a small, empty-chair drama to bring what got warmed up in them to completion. This can also be seen as a sort of action sharing, as the goal is similar: to bring closer to those who witnessed or watched the drama.

In the next chapter, I'll talk about simple role plays that can help clients to clarify specific issues that are part of passing pain through unconscious, dysfunctional relational dynamics, down through the generations.

What to Watch Out For

Remember, moments of reliving can move very slowly. These moments can be frustrating for group members, auxiliary egos, and even directors. Consequently, those in the group can act on their own feelings that are getting triggered "on behalf of" the protagonist. They can double feelings that have more to do with themselves than the protagonist, and auxiliaries can bring in their own ideas that may or may not fit the role they are being asked to portray. Sometimes role players can become overly enthusiastic and pull the drama to places that take the protagonist away from their own reliving. Maybe the role players want to help. Maybe they're triggered themselves and want a chance to dump their own stuff from the position of the double. Maybe they are feeling thrown off balance and go into their heads and use that favorite of defenses, intellectualism, or maybe they just love releasing feelings on stage. Whatever the motivation, the director needs to maintain a safe space for the protagonist, who may be in a state of reliving, and provide plenty of time for sharing so that group members can release what got warmed up inside of them.

I find that this happens more frequently in larger dramas with more characters, which is one of the reasons I like small role plays that have been warmed up and focused through sociometrics.

To summarize, if too much latitude is given to role players, a few things may happen that can get the drama off track:

- The auxiliary role player may make things up that don't really fit, and the protagonist is brought out of their psychodramatic trance state—in which an almost dreamlike, deeper brain repatterning is occurring—and back to the surface of the mind. While in a very vulnerable state, they are taken out of the affective moment and put into their heads. The protagonist is then forced to figure out what applies and what doesn't, which means they have to move to the more surface parts of their thinking rather than deeper states.
- The auxiliary role player starts to control the drama.
- The director gives the auxiliaries lines to say that skew the drama into a particular direction or that prevent deeper and more subtle relational dynamics from emerging.

- The director allows group members to double for role players rather than sticking to the classical form of doubling only for the protagonist in their role of themselves or reversed into the role of another.
- The doubles outpower the moment of reliving; they become too loud, too directive, or even advice-giving or interpretive from the position of the double.
- Director, auxiliaries, and group members who double act out their own transference issues while supposedly doubling for the protagonist.
- The director sees catharsis and rage release as an endgame rather than as a part of the process of restoring psychological, emotional/limbic, and relational balance and integration.
- The protagonist tries to please the director and the group members rather than acting on their own inner signals, which reinforces codependency.

While a good director must be aware of the needs of the group and auxiliary role players, the director's first responsibility should be to protect the protagonist, who is putting their inner world on the stage for all to see and interact with.

CHAPTER SIX

Shadowboxing with Ghosts: The Endless Cycle of Trauma and Addiction

The need for the drama can be temporarily choked, for instance, by sleep or shock therapies. But the fundamental need for the realization of certain fantastic imageries cannot be "shocked away." . . . we need to undertake a "war on ghosts."
—J. L. Moreno, *Psychodrama Volume I*

Robert Anda, MD, of the CDC and Vincent Felitti, MD, of Kaiser-Permanente paired up in a long-term study to research what health factors drove healthcare costs up. What made people go to the doctor more often and make claims on their insurance? Through collation of reams of data, it emerged that growing up with emotionally and psychologically painful or traumatizing experiences in childhood was one of the strongest predictors of health problems later in life, hence, the coining of the term *adverse childhood experiences* or ACEs. Although the researchers were in no way looking for it, Anda recounts that parental addiction kept popping up over and over again as one of the most damaging and lasting forms of childhood stress. Because if a child grows up with addiction, that is probably not the only risk factor in the home; ACEs, it turns out, *tend to cluster.* "Once a home environment is disordered, the risk of witnessing or experiencing emotional, physical, or sexual abuse actually rises dramatically," says Anda. Addiction, not surprisingly, is statistically correlated with neglect and/or verbal, emotional, physical, or sexual abuse. And, "unlike other traumatic events or natural disasters, effects of ACEs tend to roll through the generations," disappearing after kids leave home and later reappearing as health issues, delinquency, and/or learning problems—or as mental health issues, eating disorders, or process or behavioral addictions such as sex, work, internet, exercise, or spending.

It's often been said that addiction "skips a generation." But trauma does not. And as often as not, kids who grow up with addiction have both events and relational dynamics to untangle and heal from when they become adults. They remember being locked out of the house, beaten up by a drunk parent, or sexually abused. But the daily insults and hurts by a using parent may well be woven together with that parent's sober, compensatory behavior, in which they were suddenly all that the child would want them to be—generous, attentive, and loving. So the child can't figure out which is which, and if their other parent is as caught in the web of dysfunction as they are, then there is no one to explain it to them, no one to check out reality with and get grounded.

Treating the Dyad, the Magic of Role Reversal

We talk about other people living "rent-free in our head." But what if what's living rent-free in our heads is really our relationship with a person, and there are two of us there in a dyad? What if in our heads we're a babbling-back-and-forth pair of people—bragging, laughing, crying, shouting, hugging, arguing, running away, and then kissing and making up again?

Or what if one of the people in the relationship, with us in our head, is drunk?

Children who are living with any form of adverse childhood parenting, whether dysregulation from mental illness or addiction, are faced with a conundrum: how do I access the parent I love and need while staying safe from the parent who is scaring me? Adult Children of Alcoholics (ACAs) regularly experience connection-versus-disconnection from their alcoholic parent, and even from their other parent, who may also be unavailable or suffering from mood issues. Their attempts at reconnecting can meet with reciprocal love at one time and just the opposite at other times. And nothing they can do can change that. In an attempt to feel less anxious and unsafe connecting, they may develop a false self that is designed to be more acceptable to those they live with, and that garners more approval. This can begin the process of shaping the developing self to manage other people, sometimes referred to as people pleasing, false self-functioning, or codependency. But the larger and more complex the false or inauthentic self grows, or the longer we self-medicate to deaden inner pain, the more distant we become from the self we are trying to protect.

Trying to unconsciously feel and sense our way into a coregulated state with someone who is drunk or high on pills, which is the child of an addict's regular experience, interferes with our ability to internalize and strengthen our own skills of self-regulation and the neural pathways that support it.

Unconscious Expectations

When we drag this kind of childhood lens into the way we see our adult relationships, we often as not misread what's coming toward us (Porges, personal communication, 2021). This is a very important juncture at which adult conflicts can go off the rails: we transfer onto another person the characteristics of those people who hurt us in childhood and then engage our childhood defenses to "stay safe" to avoid what we perceive as pain coming toward us, whether or not it's real. We project and transfer old pain onto new relationships. We imagine we'll get what we got and may even push someone until we bring a behavior that we *unconsciously expect* toward us. We recreate the past in the present. We shadowbox with ghosts.

The ability to use the double to help someone to get in touch with what's really going on inside of them in a painful relational exchange and role reversal—so that they can concretize the other person, so they can show us, and even more importantly themselves, what drunk behavior looked and felt like—lets the ghost come to life and enter the reality of the stage, where they can be finally dealt with in an embodied form.

Inebriation and Disorganized Attachment

All children are faced with the developmental task of integrating their normal feelings of love and hate toward their parent and accepting their parents as flawed humans whom they can still love and need. But for the child of addiction, this can become a complicated and complex task. With one side of their parent, the Dr. Jekyll side, they may well feel securely attached, while the other side, Mr. Hyde, frightens them to their core. One is welcoming and loving, funny and available, and the other is cold and selfish, abusive and rejecting; one is a person and the other a monster, the avatar of a drug. So ACAs may have a trauma bond or an anxious-ambivalent or anxious-avoidant attachment with the drunk or mentally ill or dysfunctional (read: scary) side of our parent, while feeling a rather secure attachment with the sober one.

This can cause the more frightening side of the parent to be thrown out of conscious awareness and remain disintegrated within the child's psyche, which is why, I believe, we reenact, recreate, or project and transfer the side of the parent that most disturbed us. In other words, we relegate the drunk, abusive (or dysfunctional/mentally ill) parent to our unconscious while maintaining a relatively comfortable connection with our more desirable parent. If they stayed unconscious, that would all be fine, but they don't; they live within us in a ghost-like manner, and we unconsciously drag them with us into our adult intimate relationships. Under the black light of the therapeutic moment or stage, these invisible wounds and transference figures can reappear. We can begin to identify and separate our adult relationships from ghosts of the past.

Mary Ainsworth, mentee and later colleague of Jonathan Bowlby, who did seminal work on attachment at the Tavistock Clinic in London, created what she called "the strange situation" to explore early attachment styles. She identified three types of attachment styles that she has named: 1) secure, 2) anxious/ambivalent/insecure, and 3) anxious/avoidant/insecure. ACAs, in my observation, often experience the latter two forms with their alcoholic parent, and sometimes with their other parent as well, who may be distressed by their spouse's addiction or have their own mood disorders that predate it.

The Still Face Experiment

The still face experiment done by Dr. Ed Tronick in the 1970s demonstrates and makes attachment wounds visible with poignant clarity. It has essentially two parts. The first is the mother connecting joyfully with her child, and the child connecting joyfully with the mother. Both are reading each other's facial expressions, sounds, and gestures and responding in a mutually attuned fashion. They are in what Stanley Greenspan describes as a mutually satisfying "feedback loop," both initiating and completing, opening and closing repeated loops of communication.

In the second part of the still face experiment, the mother momentarily turns away, and when she returns, she is expressionless. When her child makes the same attempts to communicate that were so successful before, the mother remains implacable and unreachable. She offers nothing. Initially the baby looks around the room in confusion, *Where did my mother go?* She points, which got her mother's engaged response before, and nothing happens. As she continues to try to communicate with no success, she becomes increasingly agitated, despondent, and begins crying and calling out. Her central nervous system goes into a sort of collapse, and she loses control of her posture. Eventually she gives up and stops trying to connect; she no longer tries to get her mother's attention. She turns away. She is alone in the presence of her mother.

Then, as mysteriously as the mother turned into someone she didn't recognize, her mother returns all smiles and attention. With the reappearance of her "good enough mother," a term coined in 1953 by Donald Winnicott, a British pediatrician and psychoanalyst, the baby recaptures her previous contentment and joyful expressions.

"Babies use their primary attachment figures to work out and integrate their emotions and intensions . . ." says Ed Tronick (2016). "We see the powerful impact that the simple lack of emotional response has on a child and the emotional gymnastics the child goes through to deal with this lost connection. We need loving contact like oxygen. . . . we really don't have many ways to deal with the pain of disconnection." Sue Johnson picks up the thread, "now let's look at how the exact same drama plays out in a couple, the moment when emotional connection is lost."

Isn't this a mirror of the experience of the child of an alcoholic, drug addicted parent, or mentally ill parent? The child, looking to find himself in the face of the one he loves, who functions as a constant object and external regulator, has this experience of losing himself and finding himself over and over again depending on the state of mind his parent is in. His nervous system alternates between bracing for danger and opening up, between what Erik Erikson, in his stages of psychosocial development, referred to as trust vs. mistrust. But eventually, he finds out he cannot rely on either state and so shuts down or hides in plain sight through some version of false self-function or denial of his authentic, spontaneous self. He moves into a second stage of Erickson's model of development, autonomy vs. shame. Because he cannot be fully embraced as himself in the arms of those he loves, he feels shame (Erikson 1950).

Later as adults, when we get stuck in these sorts of patterns of feeling hurt or rejected, we may return to that child state. We may experience our partner as big and ourselves as little and powerless. We can lose track of our adult self because our child self is getting triggered.

The next part of Tronick's film shows a husband and wife having a fight in which the husband shuts down and withdraws communication and connection, and his wife slowly, then more quickly, becomes distressed as one-by-one her attempts to reconnect are rebuffed. "Disconnection hurts," says Tronick, "and how we handle these inevitable moments of disconnection defines how these bonds work out for us. We often don't see the impact on our partner of our lack of response to their emotional call." How the couple handles and works through these disruptions in empathy toward a mutually satisfying connection may determine how well their relationship goes and grows.

Projection and Transference: How Pain Gets Passed Along

As ACAs or children of adverse childhood experiences, we may choose partners with whom we recreate those parts of the dynamic with our parent that hurt us the most because of the dynamics we relegated to our unconscious, and they emerge through our actions without our awareness. A son who felt humiliated by his drunk mother but who could not bear to feel the humiliation may have foreclosed on that painful feeling in childhood or adolescence. But later, as an adult, the feeling of being humiliated or the perception of it, even if he is misreading another person's intent, may trigger that unconscious pain. He'll conflate his unconscious "mother" pain from the past with the pain being triggered in the present moment, say, with his wife. Then, with no awareness of the unconscious nature of his pain, he may project it onto the person he's perceiving or misperceiving as humiliating him and become defensive, angry, or belittling of that person. In other words, he'll see his wife as the sole person causing him discomfort. Or he may withdraw and become sullen, shut down, or a combination of both—a withdrawal and then a burst of anger or rage. Defenses that got seared into place will resurrect themselves in the blink of an eye, and the past becomes seamlessly imported into the present. Entering these inner rooms, gathering up those pieces of our personal stories, and stringing them into meaningful and understandable sets of observations and reflections is the work of therapy.

With help, the unconscious portion of his part of the dynamic can change when understood, because he will no longer respond without awareness of what he's transferring from his past onto his present; he will have a choice in his own behavior. He can separate his pain from the past from his pain in the present and understand his overreaction as being part of previous unprocessed wounds.

This is why sociometrics focus so much on learning to translate the disequilibrating emotions that get triggered into words and sharing them with others, then listening as others share their own feelings. We need to build emotional literacy and intelligence. Once we can feel, name, and talk about our unconscious pain, we can process it. For example, in the trauma/PTSD symptom floor check, each time a participant chooses a symptom, they share about why they chose it and how it relates to or plays out for them. This is another way to separate the past from the present.

Grandchildren of Addicts (GCoAs)

I wrote *The ACoA Trauma Syndrome* (2012) to make the connection between being an ACA and developing PTSD, the thesis being that the unconscious pain and trauma of growing up with addiction surfaces in adulthood as a post-traumatic stress reaction; years after the original stressor is removed, we behave as if it is still there. Childhood relational pain shows up and is re-experienced and recreated in the area of adult, intimate relationships like partnering and parenting, so ACAs risk passing along anxiety engendering attachment styles. And in that case, the child of the ACA, the grandchild of the addict (GCoA) doesn't have any clear addiction to point to, to understand why their ACA parent is still so preoccupied with their families of origin, why they can be both loving and rageful, competent and so very complicated. As Judith Herman pointed out in *Trauma and Recovery,* "The terror of the traumatized infant intensifies the need for protective attachments therefore the traumatized person frequently alternates between isolation and anxious clinging to others," and Janet Woititz, author of *Adult Children of Alcoholics,* says that children of alcoholics "don't have relationships they take hostages." Adult children of alcoholics' parenting style can be a confusing mix of clinging and being unattuned because of their own unmet needs and unresolved pain. In fact, ACA parents can be very loving, but they also carry the ghosts of their pasts and that impacts the way they parent. Then the GCoAs wind up carrying their parents' pain *for them and from them* because their parents haven't dealt with their own ACA pain. They too are left shadowboxing with ghosts from the past, but no one is acknowledging that this is what is going on.

As I said previously, although addiction may skip a generation, trauma does not, so pain just keeps recreating itself. It is through the epigenetics of trauma and addiction that the pain simply passes from one generation to another, then the wheel of trauma and addiction makes another sinister turn through the generations. Another generation, the grandchildren of addicts, are at risk for self-medicating unconscious pain from unresolved addiction in the generations before them.

As adults, when we experience these disconnections with our intimate partners, we stand at a potentially intimidating size but feeling like a hurt, dismissed little kid. We fall back on the defenses we used to stay safe as a child and have little sense of the impact that our shut-down, anger, or tears has on our partner. Soon we're two children in adult bodies having a fight, and neither party can access mature enough states of mind to figure out how to climb out of it this dysfunctional interaction.

Through simple role plays, we can embody these moments of disconnection and make them more explicit and easy to understand. I often embody the transference (ghost) figures that we're dragging from out past and bring them onstage to stand behind the person we're trying to work something out with in our present. Just seeing this on stage can help clients to separate their childhood relationships from their adult ones.

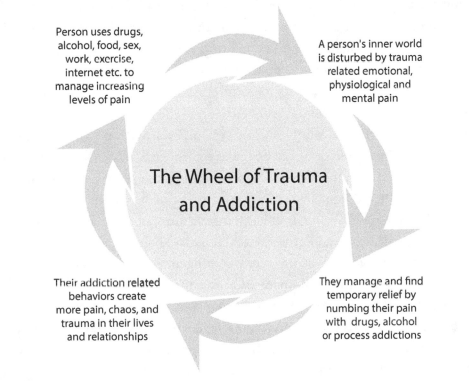

Person uses drugs, alcohol, food, sex, work, exercise, internet etc. to manage increasing levels of pain

A person's inner world is disturbed by trauma related emotional, physiological and mental pain

The Wheel of Trauma and Addiction

Their addiction related behaviors create more pain, chaos, and trauma in their lives and relationships

They manage and find temporary relief by numbing their pain with drugs, alcohol or process addictions

Modeling Drunken Thinking, Feeling, and Behavior

If you grow up with an alcoholic parent, you are modeling two people: the drunk or using parent and the sober one, Jekyll and Hyde. And you are madly trying to weave the two into some sort of a coherent whole. But try as you will, you just can't. So when treating ACAs or addicts (who themselves are often ACAs), we not only treat what is now understood as early attachment trauma; we often treat the kind of trauma that is unique to having a parent who is addicted.

It hurts to watch the parent you love act like a drunk, disorderly, embarrassing person. It hurts when they yell at you. Or your friends. Or your pet. When they run you down, call you names, slobber all over you, weird you out, and do all of the stuff that drunk people do. So you hide that too—from your relatives, from your friends, from your parents, teachers, neighbors . . . the mail carrier. You hide and you hide and you hide some more. And because you turn away from pain, you don't process it. You shut it down, you try to pretend something didn't happen almost at the same time as it's happening. So you hide if from yourself, too; or maybe mostly.

As I have said previously in this book, we relegate to our unconscious what hurt us most. That's what we act out; we unconsciously recreate what we internalized without knowing we even took it into our psyches and into our selves. Then we live it out exactly as it lives inside of us. Like brilliant actors, we reproduce the kinds of behaviors that we have witnessed and absorbed.

In stunning portrayals, ACAs reenter the psychic realm of drunken ghosts. We recreate the behavior we modeled from our parent while he or she was drunk or high on pills or drugs, even though we may be completely sober. When triggered, we take on the vocal tone, the body posturing, the thinking, and sometimes even the words of a parent when they were drunk or high. To complicate matters even further, the spouse of our addict may also have been locked in the "wet brain" of alcoholic thinking, feeling, and behavior, so the behaviors and thinking we recreate from them are still those of an alcoholic family system, even with no alcohol present. And we reenact it all with a seamless precision that can take your breath away. The tenor of our voice, our subtle motions and expressions, the rage and ridicule, and/or the set of our jaw can be an uncanny replica of what we saw, heard, and sensed. When this happens, whether in real interactions or through role play, I feel like I'm seeing double, almost rubbing my eyes and doubting what's right in front of me. But there it is: the addictive (or co-addictive) behavior of the family system that is so accurately portrayed that you feel as if you're watching an episode of *The Twilight Zone*, or that you're right smack-dab in the living room all ACAs seemed to grow up in.

I have always felt that this is one of the reasons that psychodrama is so popular in the addictions field: it is the only form of therapy that can recreate the emotional intensity that ACAs grew up with; it gets to those inner states and brings them to the stage so we can see what we carry inside of us so that the drama, through catharsis, can, as Aristotle advised in his *Poetics*, help us to rid ourselves of the pain we carry.

Talking to the Wrong Person, at the Wrong Place, at the Wrong Time

Sometimes ACAs have parents who get sober or are at least less dysfunctional. So when the ACA tries to talk with their parent about the hurt and confusion that the child inside of them still feels, they often feel like they are talking to the wrong person, at the wrong place, at the wrong time. The child in them may need to scream, kick, and cry, to experience a catharsis of deep pain, but when they want their now-sober or more mature parent to listen to this old pain, it doesn't always work so well. Even parents in recovery can find the extent of their adult child's pain unbearable, and they don't receive it well. Whether it's because it activates too much guilt, they don't remember or realize how much pain they caused, or they just don't want to be reminded varies, but ACAs still need to heal their childhood wounds so that they can move on and create healthier relationships in adulthood.

So the ACA may find themselves in a bind: *do I risk disturbing the more satisfying relationship I have with my now-sober parent by bringing up a past they don't necessarily even remember, or do I step around this elephant in the living room and just make the best of things?* Another bind that ACAs find themselves is that they have a long-time pattern of avoiding feeling their attachment pain, and they may have a pattern of projecting it where it doesn't belong because it's still quite unconscious.

The dilemma of ACAs is that we carry pain and anger from what amounts to a previous relationship from a previous time in life and with an almost previous person. Psychodrama lets us concretize and talk to the right person, at the right place, and at the right time through surrogates and role play. When we do psychodrama with an ACA, we're also working with the child who lives inside of them. Through role play, we can let the child speak fully and freely to an adult who represents *not the parent they have now, but the one they had then.* The child in them can rage, cry, and release their pain in a safe, therapeutic environment with support. They need to have their reality of that time and place witnessed and validated so that they can empathize, hold, understand, and grow up this part of themselves. They need to extricate the child who is frozen at a point in time from the past and walk them gently toward the future. As directors, we help these protagonists to reenter relational dynamics from childhood and slowly become conscious so that they can clearly see the defensive postures they used to stay safe then, and that they may be continuing to use now, and shift them into more nourishing and mutually satisfying forms of relating (Porges, personal communication, 2022).

Our complexes, drives, and longings have their locus or origin at some particular point in time. Through a specific, strategic role reconstruction, our inner adolescent can face the drunken father and release the torrent of emotion toward him that we're holding on to. Or our inner toddler can talk to the mother with an impassive, unempathetic face. We can explore the relational forces that caused us trauma at that time in our lives without pathologizing our entire self or the entire relationship. We can heal the particular role relationship from the time, space, and circumstance that needs healing and leave the rest of the role relationship—the better, healthier relationship of today—undisturbed. In this way, role reconstruction has the power to allow us to reenter a specific moment in time laparoscopically: relive it, say what we didn't get a chance to say, do what we didn't get a chance to do, and process the pain, anger, or disillusionment we have in association with it. In other words, we need to talk *as the child we were then to the parent we had then.* It is not that this is the only healing we may need on the subject, but it is an intervention into those less-than-fully-conscious relational patterns that form seeds of reenactment dynamics.

We can even have a re-formed auxiliary or a **moment of repair**, when we can choose the father we wish we'd had so that we can gain a felt sense of what it might have been like had it gone differently. Or, we can reshape a family scene, to be like the family as we wish it had been, placing ourselves where we wish we had stood and others where we might have longed for them to be. We can apply these same ideas to an enabling, dysfunctional, or mentally ill parent with whom we may also have lost a healthy connection.

Even if we don't want to return to a close relationship with a present-day parent, we're in a better position, if we get some healing, to let our relationship with our parent of today be whatever it is without feeling as trapped by it within ourselves.

Back to the Dyad: The Importance of Role Reversal

What we cannot feel in relationship to our primary caregivers, we too often learn to shut down within ourselves, and this is at the core of why we cannot use the inner presence of these attachment relationships—the introjects—as a path toward self- and interpersonal regulation.

We need to experience, and hopefully find healing for, both sides of the relational dynamic, maybe not in real life, but at least as it lives inside of us. This is where role reversal, which is unique to psychodrama, comes in and is a kind of therapy like no other for attachment issues. It turns out we don't need to say everything to the actual person who hurt us in order to heal; we just have to say it so that we can feel our own feelings, so that we can shape and reshape the role relationship, as it lives within us.

At the 2012 Republican National Convention in Tampa, Clint Eastwood gave a short speech where he used the technique of the empty chair to talk to Barack Obama. In the week following Eastwood's presentation, J. L. and Zerka Moreno's son Jonathan D. Moreno, professor of medical ethics and health policy at the University of Pennsylvania, published an article in the *New York Times* commenting on the actor's use of this technique developed by his mother Zerka Moreno, to support "so narrow a political vision." He openly criticized the actor, because for the empty chair to be effective, at least therapeutically, Eastwood would have had to include the other half of the dyadic equation that he had left out. "He neglected to 'reverse roles' and put himself in the place of Obama. This forgetting to reverse roles plagues many derivative forms of psychodrama but through the therapeutic theory and lens of psychodrama, it's a big mistake!" (Dark Hasidism, Rafael Baliardo 2020).

While a complete role reversal is not realistic, or perhaps even possible, the ability to mentally and—in the case of psychodrama—physically reverse roles with another person is experiential empathy training. The beauty of experiential role reversal is that we are forced to actually respond as another person might respond, which means that for a moment we're called on to think through their mind, feel through their heart, see through their eyes, and talk as them. Otherwise, it's not a true role reversal, just an imitation, a caricature.

Paradoxically, leaving the self by choice and intention through role reversal has the effect of strengthening rather than weakening it. As we enter the role of another, something surprising happens: we ourselves are made larger and stronger. Seeing ourselves as if through the eyes of another allows us to see not only them, but ourselves with greater clarity and objectivity. It makes us less invested in protecting our own space and more aware that we are sharing space with others. In terms of a relationship dynamic, it pulls back the thin and illusory veil that separates two people and lets us see how truly interconnected we are.

Talking to the Right Person, at the Right Place, at the Right Time

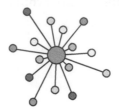

Note: If over time, the child's urge to connect was not met with an equally engaged attempt on the part of the parent, the child may have learned to withdraw or hide their deep need to be close. They may have over time lost touch with what a reciprocal, satisfying, intimate connection feels like or developed some hypervigilance around their desire to be connected. Or they may have developed a false self that was more acceptable to those around them and successful at garnering love and approval. This exercise seeks to bring more of this loss of connection to a conscious level.

Goals:

1. To give healing to the inner child.
2. To let the inner child talk to the parent they had at the age when a complex set in.

Steps:

1. Invite the protagonist to choose role players, one to play their wounded inner child and the other to play their parent at that period or age.
2. Ask the protagonist to set the scene by placing both their inner child and parent in the scene in whatever size relationship feels right. Say "set up a typical scene in which there was a painful interaction. It can be a model scene of a type of re-occurring dynamic." If the role players are not available you can use an empty chair.
3. Ask the protagonist to say something as their inner child self *then* to their parent *then*. After they have done this, they can reverse roles and become their parent and continue with the scene using doubling and role reversal throughout.
4. Whenever the scene draws naturally to a close say to the protagonist, "say the last things you want to say for now as your child self to the parent that you had then."
5. Return to seats and share and de-role psychodramatically (see Chapter 3: Psychodrama Basics).

You can do several of these in a row with group members then share, or you can share after each role play depending on the needs of the group.

This can also be done as experiential letter writing, in which case you would begin by writing a letter as your inner child at a particular time and place to the parent you had at that age.

Transference

Transference is a phenomenon named by psychoanalysts to describe how feelings from a relationship, usually in childhood and usually with parents, get redirected and transferred onto relationships in adulthood. We may unconsciously layer onto someone in our present qualities and characteristics of someone from our past, and we expect or even draw toward ourselves behaviors from them, both positive and negative, that we experienced previously.

Separating the Inner Child from One's Own Child

When ACAs or children of dysfunctional families become parents, they may confuse the natural pain of growing up in their own child with the unnatural pain that they experienced as children with addicted or mentally ill parents. The child that lives within the parent can get triggered by the age or stage that their own child enters. If the parent doesn't make this conscious, they are likely to layer their own pain from the past onto their child in the present. They will confuse their own unhealed historical pain with whatever their child is or even isn't going through, and set about fixing in their child what needs fixing inside them. The pain that their *inner child* carries will get projected onto the *child they have today*.

Addressing this psychodramatically is straightforward. Simply use two chairs, one to represent the parent's inner child and one to represent their child of today. This can be done as an exercise in a parenting group or worked into a psychodrama, should it naturally come up. For example, if a parent is doing a drama of talking to their child and the director senses that a confusion is taking place, the director might suggest, "Would you like a chair or a role player to represent the child inside you so you can talk to them directly?" By separating the roles on stage, the protagonist can uncouple them in his or her mind.

Parent Role Play: Separating the Inner Child from One's Own Child

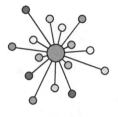

Goals:

1. To help parents to understand that we can sometimes confuse our inner child with our kids and project onto them what needs attention in ourselves.
2. To give a strong visual and experience of separating the protagonist's inner child from their actual child.

Steps:

1. Set up three chairs. In the first one, seat the parent who is currently in treatment. In the two chairs facing the parent, seat their actual child and their inner child.
2. Invite the parent to talk to their inner child or their actual child as feels natural. You will be doubling for the protagonist in the role of themselves, or in any role they have reversed into, and inviting group members to double. As director you will be calling out role reversals where appropriate. You can also use the soliloquy and role reversal interview as you feel it's useful.
3. Encourage the protagonist to have full interactions with their inner child and their actual child; they can feel like two dramas within one role play.
4. When it feels like the drama has drawn to a natural closure, invite the protagonist to say the last things they want to say to their inner child and then to their actual child.
5. Move into sharing or simply allow another group member to do this same set up until as many who wish to have worked. Share with the protagonist either after each one or after a few protagonists have worked.

Variations:

This can be followed up with more dramas or experiential letter writing with the inner child, the actual child, or the parent or any other parts of self or people it warms the protagonist up to.

Ghosts: Dealing with Transference Figures

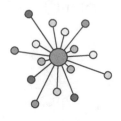

Goals:

1. To clarify transference figures from the past who are being reenacted in present day relationships.
2. To work out unfinished business from the past.

Steps:

1. Ask group members to think of a "presenting issue," e.g., a relational conflict that they repeatedly find themselves in with a spouse, child, friend, partner, authority figure or coworker.
2. Invite any group member to set this scene onstage, finding a role player to represent the person they are having a conflict or issue with.
3. Next, invite the protagonist to begin the scene from their own role, talking to the person with whom they are currently experiencing a conflict with. Encourage them to speak fully, incorporating role reversal and doubling.
4. When it seems that the scene is recreating the dynamic that keeps repeating itself, ask the protagonist, "Where and with whom did this type of conflictual interaction begin for you?"
5. Once the protagonist identifies that person, ask them to choose a role player or use an empty chair to represent that person with whom the conflict began, or the "ghost figure."
6. Locate the "ghost figure" behind and to the side of the person that the current conflict is with.
7. Invite the protagonist to talk to both the "ghost figure" or the other person as they choose, using role reversal and doubling throughout.
8. When the scene draws to a natural closure, invite the protagonist to say the last things they want to say from the role of self for now, both to the person they are in a current conflict with and to the "ghost figure."

9. Next "redo" the role relationships on stage using space to represent distance, closeness, etc. Invite the protagonist to put these two role players in a new and different relationship to themselves.
10. Next, ask the protagonist to do a new ending for each person, now in a different relationship to their role of self and to each other.
11. Let the group members de-role and share with the protagonist what came up for them.

Variations:

If the group is warmed-up to do so, you can do two or three of these and share after all have finished. In this case, have group members de-role first by saying, "I am 'so and so,' not the role I played. Playing the role, I felt . . ." (They share how it felt to be in that role). Then if anything came up from their own lives, they can share that after brushing off the role. "What came up for me in my own life was . . ."

Then all group members can share with the protagonist(s) what came up for them, from their own lives, witnessing the dramas. No feedback please in drama, only sharing from one's own life.

The Sociometric Protocol

Floor Checks

The Trauma Timeline/Resilience Timeline

Social Atoms

Experiential Letter Writing

Spectrograms, Locograms, and the "V" of Self-Regulation

On the following pages you'll see the basic protocol for bringing sociometrics into your work. See Chapter 14 for a discussion of how best to fit them into your own treatment setting.

CHAPTER SEVEN

Floor Checks: Get On Your Feet!

In a group, each person becomes the therapeutic agent of the other.
—J. L. Moreno

Floor checks came about almost by accident—or, more likely, by necessity.

It happened one day with Carlos, a trainee of mine who worked with a Latino population, helping them put broken lives back together. He came to group looking forlorn—none of his usual poise and pleasantness, his head hanging so low that his chin seemed to be making a groove in his chest. As I always do, I waited to give him a chance to come forward. Finally, I couldn't ignore it any longer and asked, "How are you doing, Carlos?"

"They want me to do therapy with thirty-five people," he said with an air of resignation and almost disbelief. "I can't do it. Thirty, thirty-five people and only me? They want me to help them . . . it's too many. I can't do it."

But I was his trainer, and I admired what he was trying to do. I regarded him highly as a clinician. He had such heart and passion for helping people. He was an addict himself who had gotten help and then become a Certified Addictions Counselor, and sought out further training because he was curious, had a feel for the work and truly wanted to be part of the solution. A very spiritual and committed man, his mission was to help his community find the peace and healing he had found. And my mission was to support his mission.

I thought that if ever there were a legitimate time to experiment with the ideas that had been germinating within me in my treatment and training groups, it was now. The budget cuts in New York state were affecting so many people. What did we have to lose by trying? Nothing was working anyway for these huge groups and their overwhelmed therapists; the situation required creativity. In order to work with these large numbers, I obviously had to access and rely on the healing power of the group itself, as there was only one therapist for thirty-five clients.

I leaned into two ways of working, one from Moreno, the other from Maria Montessori.

As a trained Montessori teacher, I admired Montessori's way of working with large groups of children through positioning the teacher as a "catalyst" between the learning materials and the structured learning environment and the child. As a trained psychodramatist and sociometrist, I leaned into Moreno's seminal idea that "in a group, each person becomes the therapeutic agent of the other."

I knew I had to create processes that connected group members with one another in a healing process. I knew the "learning environment" needed to be structured enough so clients could teach themselves and learn from each other. I knew I needed a process that could help clients access each other and become healing agents for each other. And lastly, the therapist needed to be removed from seeing themselves as the source of healing and knowledge. They needed to act as a catalyst between the group and the healing/learning environment. Their job was to keep the room safe, the group engaged with one another, and the process moving.

Whatever I came up with also had to require less training than psychodrama did because the need was so pressing, and those therapists who needed new tools didn't have years to train. So I leaned into sociometry. As Moreno was known to say, "We get them into the door with psychodrama, we heal them with sociometry." Psychodrama is riveting and moving to those watching, but the healing that goes on in sociometry is present-oriented and accomplishes the reconnection with the inner self and the relearning and practice of how to be in close connection with others that is so crucial to trauma healing and templating new behaviors. As Porges might say, we need to help clients to move from upregulated, defensive states to more relaxed prosocial states, and floor checks do just that.

I had recently been doing "feeling checks" in my work in treatment facilities and found them somewhat flat and too often inauthentic, so I thought I would play with those. My reasoning in this first exercise was that feelings were what seemed to get everyone into trouble because they caused addicts to relapse or anyone with a trauma history to blow up, withdraw, or shut down. We also need feelings to love, to feel passion, or to know what's going on within us, so I always saw becoming emotionally literate as an important part of any therapy. Managing feelings seemed a good place to start.

I knew Carlos had these large groups, and that was overwhelming to him and he didn't know what to do with them. So I showed up at the next group with a lot of feelings—the ones clients tended to come up with most often, scrawled on pieces of paper one at a time—and of course I added the ever-present designation of "other." In sociometry, we never feel we have thought of everything; "other" is where clients can write in their own feeling or symptom. I scattered the cards around the floor as a sort of check-in for the group. But unlike a typical "feeling check," I got people immediately out of their seats, tuning into their inner world and choosing a feeling from what was on the floor, then engaging with others. I asked criterion questions to move the process along. As I watched what people said, I was amazed—the spontaneity and creativity of the group just flowed. Feeling checks were no longer one word: "I'm *happy*," "I'm *excited*," "I'm *anxious*," rather they became imbued with more vulnerability. Clients were saying the most truthful and riveting things, so I kept asking questions, thinking they would surely get sick of the process, but they didn't; with each question, they just kept going deeper. Then I said things like "What questions would you like to see the group explore? Just call them out." So they did, and as they did, buy-in was created: they were part of driving the action.

Over the next couple of months, an odd thing happened: I began hearing about others who were using feeling checks. I hadn't shared this experiment with anyone, fearing that psychodramatists would find it too structured for their taste. I was doing this simply because I knew it was needed and I wanted to help Carlos. But my trainees had apparently taught colleagues about them, and they had further shared it. It was lovely and surprising.

But as the **feeling floor check** circulated in this grassroots way over a period of only weeks, I began to think that I might try using floor checks to teach concepts as well. Because the feeling checks were working so well, I burrowed into studies and research done on emotions. I realized that I was developing a process wherein the emergent skills being learned where those of emotional containment, emotional literacy, emotional intelligence, and emotional regulation—the basics for healing trauma and addiction.

Part of the program development I was doing was creating lectures to educate clients as to trauma symptoms they might be experiencing. I observed that clients sometimes found the symptom lists overwhelming—especially the talks on trauma—and people tended to turn off after six or seven symptoms, which meant that they couldn't learn about the others. I thought I might try putting PTSD symptoms around the floor on pieces of paper, as a sort of psychoeducational prepared environment, and create questions that could do two things: 1) give them the freedom to choose for themselves which symptoms they might be experiencing, and 2) connect them with each other so that they could share in more intimate dyads and clusters as to how those symptoms might be showing up in their lives.

Something truly fascinating began to happen. There was a quiet explosion of alive and rich case studies popping up all over the room as people got in touch with the symptoms that they themselves were experiencing and shared how they were playing out in their lives. The education that needed to happen in a treatment center was pulled off of the chalkboard and put onto the floor in a live, experiential, relational process. No more canned case studies or lectures. Clients were creating the process together as each person shared moving examples of how symptoms manifested in their lives. The material came alive, and participants were making it relevant to themselves and to each other. The learning was palpable; they could mill around and could choose for themselves where they did or did not identify, cutting their own path of healing and discovery as they did. They became curious about their own inner worlds and more open to and engaged with the inner worlds of others.

In the floor check everyone was on their feet, grounded and oriented in the room, and there were many incremental, unthreatening opportunities to share. Sticky issues became normalized and made visible and real by spontaneous case examples that popped up around the room through everyone's individual sharing.

Floor checks seemed to help clients to find their way through internal places that glued them to the past and come forward into the present-oriented, relational moment as they interacted with others over shared issues. It was a process that helped the client come to the threshold of their own ever-evolving awareness, a form of experiential therapy that activated the social engagement system in easy but slightly challenging ways so that clients could relearn how to connect in comfortable ways and take that learning with them into their lives.

This process warmed clients up to doing healing work. It can be befuddling for clients to be asked to come up with what they want to "work on" before they have had time to let deeper themes and inner states emerge within them. The very nature of the instinctual trauma response means that much trauma-related pain is fairly unconscious. Floor checks and the trauma timeline appeared to offer interesting ways to wade into this material and let it become slowly conscious.

Once I felt comfortable that the kinks were worked out and I had spent a couple of years testing floor checks in my groups, trainees' groups, and in small treatment settings, I took them on the road and trained therapists around the country to do them. Again, the consistency and predictability amazed me. Whether I was in California, Arizona, Tennessee, New Jersey, Utah, or New York, the process looked the same at all of its various stages. The group was engaged and connected, and group size was now a seemingly moot point. With groups of thirty to thirty-five, it was now entirely possible to provide both an educational and a healing experience. When I began using them with groups of one to two hundred, I was pleasantly surprised to find out that they worked wonderfully, but doing them with a group of a thousand for the state agencies of New Jersey blew my mind. Probably two-thirds of that group participated, but the process worked just as it always did, except the clusters were larger and there were more of them. Healing was in the hands of the group. As long as I provided the structured process that allowed group members to connect around mutually involving material, they were able to heal themselves and each other. I felt as if I were looking from the ceiling down at a Swiss clock, as there on the floor, grouping after grouping formed, clustering around the words/symptoms/issues written on the floor cards and moving, with each new question, into new clusters. There was chatter, movement, and laughter and tears, just like there always had been. Had I closed my eyes, I would have thought I was at a party. And in each other's presence, there was member-to-member co-regulation happening naturally.

To Review the Process and History a Bit

If you only add floor checks and timelines to your work, you will have added an experiential component to programming that will change your work and the experience of your groups. You will find that your groups are on their feet, grounded in the room, making choices, and engaging and bonding with each other. For this reason, I want to go over my thinking behind floor checks so that they will be fully understood.

First, in creating them, as a therapist, I had to let go of the notion that healing had to come from me. To do this I used what I knew well: Moreno's process of experiential healing and Montessori's processes of experiential learning. I also incorporated the ideas of healing through identification and sharing, core to twelve-step programs and the idea of mammalian limbic resonance present in all groups, including groups of animals.

Maria Montessori was a pioneer in turn-of-the-century Vienna, as were Moreno and Freud. She was the first woman doctor of her time; she was given children to teach who were thought to be unteachable in a poor section of the town, much like Moreno found work with prostitutes. She taught them to read, write, and do math, which was seen as remarkable, thus breaking down the stereotypes of her time. Montessori developed the idea of a prepared learning environment, in which there were learning materials created for children and they were free to choose what they wanted to work on at any given moment. She believed children went through "sensitive periods" in their learning and that they needed to access learning materials that were right for them at those times. I feel that recovery is a sensitive period for learning life and emotional processing skills, and treatment centers are like recovery schools. The role of the teacher in Montessori's classroom is to act as a catalyst between the child and the environment or the learning materials. It was an enlightened, efficient, and practical approach that allowed her to work with large groups of children.

Adapting her ideas, I saw my prepared environment as the research-based **floor cards**, which became the learning materials, and the therapist's role was to act as a catalyst between the clients and the learning materials and to keep the process safe and moving.

Twelve-step communities are all about healing through this kind of connection by sharing our "experience, strength, and hope" with like-minded people. Groups are divided into categories that are essentially sociometrically aligned according to "issues" or subject matter. There are separate groups for alcohol addiction, drug addiction, food issues, compulsive sexual activity, money issues, codependency, and so on. Family members of addicts can also find groups of people who are going through what they are going through. These groups are profoundly healing, are easily accessed, and can be part of ongoing healing and creating a new design for living. Twelve-step work had taught me, a day at a time, about the powerful healing forces at work in a group of like-minded people. I just had to make the mental adjustment that I was not necessarily the most important person in the room in terms of delivering therapy; as the youngest of four children myself, it wasn't hard for me to do. I preferred it, in fact.

I have to admit that I had one more inspiration: horses. My neighbor in the country raised racehorses, and once a year we all heard the heartbreaking sound of a mare and her colt or filly whinnying across the paddocks to each other when they were separated. One year it stopped, and my neighbor shared with me that they had begun separating them one at a time. When they did this, the horses were able to manage the process and co-regulate on their own. The new mares adopted the new colt or filly, and the mares who had lost their little ones adopted those still near to them. It was a stunning example of the power of mammalian co-regulation. I have learned that groups of people, also mammals, behave similarly. So in doing floor checks and timelines, I know limbic resonance is always taking place, groups regulate each other and they contain the affective atmosphere, the process.

Moreno's locograms gave me the original idea of using the floor as part of the process. But locograms allow for only four choices and there is no educational component, so the locogram process is very quick. By extending the potential choices to twelve or sixteen and integrating research to use as the "prepared learning environment," I could make Moreno's adage that in a group each person becomes the therapeutic agent of each other work in a whole new way. And if I added role plays, they were focused, and the protagonist had already done much of their healing. This made the warm-up and sharing primary, and longer parts of the process and the role plays secondary and shorter. Floor checks and timelines answered the needs of the treatment world I was working in. I have also shared floor checks with people who use them in the business world, faith-based institutions, and for networking. All you do is change the learning materials on the floor cards and create criterion questions that are specific to the population you're working with.

Reducing Questioning and Intellectualization

Another safeguard that appeared as a bonus to me was that this process automatically reduced the kind of questioning that therapists sometimes did in a misguided effort to get to the truth, to get underneath the trauma. I had been experiencing this in my own work and was validated when I came upon Bessel van der Kolk's admonition not to go after trauma through too much questioning. Too much questioning could shut people down or make them think they had to come up with a good answer. On the other hand, connecting with each other over specific criteria seemed to wake them up and put them in touch with their inner world in a nonthreatening way. The criterion questions were impersonal—thrown out to the whole group, and participants were free to choose their own answers. The groupings felt supportive, and co-regulating; participants could share vulnerably and take in what others were saying without feeling put on the spot. It could become playful and game-like as people moved about the room on their own volition—they joked, hugged, patted each other on the back, and shed tears—all in the same grouping.

I began to realize that I had something that really held together. I had never seen anything quite like it. I had found a way to make psychodrama and sociometry into informed experiential, psychoeducational processes that were easier for clinicians to learn and use. And this solved some of the lack of training issues that I was always dealing with, in training clinicians to do experiential work safely.

I am often asked if floor checks are the same as locograms; they are not. Floor checks incorporate research. While locograms are a wonderful way of checking in and getting snapshots of where the group is, floor checks are an extensive psychoeducational process. The research-based floor cards in floor checks are many in number and allow for repeated choices and for clustering, sharing, and listening; they provide for ever-evolving, varied, and ongoing small groupings. They allow the client to get what I call "safely triggered"—to experience emotion coming up around a targeted criterion specific to treatment and recovery; to share it, listen, let it go, and move on; then not and shed its intensity and recalibrate for a moment within themselves. Group members find each other by choosing similar criterion questions that stimulate mutual identification and safe connection. Then they choose again and follow the same process. And all of this time they are learning the material that needs to be taught throughout treatment. The size of group is really no issue; I have done floor checks successfully with groups from eight to seven hundred members. Groups of one hundred to two hundred are so lively that no one wants to stop doing them. When I interrupt them to ask a new question, I always love it when the group silently colludes to ignore me. At a certain point in the process, they are more engaged with each other than me. They no longer want to get it right for the leader; they want to get it right for themselves and each other. They are immersed in their own process.

Giving Information: Creating Buy-In

An advantage of floor checks and sociometrics is that they develop curiosity, intellectual buy-in, and a willingness to own one's truth of the moment. They make clients stakeholders in their own recovery process, helping them to move past their resistance. Addicts enter treatment through many portals—interventions, pressure from the workplace, pressure from family members, internal pressure, and more. In other words, they don't necessarily come skipping through the door dying to work on themselves. They may feel some resistance and suspicion and carry unconscious pain that they have been managing with substances and addictive behaviors that we, as professionals, are asking them to give up. Providing information so that clients can wrap their minds around their own disease process reduces anxiety.

Personally, if I go to the dentist's office to get a tooth pulled, I want as much information as possible in order to manage it. As an intelligent person, I want to be given sufficient information so that I can make an informed decision as to, say, what kind of pain management I will choose.

Should it be sodium pentothal or Novocain? Until I can wrap my mind around the particulars of what I am dealing with, I am not fully onboard. Information makes me less anxious about what's to come and more open to being cooperative with the doctors and nurses who will, after all, have their hands in my mouth. Why should therapy be any different? Our process as therapists is at least as intrusive.

This may be part of why the addictions field intuitively found its way to psychoeducation: it helps people to take ownership of their own recovery process. Sociometrics allow clients to feel more in charge of what they wish to explore. It's frightening and unnecessary to be told you have all sorts of problems you need to get over. Sociometrics chunk symptoms down into manageable portions that teach and heal simultaneously, so that clients can feel included in their own healing, respected, and informed.

Adapting Floor Checks to Fit Your Population

Adapting floor checks is a simple matter of creating floor cards and criterion questions that are appropriate for the populations you are working with. Floor checks can be made specific to any gender, age group, race, religion, language, workplace, or to any situation. You can create floor checks that reflect the interests of the group by changing the words on the floor cards that will be explored. The process remains the same, but the floor cards can change. The material being shared always arises from the group members themselves, so floor checks are culturally, racially, and gender sensitive. The group itself provides content, and that content is naturally specific to that group. Then therapists or group members can come up with their own criterion questions around these issues or subjects that they might wish to explore. There is an intellectual rigor that is very satisfying for clients in understanding the symptomology of any given exploration, be it grief, PTSD symptoms, or the many ways in which fear, anxiety, or anger might manifest.

Feeling Floor Check: Examining and Expanding My Feeling Palette

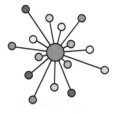

Goals:

1. To expand a restricted range of affect that can be the result of trauma.
2. To allow the group to become comfortable identifying, articulating, and sharing emotion.
3. To allow the group to connect with each other around vulnerable emotions, share, and take in sharing and support.
4. To teach and develop emotional literacy and emotional intelligence.
5. To help clients learn to "tolerate" and talk about painful emotions so that they are less likely to act them out and relapse over them.
6. To help clients learn to "tolerate" and talk about positive and self-affirming emotions so that they are less likely to relapse over them.
7. To mobilize the social engagement system in service of healing and developing the skills of self-regulation and c-regulation.

Steps:

1. On eight-by-ten-inch pieces of paper, write "feeling" words such as angry, sad, mistrustful, anxious, despairing, self-conscious, content, hopeful, ashamed, guilty, frustrated, desperate, happy, etc.
   - Angry
   - Sad
   - Mistrustful
   - Anxious
   - Despairing
   - Hopeless
   - Self-conscious
   - Content/happy

- Hopeful
- Ashamed
- Engaged
- Withdrawn
- Guilty
- Frustrated
- Desperate
- Other

Mark one paper "other" so clients can write in their own emotion. You may leave a few pieces of paper blank for the group members to write in their own feeling words if you choose.

2. Place the words a couple of feet apart from each other, scattered around the floor.

3. Ask participants to "stand on or near" the feeling that best describes their mood of the moment.

4. Say, "Whenever you are warmed-up, share in a sentence or two as to why you are standing where you're standing."

5. After all who wish to have shared, allow the group to repeat the process and stand on another feeling that they might also be experiencing (*note: learning to "hold" more than one feeling at a time helps clients to tolerate living in "gray" rather than "black and white"*), then share as before.

6. At this point, you can vary the next criterion questions by asking the following:
   - Which feeling do you avoid feeling?
   - Which feeling did your family avoid feeling?
   - Which feeling did your family of origin struggle with or get stuck in too much of the time?

7. If the group still has energy to continue to explore more questions, you can further vary criterion questions by asking the following:
   - Which feeling do you have trouble tolerating in someone else?
   - Which feeling would you like to experience more of in your life?
   - Which feeling used to drag you down but now you have learned how to manage it better?

8. If you'd like to extend the process you can invite the group members to "place your hand on the shoulder of someone who shared something with which you identified." Group members can share directly with the person as to why they chose him or her. The entire group can do this at once, which can create a nice feeling of connectedness in the room or even a bit of a buzz.

9. Or simply sit down and share about the entire process and what came up throughout.

Role plays may emerge at any point in this process if the therapist is comfortable leading them, they can do so. Role plays can also include body awareness. Therapists can learn to observe the body and face in order to see if emotions are coming up first in the body that can be given a voice. And as clients do role plays, they can become aware of how their body feels, and the therapist can say, "If that part of you had a voice, what would it say?" Role plays can be done with inner parts or body states, e.g., my anxious self, my hypervigilant/triggered self, or anyone the protagonist wishes to talk to. They can also be done with a child self or a future self.

Symptom Floor Check: Learning About and Assessing PTSD Issues and Emotions

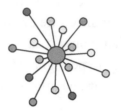

Goals:

1. To educate clients as to the range of symptoms that can accompany relationship trauma.
2. To provide a format through which clients can decide for themselves which symptoms they feel they identify as experiencing in their own lives and relationships.
3. To create opportunities to hear about how symptoms manifest for other people and in other people's lives and relationships.
4. To encourage connection, sharing, and support around facing difficult personal issues.
5. To educate clients as to how to trade a pathological symptom for a healthy trait.

Steps:

1. On large pieces of paper write these symptoms or characteristics of relationship trauma:
   - Cultivation of a false self
   - Hypervigilance/anxiety: waiting for the other shoe to drop
   - Overreactions/hyperreactivity/easily triggered
   - Problems with self-regulation
   - Learned helplessness/collapse
   - Emotional constriction
   - Relationship issues
   - Somatic disturbances: body aches and pains
   - Learning issues
   - Loss of trust and faith in relationships and an orderly world
   - Traumatic bonding
   - Unresolved grief
   - Depression with feelings of despair
   - Distorted reasoning
   - Loss of ability to take in caring and support from others

- Tendency to isolate or withdraw
- Cycles of reenactment: repeating painful relationship patterns
- High-risk behaviors: speeding, sex, spending/debting, working
- Survival guilt: shame
- Development of rigid psychological defenses: denial, dissociation, splitting, minimization, intellectualization
- Desire to self-medicate with drugs, alcohol, food, sex, money, work
- Other

2. Place the papers with symptoms on them a couple of feet apart scattered around the floor.
3. Ask participants to stand on or near a characteristic that they identify as being a problem for them in their lives.
4. Ask participants to walk toward one of these symptoms they have trouble containing or they act out around.
5. Once group members are standing on the characteristic that they identify with, invite them to share a sentence or two about why they are standing where they are standing.
6. Next invite group members to stand on or near a trait or symptom that they feel was present either in someone in their family of origin or in their family of origin as a whole that created problems.
7. Once group members are standing on the characteristic that they identify with, invite them to share a sentence or two about why they are standing where they are standing. A resilience-building question might be, "Which characteristic do you feel used to be a problem for you but you have worked your way through?" (see variations for more suggestions).
8. After group members have shared about one, two, or three characteristics say, "Walk over to someone who shared something that you identified with or that moved you, place a hand on their shoulder and share with them what moved you." *Note: the sharing will be taking place in dyads and subgroups that will naturally and spontaneously form as a result of this question.* The therapist may vary questions, e.g.:
   - "Which symptom do you have the toughest time dealing with in other people?" or
   - "Which symptom seemed to be the most present in your family or origin?" or
   - "Which symptom do you feel you recreate the most on your present day life?"
   - A resilience-building question might be, "Walk over to someone from whom you feel you could learn something and ask them for help."

9. At this point the group may be ready to sit down and share about the experience so far or move into role plays.

Variations:

You can follow up by putting two chairs in the center of the stage and inviting group members to "place a symptom or someone they associate with a symptom in the chair or represent them with a role player and do a short role play including the techniques of psychodrama."

And/or invite group members to "upgrade" their symptoms, to trade in one for a trait they would like their symptom to morph into, e.g., "I would like to trade learned helplessness for a chosen position of surrender," or "hypervigilance for awareness," or "a loss of trust and faith with renewed faith in Higher Power," and so on. As they do this, let them write their "upgrade" on a sheet of paper and place it next to or on top of the symptom. Allow them to do this for any symptoms with which they identify.

During sharing you may invite clients to share what qualities they feel they developed through adversity or what the silver linings are for them in having gone through a particular circumstance.

Journaling:

1. **Letting the Child Speak.** Mentally reverse roles with yourself while in the throws of any one of the trauma characteristics and journal from that place. For example, "I feel helpless . . . I get this way whenever . . ." and so on, or "I am feeling so emotionally constricted I just want to . . ."

2. **A Moment of Repair.** Journal about a time when repair occurred; write about how you felt during or after a moment of repair (apology, reconnection, repair of some sort) within the relationship and what positive lessons you learned about relationship repair from it that you might still be living out in your life.

Fear and Anxiety Floor Check

Goals:

1. To allow the group members to broaden their concept of the many ways in which fear/anxiety manifest.
2. To give the group a chance to get safely triggered, to talk out rather than act out, and to develop new ways of behaving when triggered.

Steps:

1. On large pieces of paper, write the following symptoms of anxiety:
   - Constantly feeling overwhelmed or under the gun
   - Somatic health issues
   - Fear of retribution or punishment if life works out
   - Caretaking too much
   - Talking too much
   - Sleep issues
   - Tightness in chest or muscles, back aches or headaches, body aches
   - Hypervigilance, always waiting for the other shoe to drop
   - Fear of panic attacks
   - Irrational fears or free-floating anxiety
   - Over controlling people places and things
   - Phobias, creepy crawlies, agoraphobia, etc.
   - Guilt
   - Chronic regrets or feeling you have missed out
   - Transference
   - Projection
   - Blaming
   - Withdrawing, shutting down
   - Other

2. Scatter the papers a couple of feet apart.

3. Ask participants to "stand on or near" the manifestation of anxiety they identify with the most.

4. Once group members are standing on the emotion that they identify with, invite them to share a sentence or two about why they are standing where they are standing.

5. Invite members to make another choice and repeat the sharing. Most of us have more than one way that anxiety manifests.

6. As you progress, repeat this process by choosing any criterion from the following list or create your own questions that feel relevant to the group you're working with. Group members may also come up with questions that they may wish to explore. *Note: The group may be saturated after three or four questions, and then you can move on to the next step.*

   • Which form of anxiety is generally your go to in terms of how it shows up for you in your life and/or relationships?

   • What type of anxiety do you have the hardest time coping with or fear the most?

   • Which form of anxiety do you have trouble containing or tolerating and how does that manifest?

   • Which form of anxiety creates problems for you in relationships?

   • Walk over to the anxiety that you have the hardest time dealing with in someone else?

   • Which form of anxiety did your family get stuck in a lot?

   • How vulnerable do feel opening up and sharing about anxiety?

   • Which form of anxiety was a problem but you have learned to cope successfully with?

7. After group members have shared about one, two, or three qualities say, "Walk over to someone who shared something that you identified with or that moved you, stand next to them, and share with them what moved you." *Note: the sharing will be taking place in dyads and subgroups that will naturally and spontaneously form as a result of this question.*

8. At this point the group may be ready to sit down and share about the experience so far or to move into role plays talking to a person they feel warmed-up to encounter or to a part of self.

Variations:

Group members can share so that the entire group can hear them or, if the group is large, they can share with those who are standing on the same characteristic that they chose. When they share "around their characteristic or symptom," they will be sociometrically aligned by symptom, i.e., all those experiencing a particular symptom will be sharing with others experiencing that symptom. This subgrouping can make sharing feel safer and can allow clients to feel seen, supported, and more open. The symptom-choosing can go on as long as it is useful, depending on the needs of the group. Generally, the group is saturated by the third choice and needs to move into sharing or role plays.

Anger/Resentment Floor Check

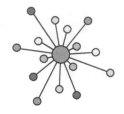

Goals:
---

1. To allow the group members to broaden their concept of the many ways in which anger manifests.
2. To provide a sociometric exercise for the exploration of anger.

Steps:
---

1. Print out anger floor check words such as, cynicism, negativity, criticism, sarcasm, digging in heels, passive aggression, whining, rage, acting out behaviors, violence, stonewalling, withdrawal, cut off, coldness, other, and so on.
2. Scatter the papers a couple of feet apart.
3. Ask participants to stand on or near the manifestation of anger they identify the most with.
4. Once group members are standing on the emotion that they identify with, invite them to share a sentence or two about why they are standing where they are standing.
5. As you progress, repeat this process by choosing any criterion from the following list or create your own questions that feel relevant to the group you're working with. Group members may also come up with questions that they may wish to explore. *Note: The group may be saturated after three or four questions, and then you can move on.*
   - Which manifestation of anger do you avoid?
   - Which manifestation of anger did your family avoid?
   - Which emotion are you working on feeling more of?
   - Which manifestation of anger have you gotten better at since you've been here?
   - Which manifestation of anger did your family get stuck in a lot?
   - Which manifestation of anger do you have trouble tolerating in others?
   - Which manifestation of anger do you have trouble containing and how does it look when you can't contain it?

- Which manifestation of anger have you become more aware of in yourself recently and are learning to cope with in healthy ways?

6. After group members have shared about one, two, or three qualities say, "Walk over to someone who shared something that you identified with or that moved you, stand next to them, and share with them what moved you." *Note: the sharing will be taking place in dyads and subgroups that will naturally and spontaneously form as a result of this step.*

7. At this point the group may be ready to sit down and share about the experience so far.

Variations:

Group members can share so that the entire group can hear them or, if the group is large, they can share with those who are standing on the same characteristic that they chose. When they share "around their characteristic or symptom," they will be sociometrically aligned by symptom, i.e., all those experiencing a particular symptom will be sharing with others experiencing that symptom. This subgrouping can make sharing feel safer and can allow clients to feel seen, supported, and more open. The symptom choosing can go on as long as it is useful, depending on the needs of the group. Generally, the group is saturated by the third choice and needs to move into sharing, journaling, or psychodrama. On tiandayton.com under "guided imageries," I have a guided imagery for processing anger. This can be helpful to group members if they will learn how to process their own anger, and they can also do the guided imagery on their own when they leave treatment.

During sharing you may invite clients to share what qualities they feel they developed through adversity or what the silver linings are for them in having gone through a particular circumstance.

Depression Floor Check

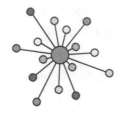

Goals:
---

1. To educate clients as to the range of symptoms that can be part of depression.
2. To provide a format through which clients can choose for themselves which symptoms they feel they identify as experiencing in their own lives and relationships.
3. To create opportunities to hear about how symptoms manifest for others so as to normalize negative feelings about the self.
4. To encourage connection, sharing, and support around facing difficult personal issues.
5. To create opportunities to reach out and connect in healthy ways.

Steps:
---

1. On large pieces of paper, write these symptoms of depression:
   - Anger
   - Sadness
   - Withdrawal
   - Social isolation
   - Obsessive thoughts/dark rumination
   - Trouble sleeping
   - Lack of energy
   - Anxiety
   - Irrational fears
   - Trouble concentrating or remembering
   - Loss of appetite
   - Aches and pains that don't go away
   - Fatigue/exhaustion
   - Shame/guilt
   - Digestive issues
   - Headaches

- Changes in weight
- Back pain
- Agitated/restless
- Sexual problems
- Diet/nutrition
- Smoking/self-medicating
- Self-harming
- Other

2. Place the papers with symptoms on them a couple of feet apart.

3. Ask participants to stand on or near a characteristic that draws them, that they experience as a way that their depression manifests in their lives.

4. Once group members are standing on the characteristic that they identify with, invite them to share a sentence or two about why they are standing where they are standing.

5. As you progress, repeat this process by choosing any criterion from the following list or create your own questions that feel relevant to the group you're working with. Group members may also come up with questions that they may wish to explore. *Note: The group may be saturated after three or four questions and then you can move on.*
   - Which form of depression manifests for you the most?
   - Which manifestation of depression triggers you the most when you encounter it in another person?
   - Which manifestation do you have the hardest time sitting with or containing and what do you do at those times?
   - Which one of these issues have you been successful in dealing with, i.e. you used to struggle with it more before than you do now?
   - Which of these issues do you feel you inherited from the dynamics on your family of origin?
   - Which of these issues do you feel most hopeful about?
   - Which of these issues do you feel most hopeless about?

6. After group members have shared about one, two, or three characteristics say, "Walk over to someone who shared something that you identified with or that moved you, stand next to them and share with them what moved you." *(Note: the sharing will be taking place in dyads and subgroups that will naturally and spontaneously form as a result of this question.)*

7. At this point the group may be ready to sit down and share about the experience or move into role plays.

The therapist may vary questions, e.g., "Which manifestation do you have the toughest time dealing with in other people?" or "Which manifestation seemed to be the most present in your family or origin?" or "Which manifestation do you feel you recreate the most on your present day life?" A resilience-building question might be, "Walk over to someone from whom you feel you could learn something and ask them for help."

During sharing you may invite clients to share what qualities they feel they developed through adversity or what the silver linings are for them in having gone through a particular circumstance.

CHAPTER EIGHT

Reclaiming Lost Parts of the Self: The Trauma Timeline and the Resilience Timeline

Some people's lives seem to flow in a narrative; mine had many stops and starts. That's what trauma does. It interrupts the plot. You can't process it because it doesn't fit with what came before or what comes afterward. A friend of mine, a soldier, put it this way. In most of our lives, most of the time, you have a sense of what is to come. There is a steady narrative, a feeling of "lights, camera, action" when big events are imminent. But trauma isn't like that. It just happens, and then life goes on. No one prepares you for it.
—Jessica Stern, *Denial: A Memoir of Terror*

I first described the trauma timeline in my book *The Living Stage* in 1994. It has moved through many permutations —adding resilience factors and empowering moments to name a couple— but ultimately, I have found it more useful to break those out into separate timelines. The reason I have used it as the trauma timeline is because this approach has yielded the most consistent and reliable results.

In the 1980s, when I began working with trauma, I encountered what felt like a hurdle. The grief work I had been doing was successfully addressing pain associated with loss, but still, for those working through trauma, there was an absence of a sense of context. More often than not, when clients talked about their trauma, their minds got foggy. There was little "where and when": some memories were highly specific, while others were indistinct, vague, confused, and fragmented. The way the thinking mind shut down during frightening encounters, dynamics, or events meant that there wasn't the kind of intellectual processing that allowed for a clear time and place to be identified. And defenses, such as dissociation against integrating painful events or interactions, meant that traumatic times were often not processed, filed away, and categorized in the mind. Rather, they appeared strewn throughout the mind/body in a curious combination of sense memories, emotions, and occasionally crystal-clear recollections.

Part of the problem seemed to me to be that at this time trauma work was focused on events or abuse; people were trying to make sense of their trauma by naming events that were traumatic. But the kind of trauma I was seeing was generally relational. Certainly, there were events and scenes that stood out to clients and merited exploration, but their problem was how the people they grew up with impacted the way they saw themselves, how those people shaped who they were on the inside. It was the meaning that they made out of the relational experiences of their lives that they were still living by, and importing into their partnering and parenting, that I was interested in exploring with them. It seemed to me that those with PTSD had become fixed on perceptions about life and relationships that they developed when they were young, that came to feel unalterable and were difficult to get underneath.

Essentially, this is what we talk about throughout this book: how to use psychodrama and sociometrics to get underneath these interpretations and change them. I found a pitfall here that therapists often fell into, particularly in treatment centers when there is pressure to do a lot of work in a short amount of time. Because it can be so frustrating to sit with these complex defenses, we either want to push clients beyond their capacity—to make them see too much, too fast—or we do too little, feeling helpless and collapsed along with them, and we sort of go along with anything they say. Or—and this one is common—we get heady and interpretive and essentially try to glue them to a new set of perceptions, reversing course and offering equally unattuned and impersonal "solutions" to their pain.

I began asking clients to make what I called their trauma timeline. Initially I simply wanted to give them a way to allow the moments, circumstances, or relational dynamics of their lives to find their way out of the malaise of what appeared to be foggy and indistinct recollections and to be put down on paper so that they would feel less confusing. I wanted to open the door for context to emerge around what appeared to be disembodied events or dynamics that felt as though they had occurred outside of normal time and space.

I tried every sort of permutation and time separation, but the most efficient proved to be simply to draw a line on the long side of a piece of typing paper and divide the line into five-year intervals. I would say something not overly specific, such as "Just write in moments, circumstances, or periods in your life or relational dynamics that caused you to disconnect with parts of yourself, that you still feel pain around." As group members did this, they became absorbed by and curious about their own story.

I was surprised at how my trainees used it and reported that it provided a way into the work that was not so overwhelming that people felt they had to shut down. Rather, it appeared to help them to open up. Its flexibility made it user-friendly, as it could be done on paper in virtually any therapeutic setting, from groups to one-to-one. And it was developmental, as trauma was entered according to age. It allowed clients to see a trauma narrative emerge almost on its own. They were no longer overwhelmed by being asked questions like, "Can you tell me about your trauma?" that put them in a position of trying to come up with an answer that they couldn't come up with, as much of their "story" was still unconscious. Rather they just watched as these moments and dynamics found their way onto the paper, and their trauma talked to them.

I kept the questions I asked very flexible, for example: "Just enter what hurt enough that you had to shut down around it, or that led you to suck in a breath that you haven't let out fully, or withdrew into yourself." Some of the most common observations clients made were things such as "I didn't realize that period in my life didn't have much trauma in it. Because I could never talk about it, I guess it felt like I had trauma all the time." There it was, right in front of me: the way that unresolved trauma doesn't let you go, that you continue to relive it whether or not there is more trauma, that it feels as if it's still there. "I see how I reenacted what went on my childhood. I just recreated it here, and here, and here. . . . I just kept it going." I was fascinated by what people were saying. Others in good recovery might say, "Even though traumatic things have happened since I got into recovery, they didn't feel as traumatizing. The pain didn't last because I was processing it as I was feeling it."

Before I knew it, I was hearing about people using the trauma timeline as a basic part of their treatment protocol. It has popped up as part of other systems' approaches, in books, and even on YouTube. It became embraced as if it had always been there. So now I am rolling it all back and explaining how it began and how and why I developed it.

Some clients' timelines may begin before they were born. A child of intergenerational trauma may carry a powerful family or racial history that feels bigger than their present family. They may need to walk backward into time to gain the information they're looking for or extend their timelines backward on the paper. Or the timeline may need to stretch forward into the future if clients carry a sense of overpowering expectations, either positive or negative, that in some way inhibit their ability to live productively in the present. Perhaps they have parents who loom large, either because of their super successes or their large failures, and that legacy feels all-consuming.

Laying events out on a timeline can also help a client to connect with the self they were before their lives took a painful turn. Connecting with a previous, more trusting and lighthearted self can be an important part of healing and can bring up a lot of feelings, ranging from sadness at years lost to awakening an innocence and sense of goodness within. I am well aware that some clients don't have any period in their lives to return to that feels free of trauma. But over the years I have come to realize that childhood itself has protective factors built into it that somehow shelter a self that remains precious and even pure, so reconnecting with that part of the self is also very worthwhile.

As people lay their trauma history on a timeline, their ways of coping may emerge as well, and they may have a sense of some of the strengths that they developed through adversity in addition to coping strategies that got them into trouble. A resilience timeline can be made to reflect on and consolidate these gains.

Developing a Connection between the Wounded Self and the Mature Self

Creating a connection between the child self and the adult self is one of the desired outcomes of working with the trauma timeline. Traumatized people sometimes talk from their childhood wounds to the world and then feel disappointed when the world doesn't want to hear them. In this way they recreate their childhood pain in their adult relationships. We need to train clients to get their child self to talk to their more mature adult self before blurting out all their childhood wounds at the world and expecting the world to understand. Strengthening the inner dialogue between the thinking, rational adult and the child mind is critical for the adult mind to help the child mind to right-size emotions. When clients talk from their wounds, they tend to be hurt and childlike and needy, and they want someone else to be the adult. This doesn't work so well in the workplace or in adult relationships, and certainly not when talking to our own children. We need to train people to talk from their wounded inner self to their adult self first, and then give time for the inner adult to translate feelings into grown-up language. We need to make ourselves hearable if we want to be heard.

The timeline is a great way to do focused role plays. As clients "walk their timeline" in their adult bodies, they can encounter their developing "selves" at any age. If at any point they wish to have a conversation with themselves, they can do so by simply talking to an empty chair, enrolling someone to play them at that age, or they can write a letter to themselves at any particular point in time and do experiential letter writing.

The Resilience Timeline: Reclaiming Strength and Initiative

The resilience timeline is done to consolidate gains and to bring awareness of what went well in our lives—how meeting and overcoming challenges, has helped us to develop strength and perseverance. Consolidating these assets and owning them as a part of us, along with getting in touch with and expressing gratitude for those who helped along the way, builds resilience. This can be a beginning of living and processing emotion differently.

Both individuals and group members may get in touch with ways in which they coped effectively with trauma that strengthened them, gave them hope, and helped them develop personal ingenuity and dynamism. They may recall people and circumstances, such as faith-based communities, schools, teachers, friends, neighbors, or extracurricular interests, that acted as buffers against pain. Doing a resilience timeline can also lead to doing dramas of talking to the self at any stage who faced challenges or made good choices or of thanking someone for protecting them, for being there, or setting a different example. These dramas are a wonderful way to support what Wolin and Wolin (1993) cite as "survivor's pride," a quality that those who have overcome challenging circumstances often report having in some form.

If the timeline reaches back into the past, those drawing or walking the resilience timeline may want to draw strength from family heroes, from a history of overcoming terrible odds, or from relatives who were before their time but were important to their identity and who made meaningful contributions to the world. If it stretches forward into the future, clients can talk to a future self, they can do a role play with someone representing a more accomplished or recovered self they want to become. As with anything in psychodrama, past, present, and future can always be included on the stage and brought into the here and now of the healing moment.

Adding Gratitude Letters or Role Plays

The resilience timeline allows for the expression of gratitude to be embodied; a role play can be done or a letter written and read thanking someone who the protagonist feels helped them along their way. Doing an experiential letter-writing exercise with someone you wish to thank is a good exercise to incorporate somewhere in treatment and can be a follow-up of the resilience timeline. In a study conducted by Dr. Martin E. P. Seligman, a psychologist at the University of Pennsylvania, tested the impact of positive psychology interventions on 411 people. They were asked to write and personally deliver a gratitude letter to someone who they had never properly thanked for his or her help or kindness. These participants showed a very significant increase in happiness scores. The impact of simply writing a gratitude letter was greater than that from any other intervention, and the benefits lasted for a month.

If you use gratitude letters or role plays as a follow-up to the resilience timeline, keep in mind that this can stretch over days. The resilience timeline can be used as the process that brings the awareness of whom to thank. The letters can be written and read in a follow-up group or as homework in one-to-one.

The treatment world and twelve-step programs have long advocated for the use of "gratitude lists" as a regular part of recovery. Research has now caught up with what they knew intuitively and through treating addicts and those affected by addiction: that gratitude is an important part of healing the mind and heart and staying sober. Two psychologists, Dr. Robert A. Emmons of the University of California, Davis and Dr. Michael E. McCullough of the University of Miami, have done much of the research on gratitude. In one study, they asked all participants to write a few sentences each week, focusing on particular topics. One group wrote lists of things they were grateful for that week. The second group wrote about their daily irritations or things that bothered them, and the third compiled a neutral list of events that had affected them with no positive or negative emphasis or rating. After ten weeks, the group who wrote about gratitude felt better about their lives and were more optimistic. Interestingly, they also exercised more and had fewer doctor's visits than those who focused on their daily aggravations.

Trauma will not be resolved overnight or once and for all; rather, through this process clients will learn the skills of translating powerful, unconscious feelings into words in order to talk about feelings without imploding, exploding, or self-medicating. Painful memories will continue to come forward for a long time, and new life challenges will arise. By leaning into our good habits and positive life choices, we strengthen those as well. The idea is to learn to process emotions consciously rather than repress or split off pain, to use pain for personal growth rather than a reason to withdraw.

FROM PAGE TO STAGE: THE FULL TIMELINE PROCESS
Writing the Timeline

As with all of my processes, the trauma and resilience timelines are broken down into stages of use, and each stage can be used as a stand-alone process. The written timelines, for example, can be done in group, one-to-one, or on Zoom, and they can become an experiential group process. If timelines are only done on paper and shared, they are still a significant, stand-alone intervention.

As clients bring split-off emotion to a conscious level and articulate and share painful feelings and memories that may have been previously inaccessible, they are able to attach words to their experience and reflect on it. They can put their experiences into the context of their lives with new understanding and awareness of the who, what, when, and where.

Making the Timeline Experiential for a Group

It is a simple process to move the timeline from page to stage and make it a powerful group experience. The easiest way I found was to put numbers on the floor from, say, 0 to 90 to cover all ages in the group, then to invite group members to "come and stand next to an age where you feel you still need to do some work" or to "walk over to an age where you feel stuck, where you have something that needs saying or you just feel you have some pull toward." I keep questions vague enough so that participants don't get hung up trying to find the "right answer." "Just go where you're feeling drawn; you can change," is the sort of thing I say. Once people are standing at the age they are drawn to, I invite them to talk to each other: "Talk to whoever is close to you, around the same age." Participants become "sociometrically aligned" with each other. In this case they are aligned according to age—the toddlers talk to each other, as do the adolescents, teens, young adults, seniors, and so forth. The participants can observe common threads as they share their struggles at particular ages with each other. This often serves as a warm-up to psychodrama, focusing the jumping-off point of the work on the age that is being explored. "Who do you wish to talk to from this age in your life? Or do you wish to talk with a part of yourself at this age?"

In the case of the resilience timeline, I might say, "Stand on or near an age when you had an insight or 'aha' moment that started you in a new direction, or when a door flew open in your mind and you could see possibilities and envision new choices and a better life. Stand near an age where you made a good choice that led to more good choices. Stand near an age where you felt good about yourself, loved, seen by someone, or like part of an activity or a community that was nourishing."

As I mentioned previously, in some cases, the timeline began *before* the client's own timeline. For example, a client might say, "I feel like I need to start way before my own birth because my parents were Holocaust survivors, and I feel like many of my issues were inherited because they brought so much unresolved pain into our family." Or the timeline may need to accommodate a **future projection**, as we call it in psychodrama: "I am twenty-eight, but I am standing on fifty because that's the age when my mother committed suicide, and I am afraid of it." Another future projection might be: "I want to talk to the self my family expects me to be by the time I'm fifty from my age today, and let him off that hook so he—I—can be who I am meant to be."

Walking the Timeline One Person at a Time

Another way that many use the timeline is to walk it one at a time. A protagonist can simply walk along the timeline and talk about periods in their life. They do a spontaneous narration or soliloquy. They can identify difficult times, and if they have addiction issues, they can also identify at what time they began to use substances, which creates a trauma and addiction connection. One example of this is a young woman's walk through the years of her own life:

> Here I'm maybe around six, and my parents start to take me to all these doctors. I don't know what's wrong with me, but everyone seems really concerned, but it feels like something big is wrong with me. I'm not like the other kids at school. I feel dumb. They give me something to take that helps. Can I talk to this part of myself? (A short role play here talking to the part of herself that felt dumb. That part reassured her that she was smart). Now I'm a teenager, I don't have a lot of friends, and I don't feel great about myself. I discover pot and drinking and this really helps. Suddenly I do have friends. And they gave me something that helped when I was a kid so I already take something. This is something new to take and it lets me belong. So for a while this makes things better, but then I get addicted. Something's really wrong with me again, everyone's worried again I'm not sure what it is. Here I'm about nineteen, I get sober, I do everything I'm supposed to do, go to meetings, get therapy, but now even though I'm supposed to be doing so

well, I still feel awful. I didn't see this part till just right now, standing here. This is a really important part, I left a part of myself behind here. Can I talk to this part of myself? (A short drama here talking to the part of herself that wanted to give up. That part wanted to come back to her and continue to grow up and move forward in life).

The drama continued and our protagonist walked into the present moment. Potential role plays emerge organically throughout this process. At any point along the timeline, a protagonist may choose someone from the group to represent themselves at an age they wish to explore, including a future age, and do a **vignette** with that part of themselves, or they can talk to others from their life who were part of important moments or interactions. This protagonist went back to school and earned a PhD. Sometimes walking a timeline can allow protagonists to tell themselves what they need to hear to move forward. They intuitively move toward the parts of themselves they have left behind, talk to them, feel their way back into a relationship, and reincorporate them into their larger self.

THE TRAUMA TIMELINE

Jot down whatever incidents or relational dynamics from your own life, that felt highly stressful, painful or traumatizing to you.

_____   **80 years**   _____

   75 years

_____   **70 years**   _____

   65 years

_____   **60 years**   _____

   55 years

_____   **50 years**   _____

   45 years

_____   **40 years**   _____

   35 years

_____   **30 years**   _____

   25 years

_____   **20 years**   _____

   15 years

_____   **10 years**   _____

   5 years

_____   **0 years**   _____

© _Tian Dayton PhD, TEP._ Relational Trauma Repair Therapist's Guide (revised edition).

Writing the Timeline on Paper

Goals:

1. To provide a visual context through which to identify the developmental progression of trauma.
2. To see where traumas may have clustered in life or where there was little to no trauma.
3. To allow clients and therapists to identify where development may have been arrested or gone off track.
4. To bring to consciousness how trauma breeds trauma, connecting related traumas so that one can see the full impact not just of one traumatic event, but of a string of relational trauma.
5. To put life experience back into a context and place traumatic experience into real rather than imagined time.

Steps:

1. Ask participants to create a trauma timeline.
2. Ask group members to recall events, moments, painful relational dynamics, circumstances, or behaviors from their lives that have felt traumatic to them and that hurt them, frightened them very much, or caused them to shut down or disconnect.
3. Have them locate these in their appropriate places along the timeline.
4. Share the timelines and invite clients to make observations as to what they see in their own timelines.
5. This can be the entire timeline experience and can be done in one-to-one or in group. Writing and sharing a trauma timeline is a deep, evocative experience in and of itself. Sharing can happen in dyads or clusters or in the large group.

Group Process Timeline:
If You Want to Bring the Full Group into the Timeline

1. If you want to take the next step of making the timeline experiential for the full group, lay out large note cards on the floor in a timeline progression at five-year intervals to match the trauma timeline.

2. Invite group members to go to a place along the timeline on the floor where they feel they have unresolved issues (they can just choose that place that they are presently most "aware" of and feeling the most intensely, as there may well be several). This will naturally align people and allow the ones who are emotionally tender around the same developmental stage to stand near each other.

3. Invite them to share with those nearest to them on the trauma timeline, thus allowing them to 1) begin to talk from that age and emotional and psychological space in time, 2) give that part of themselves a voice, and 3) receive identification and support. This will help to break the pain of isolation and is itself a full exercise. You can do this for more than one stage, until the group reaches a saturation point.

4. If the group wants to continue a timeline process any of these questions can be asked:
    *   What age do you recall someone else's problems started to become yours?
    *   What age did something happen that you feel you are still stuck in?
    *   What age did you have an "aha" or make a good decision that led to other good decisions? (Note: This is a way to blend resilience questions with the trauma timeline).
    *   What age would you never return to?
    *   What age would you like to return to?

Walking the Timeline:
If You Want to Make the Timeline Experiential for One Person

1. If one person or several people in a group want to take turns walking the timelines on their own, simply invite someone to start at the beginning and narrate their walk through the various ages of their own life (see an example on tiandayton. com). As they walk, they can simply say things like "I am two and here I was told that I was . . ."; "Here I'm about four and I remember . . ."; "When I was ten my nanny who I adored left, and I came home to an empty house. I remember sitting in the dark, watching TV and eating ice cream. I gained weight and that hurt me in sports"; "I am twelve now and I discovered beer"; "Here I'm around fifteen and I got into pot and soon after into heavier stuff." In this way participants can begin to see how trauma in their lives may have led to self-medicating behaviors. They begin to make the connection between trauma and addiction.

2. Depending on the time and situation, sharing can happen after each person's walk or after more than one person has walked; then the group can share about ways in which they identify and what was brought up for them while watching and witnessing.

Adding Role Plays

If you want to add role plays to either timeline, simply follow the protagonist's warm-up. If the protagonist passes an age where it looks like further investigation might be good, simply ask them, "Would you like to pick someone to play yourself at this age or would you like to talk to that person you just mentioned?" Then have the protagonist choose a role player and bring the role player onstage at this point on the timeline alongside the protagonist. Then proceed for a short role play, let the role play come to closure and then let the protagonist continue to walk along the timeline.

Variations:

"Dialoguing," whether on paper or in role play, is designed to teach clients to 1) learn the difference between a "child" or "adolescent" state of mind and an "adult" state of mind, 2) teach the child self to translate his or her powerful emotions into words and talk about them rather than simply act them out, 3) develop the habit of listening to the feelings your child self is trying to articulate, 4) develop a relationship between the child self and the adult self so that the adult self can help the child self to feel seen and understood, and 5) help the child self to "right-size" their emotional responses so they can communicate them more effectively and with more maturity to others.

THE RESILIENCE TIMELINE

Jot down times in your life when you felt good about yourself, made a good choice that led to other good choices, developed strengths from facing challenges, had "ahas," or valued the love or support someone gave you.

_____	**80 years**	_____
_____	75 years	_____
_____	**70 years**	_____
_____	65 years	_____
_____	**60 years**	_____
_____	55 years	_____
_____	**50 years**	_____
_____	45 years	_____
_____	**40 years**	_____
_____	35 years	_____
_____	**30 years**	_____
_____	25 years	_____
_____	**20 years**	_____
_____	15 years	_____
_____	**10 years**	_____
_____	5 years	_____
_____	**0 years**	_____

Resilience Timeline

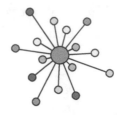

This same process can be followed for the resilience timeline. The goals in this case are to identify points of strength and resilience, to provide visual context of how good decisions and attitudes bred more good decisions and attitudes and to integrate a stronger sense of self.

Goals:

1. To consolidate strengths and gains developed from struggling successfully.
2. To identify innate strengths or inner strength that helped one thrive.
3. To identify relationships that were helpful and supportive.
4. To see where good actions were taken, good decisions made and good attitudes adopted, that helped to move one's life in a positive direction.

Steps:

1. Use the time line blank and give clients some of the following instructions.
2. "Enter those times in your life when you rose to a challenge, made good choices that led to more good choices, reached out for or received help or support from someone, felt great about something you did or thought or accomplished, showed your good qualities of kindness, and strength, and so on. Enter times in your life when you felt you drew on the kinds of qualities inside you that not only helped you get through but built strength, decency, perseverance, and grit. Identify relational moments along the way or key relationships where you felt loved, seen, and supported and you were helped to move forward in positive ways. Enter these on your timeline."
3. After clients do this, follow the same process as for the trauma timeline, inviting group members to share their timelines in group or clusters. This can be the complete process.

Making the Timeline Experiential for the Group

1. If making the resilience timeline experiential for the group, give any of the following instructions or come up with your own.

   - "Walk over to an age in your life when you made a good choice, stand there and share about it with those close to you or with the group."

   - "Walk over to age when something wonderful occurred, stand there, and share about it with those close to you or with the group."

   - "Walk over to an age when you learned to mobilize your own supports, stand there, and share about it with those close to you or with the group."

   - "Walk over to a time when you felt that you were developing qualities of resilience and strength, stand there, and share about it with those close to you or with the group."

   - "Walk over to an age when you felt supported or seen, stand there, and share about it with those close to you or with the group."

   - "Walk over to an age when someone helped you who you feel grateful to or would like to thank, stand there, and share about it with those close to you or with the group."

   - "Walk over to an age when you struggled well and that helped you become who you are today, stand there, and share about it with those close to you or with the group."

   - "Walk over to an age where you need to draw strength from that you once feel you had but worry that you have lost, stand there, and share about it with those close to you or with the group."

Making the Timeline Experiential One Person at a Time in Group

1. Another variation of the timeline that can be done over several groups, is to let clients walk it one at a time. If this is done, simply lay papers with the numbers on the floor that represent five-year intervals and invite clients to, one at a time, "walk their resilience timeline."

2. As clients move along their timeline, they identify moments of resilience, strengths they brought with them or developed through facing challenges, "ahas," good choices, times when they felt good about themselves, and people they got help from or found sustaining.

3. As individuals walk their timelines, they can do several small role plays acknowledging, seeing, or thanking themselves or someone else at any age along the timeline. The idea is to gather up moments of strength, good judgement, resilience, "ahas," and or an awareness of people who lent a helping hand. The purpose is to acknowledge

and incorporate those persona strengths and positive relational feelings. Role plays expressing gratitude to a part of self or another person can emerge from this process. Or group members may wish to talk to their self that struggled and built strength, that worked hard to get where they have gotten or that showed initiative and mobilized to make their life better.

4. The person walking can return to their seats and the group can share what came up for them while witnessing or playing a role in their timeline. Or another person can walk their timeline and sharing can happen after both or several people have worked.

Variations:

This is an ideal way to do meaningful role plays both with the self and others, that are contained and focused. Experiential letter writing can also be a great extension of this exercise as clients write letters to parts of self or others and read them to an empty chair or role player.

CHAPTER NINE

Social Atoms: Working with the Social Network

The basis of drama is the struggle of the hero towards a specific goal at the end of which he realizes that what kept him from it was, in the lesser drama, civilization and, in the great drama, the discovery of something that he did not set out to discover but which can be seen retrospectively as inevitable. The example Aristotle uses, of course, is Oedipus.

—David Mamet

The social atom places clients at the center of their own drama, their own life story, and the proxemics present in the social networks that shaped them. The social atom on paper is a diagram or picture that represents the nucleus of all individuals to whom we are emotionally related; it might also be called a relational map. The study of these atoms and the interrelations represented on them is important in understanding how our relational environment has shaped us, and eventually how we can shape our relational environment. Social atoms provide a concrete form through which we can explore, understand, or modify relationship issues.

The psychodramatic stage is then given to clients as a vehicle through which they can encounter their relational world in concrete form; they can share their story and have it witnessed. The director serves as a sort of coproducer, following the lead of the clients (protagonists), allowing them to be in charge of the relational issues that they wish to examine. The client and therapist form a therapeutic alliance in which the therapist tacitly agrees to stay within the client's internal range of motion, and together they agree to work with what is emerging. The group members are available to play roles of actual people from the life of the protagonist so that the conflict or issue can be brought to relational and given shape and form, voice, and movement.

Sociometrics are open-ended and can be done for literally anything the mind can conceive of. Here I have focused their use specifically on treatment and recovery from trauma or addiction and on personal growth. And I've shaped them according to the way that therapy has evolved in the addictions field.

I learned the version that I do from Robert Siroka, PhD, TEP, Director of the Sociometric Institute. It differs from Moreno's. "As you know, some people place themselves at the center of everything (including the social atom). I prefer the option of the person choosing their location on the page. Since it is a projective technique, it may indicate how the person sees themselves in the world. A research study looking at the position on the page might yield some correlations with dimensions such as egocentric, introversion-extroversion, etc." (Personal communication 2022).

Embodying the Social Atom

The social atom is an outward picture of an inward organization. We cast the roles we wish to represent in our scene, including roles to represent ourselves or aspects of ourselves and roles to represent those significant relationships that shaped or shape us. If someone feels large and distant, our sculpture can represent that by actually locating them at a far end of the stage or working area. Conversely, if they are close and smothering, we can show that. We can reveal support, antipathy, cliques, covert and overt alliances, and isolates by placing them at the appropriate distance or closeness to us.

The process of embodying in and of itself is both evocative and clarifying. The act of seeing ourselves in situ can be emotionally charged. One of its advantages in trauma treatment is that the embodiment itself reveals so much of what goes on within the system, without a word being spoken. Seeing embodiment on stage, allows the nature of our relationships to become more explicit than they might be through verbal description alone. Another advantage from the trauma perspective is that embodiment allows much emotional work to be done on a nonverbal level. Viewing ourselves in the context of a moment in time, or in a model scene that carries within it much of the feeling and belief that shape and drive our action, allows emotion to emerge before we're asked to describe ourselves in words. In other words, words grow out of experiencing ourselves in action.

Embodiment blurs the line between life and art: we're asked to paint a live picture of significant moments in time with those persons who shaped those moments and, in turn, had a hand in shaping us. We can step in or out of the drama at will; through the looking glass we enter a scene or psychic space or moment in time. We become, for a brief moment, the person we once were, feeling as them, seeing through their eyes, interacting in ways that were dictated by the forces evident in that moment, that home, that family, that group. We can talk to ourselves outside the drama from the self that is inside or even trapped in the moment, and that self can talk back to us, seeing ourselves as if in a mirror. Then we can walk out of that moment back into our adult selves, standing beside a therapist who helps us to look back through time and decode and deconstruct the salient features of what made us, us.

A Stand-in Representing the Self

If the protagonist needs greater distance from traumatic material, they can use stand-ins to represent themselves as they witness the content of their own drama; in this case, they can move in and out of a scene through role reversal or double for themselves, thus giving clients a safety net if work becomes too intense. They also have the opportunity with the director to pause the scene so that they can step back and get a deeper look at what might have been going on for them at a given juncture in their lives. This allows protagonists to get perspective on their own feedback loop, or what complexes might be feeding their triggers. The fact that psychodrama is a role-based method allows a client to explore damage that may have occurred in a particular role, say, that of son or daughter of a particular parent, while preserving strength and resilience that may still be present in other life roles.

The use of a stand-in to represent the protagonist allows the protagonist to view themselves from the outside. This can allow the protagonist to empathize with themselves as they witness themselves struggling with circumstances that may, as a child at least, have been out of their control. It can also help them to unlock from a stuck position in which they become triggered and immobilized. They begin to separate the past from the present. Inherent in this separation is the realization that the past does not have to be mindlessly repeated.

A Social Atom of Internal/Personal Roles

A social atom can be done to examine any internal roles. For example, a client might do an atom to explore the roles that went along with being an addict, such as "drug seeker," "euphoric one," "spiritual seeker," "self-medicator," "shamed one," "unconscious one," "all-seeing one," "desperate one," "connected one," "disconnected one," and so on. This can be done in the same five stages, choosing new roles to exchange for the old roles in stage five—roles such as "sober spiritual seeker," "self-caring one," "connected one," "exerciser," and so on. For someone dealing with ACA-type issues, roles might look more like "hypervigilant one," "over-functioner," "helpless one," "rageful/resentful one," and so forth.

A Basic Protocol for Incorporating Social Atoms into Treatment

1. I encourage treatment centers to do several social atoms throughout treatment that can be part of their overall treatment plan. These can be done on paper only, or they can follow the pattern of paper-sculpt-live.

2. Upon entering treatment, clients can do a social atom of their using/abusing life and network that landed them in treatment.

3. During treatment they can do a family-of-origin social atom, frozen moment(s), resilience-building moment(s), or any other social atoms that might be helpful. A social atom can be done to take a deeper look into the proxemics of any moment or "model scene" that the protagonist wishes to look into. Social atoms can also be done to examine "internal/personal roles" (see the previous section).

4. Before leaving treatment, clients can do a social atom of how they would like their life to look going forward. In this they can include their network of recovery supports and self-care activities.

A Social Atom of a Frozen Moment

When I started being known as someone who does trauma work, as I was doing training at conferences, I had an odd experience. Over and over again, in state after state after state, I found that people volunteered to be protagonists, and then, as the drama progressed, they froze. Because I was not particularly conscious of this shift in how people saw me, in my mind I was just the same old me. This happened during a period of at least a year or more, and I started to think I had lost my touch. What was I doing wrong? This used to be so easy—people just met themselves on the stage, they cried, they laughed, they discovered, and they felt better. But suddenly I was being met with protagonist after protagonist who stood before the characters they themselves had chosen to work with, and then froze. Once a protagonist is frozen, getting them out of it is challenging and can eat up the whole drama, because along with their frozenness come their defenses against feeling what lies beneath it.

Out of desperation, I used my New York network, who were so familiar with the way I worked, to get underneath what I was encountering on the road. I tried asking people to think of a moment when they froze and then do a social atom of that moment including anyone or anything present. It became the equivalent of something going viral. Everyone seemed to know exactly when and where that was for them: for some it was in a classroom, for others in their mother's arms, for still others when they saw their drunk parent slumped in a chair and thought they saw a monster on their lap. People not only intuitively understood these kinds of moments or relational dynamics, they owned them and became willing, even enthusiastic, about exploring them more deeply. Structuring any psychodrama after that became easy once again. People no longer froze. The word *trauma* in and of itself had become a problem, a block. It made protagonists think they were doing something they should be frightened of or that was somehow dangerous, and this mobilized their sense of danger along with their defenses. So they got scared and speechless all over again.

The beauty of working with a frozen moment, whether from a social atom or simply something that arose in the moment, was twofold. First, if the protagonist identified it, then they were in charge; they didn't feel blindsided, and they knew what was coming and wanted to look further. Second, as the director, I knew how to work with it. I took their frozenness as a signal not to do more, but to do less. Rather than feel frustrated or self-conscious, I understood that I needed to become curious, to move gently into this space. I understood that the immobilization might well be a part of the drama and that we needed to cajole, invite, and use soft and supportive tones and ways of being so that the protagonist could feel safe enough to move just a little. And that just a little might be a lot. In this kind of work, as the famous film director Ingmar Bergman said, "less is more." For this reason, I do not make a sculpture of a frozen moment, as it can be overwhelming. I use the social atom as a jumping-off point for simple role plays. I might say something like, "Is there anyone on your atom that you wish to talk to, including yourself?" The role play has been focused through the social atom, and the protagonist cam simply say what they want to say using role reversal and doubling, in a process that is more low-key.

Self-reflection can be difficult for trauma survivors who are removed from their internal experiences through psychological and emotional defenses or who are glued to relational dynamics from their past that never seem to resolve themselves. Seeing the self in context is a slow warm-up toward the emotion of the situation that can allow the client to experience themselves and themselves-in-relation in a more real and concrete manner. It is interpersonal neurobiology in a guided, experiential format, and it's aiming not only at healing pain but at templating new relational experiences. Embodying allows clients to view the contents of their inner world before they are asked to reflect on it in the abstract through words. They can see themselves in action and context, feeling their way empathically into themselves and their own relational world.

By asking clients to identify their own moments of frozenness, we're empowering them to be in charge of their own readiness to work on what they are actually choosing to work on. They are saying, in essence, "I am willing to look at this, to travel back in time to a moment, a relational dynamic, or a period in my life that I found so overwhelming that I had to freeze or dissociate in order to get through it." The advantages of this are many:

- The director does not need to deal with a client who is taken by surprise in their own frozenness.
- The client is less likely to see the director as the cause of their being overwhelmed and thus also less likely to direct the feelings of pain and anger that may be getting triggered in them toward the director, so the director is better able to be a source of support.
- The client has the feeling that they are choosing to take a bold and self-directed journey into one of their painful moments. They feel like a courageous, albeit

vulnerable, explorer into their own inner world, rather than feeling pushed toward an edge by someone else.

It is inherent when working with a frozen moment that part of the journey has already materialized—the journey toward this pain through a level of unconsciousness that may have previously blocked access. Because of this, the client is already warmed up to work. Since they are already warmed up, their work is considerably more fluid, and their pain, anger, or wounds are accessible and on the edge of awareness. There are fewer bombshells; they have chosen this journey, this moment, this method.

Another advantage of using frozen moments is that it focuses on the moment at which someone felt threatened or traumatized while leaving the social atom representing the rest of one's life or family undisturbed. It does not, in other words, pathologize an entire childhood or an entire family system, but zeros in on those moments or dynamics that were traumatizing and processes them. The feelings that went unfelt and the thoughts that went unthought get felt and expressed so that they can be reflected upon, understood, and placed into an overall framework or context of the protagonist's life. And as the protagonist reverses in and out of their own frozen moment, they develop a felt sense of finding their way out of feeling trapped.

Working with frozen moments is also better for building resilience, as the protagonist's strengths become less contaminated by the sort of iatrogenic collateral damage of aiming at the whole family system, rather than identifying the problematic parts and allowing the happy or functional parts to remain intact and left to thrive. This creates less cognitive dissonance for the protagonist, as they feel less conflicted about retaining family strengths and good feelings. Then, as the protagonist finishes their social atom work, they can reconstruct the atom as they wish it had been, templating a new sense of what to look for in the future.

A Step-by-Step Process: From Page to Stage

The following is a description of a way of using the social atom that enhances safety by guiding the process through the use of specific techniques. My thinking behind this rather controlled, step-by-step approach is that it keeps the social atom from "going live" all at once and overwhelming or even retraumatizing the protagonist. Hence, by structuring the social atom as a sculpture, adding a stand-in for the protagonist that represents them at that point in or throughout time, and having an adult self, standing outside the atom whose thinking mind is not in a frozen state, we can help the protagonist not to get overwhelmed. This templates a connection for the future, because we learn to allow our wounded self, when triggered, to first talk to our "inner adult" before we blast out the contents of our wounds and whatever or whoever acted as a trigger, projecting our pain where it may or may not belong and then being hurt all over again when we feel unseen and misunderstood. We want to train the wounded or triggered parts of ourselves to talk first to the mature adult who can then translate our feelings into something that is comprehensible and hearable for others. In this way, we give ourselves a chance to be understood rather than rejected all over again, and we have a chance to *not* recreate old relational pain in present relationships.

Doing this in stages allows it to be a more contained process. I have written an entire chapter on social atoms and how to read them in *The Living Stage*; I hope that you will read that, as it will give you a much fuller picture of them.

Doing a Social Atom on Paper

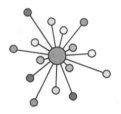

Goals:

1. To graph relational conflicts, complexes, or wished-for scenes on paper.
2. To examine significant moments or model scenes that have had long-term impact.
3. To bring the then and there into the here and now and feel feelings that went unfelt, say words that went unsaid, and move the body/mind out of its frozenness into expression.
4. To clarify the seeds of possible relational reenactments.
5. To focus a simple role play or provide a map for sculpturing.

Steps:

1. Have participants get a pencil and paper.
2. Say, "Do a social atom of any time in your life. It can be a moment or model scene when you felt great, misunderstood, hurt, frozen, or empowered. It can be a model scene of your family of origin, your network of relationships, or a life you'd like to create going forward. It can be an atom of your life right now or at any point in time.
3. Say, "Using circles to represent females, triangles to represent males, and squares to represent institutions or groups, first locate yourself on the paper anywhere that feels right to you."
4. Say, "Now locate your important relationships or institutions as close to or distant from yourself as you feel them to be, and in the size or proportion that feels right. You may include pets, in-laws, grandparents, nannies, friends, and so on. Use a broken line to represent anyone who is deceased. Write the name of each person next to his or her symbol."
5. Once all the symbols are on paper and the atoms feel finished, clients or group members can begin to share them, either in the large group, in a pair with a partner, in small groupings, or with the therapist in one-to-one. Remind clients that these

atoms are only a current reflection; they are always subject to change, and can be done for as many moments in time as one can imagine.

Variations:

The social atom can be shared without any movement toward action. Drawing and sharing a social atom is, in itself, more than powerful enough to create inner movement and awareness, and has the advantage of being easier to do than getting the whole system up and running through sculpturing and role play. If the social atom is done only as a journaling activity, it can be shared as described in step 5, which constitutes a complete process.

A Social Atom of a Frozen Moment: "Do a social atom of a time in your life when you felt frozen in place, hurt, or as though you didn't get a chance to say what you wanted to say or do what you wanted to do. It can be a moment, a relational dynamic, or a sort of snapshot or model scene of a period in your life." Doing a social atom of a frozen moment on paper and sharing it, is a more than sufficient way of making these moments conscious. Or the social atom on paper can be a warm-up to talking to the frozen self, or anyone on the atom. In other words, it can be a warm-up for a small role play or experiential letter writing.

Social atoms can be done for virtually any moment in time, past, present or future. During COVID-19, for example, we had teens doing social atoms almost every week and sharing them, as their lives felt different each week.

Clients can do a social atom of a feared or wished-for scene in the future. They can do social atoms of their work or their families. They can do an atom of a moment in time where they felt triggered in the present, then they can do another atom as they recall the "status nascendi" or the moment from their past that might be fueling their overreaction today. They can do their parent's social atom at the time they were born into their family or their parent's childhood atom.

If a parent is struggling with their child at some particular age, the parent can do a social atom of themselves at that age to see if anything from their own childhood is getting triggered and transferred onto their child in the present as an age correspondence reaction.

In couples work you can invite each member of a couple to do and share their own social atom so that they can "show" their spouse, for example, how they experienced their own family of origin. Or couples can do each other's family-of-origin social atom to see how much they really know about each other in this way.

Moving the Social Atom into a Drama or Sculpture

Steps:

1. Create a social atom on paper. Using the social atom as a map, allow the protagonist to choose role players to represent themselves and then all the people, parts of the self, states of mind, animals, and so on that the protagonist wishes to have as part of their sculpture. *Note: They need not enrole every aspect of their atom, but should be encouraged to fully represent whatever they wish to work with or even have as "part of the picture." Setting up the scene is part of the protagonist's warm-up to the material they are exploring and should be done, as much as possible, by the protagonist themselves: "Sculpt it as you see it; the stage is yours."*

2. Ask the protagonist to place the auxiliary representing themselves and each role player onto the stage, taking care to encourage them to locate themselves and the role players in whatever posture, shape, distance, or closeness that feels appropriate and like an accurate representation of that moment or snapshot of a period of time. The protagonist can have all necessary license in embodying this scene as it felt to them on the inside; for example, someone may have felt huge and looming or small and erased, and that can be portrayed in the shape or distance represented by the role players and their relative proximity to each other. In other words, the proxemics or the unspoken but very impactful relational dynamics that shaped the situation may make themselves evident by how and where they are represented on the stage. *Directing Note: As they are embodying their scene, the protagonist can be free to reverse roles with each role to show the size, shape, and relative distance from themselves represented in this moment, although this is not a necessary step. In this way, the protagonist demonstrates each role from their point of view. This allows the protagonist to give the role players some insight and "training" as to the role they are portraying. It also lets the protagonist use fewer words and explanations to get the character's essence across. I generally do not ask protagonists to give any one-liners to characters, as I feel that it is too reductive. Trauma (read: life) is not that simple, and people are complicated and say many conflicting things.*

3. Once the embodiment is up and the protagonist has chosen someone to represent themselves, invite them to stand outside their scene with you, look at themselves in this situation, and share about how it feels to see the whole system or moment at once.

4. The protagonist can talk from their adult selves to their child's self inside of the sculpture. They can then reverse roles into the scene and talk back to their adult self from inside the scene. They can talk to themselves outside the sculpture—for example, "What would you like to say to your adult or observing/witnessing self?"—and they can reverse in and out of that dialogue if it seems indicated. *Note: In healing from trauma, we want to help clients to create a dialogue between their child self and their adult self, so the adult can translate feelings and messages from the child self into mature words and communicate with the adult world from a more grown-up place. In this way they have a better chance of being listened to and of achieving healthy relating. Moving in and out of the scene, embodying a dialogue between the adult and child self, helps to solidify this connection.*

5. The protagonist can continue to reverse in and out of the scene as they need to or they can talk to anyone in their scene one at a time using doubling and role reversal as in all role plays.

6. End the scene from the role of the adult talking to the self in the scene, e.g.,: "What do you want to tell yourself in this scene from your more mature self of today?" The idea here is to begin a running dialogue between the adult and child self.

7. Repair/redo: Next, the protagonist can reconstruct the scene, moment, or period of time as they wish it had been. This reconstructed scene or moment of repair often brings up a lot of feelings for the protagonist. They feel what never got a chance to happen. They may want to end the scene by sharing how it feels to feel this moment inside the scene, then they can reverse roles and end the scene by talking to the self from of outside it and observing what it feels like to look at the scene in its reconstructed state from the outside.

Variations:

1. At some point in treatment, attention can also be paid to what the adult self needs to understand and do in order to take care of themselves so that they can take care of these "younger" parts of the self. This can be incorporated into the drama, for example: "Younger self inside the moment, tell your witnessing/observing self or self of today what you want or need from them going forward." Then reverse roles and respond to that.

2. Another embodiment that can be done in treatment is one of **resilient** or **golden moments**. A client can be invited to "do a social atom of a moment or time in your life when you felt good, when something terrific happened or you just felt strong, successful, content, happy, or joyful with yourself and/or a relationship dynamic."

3. A Sculpture of a Frozen Moment: The safest way to sculpt a frozen moment is to stand outside of it with the therapist as the protagonist talks about the feelings it brings up. Then they can, through role reversal, go back and forth talking to their "self" inside the sculpture and to their "self" outside of the sculpture.

It is very important for therapists and group members alike to understand that everyone in the group is always working. There can be an emphasis on doing "your piece of work." Please don't get stuck here; the group will take its cues from you. This emphasis puts pressure on the therapist to grind out psychodramas and on group members to be "up for" their piece of work, because it's seen as their only chance to work. This thinking is all wrong for psychodramatic/sociometric group work. As I've said throughout the book, in a good psychodrama group, everyone is working all the time.

I always try to create many points of entry so that group members see this work as theirs to share, so that they stay engaged and active through jumping in and doubling, playing a role, sharing deeply during the sharing phase of the drama, and so forth. The knowledge and healing in a well-run group don't emanate from the therapist alone. The therapist's job is to bring the group forward, to give them maximum opportunity to share, engage, and experience. Everything I have designed from floor checks on is for this purpose.

Trauma is, in a way, painful circumstances that never got repaired, or painful circumstances in which one felt alone, misunderstood, or invisible. Repair is life's way of renewing itself, and it can be done after the fact if it was not done in the traumatic moment. Life is full of such moments; it is when they go unrepaired, when they remain frozen and unconscious, that they stay locked within us in a way that creates an emotional quicksand that we can't find our way out of. The repair or "redo" can also be a form of action reframing that allows for action insight and a new understanding or meaning which can lead to greater acceptance.

CHAPTER TEN

Words Unspoken: Experiential Letter Writing

All I need is a sheet of paper and something to write with,
and then I can turn the world upside down.
—Friedrich Nietzsche

Experiential letter writing is probably one of the easiest and safest ways to do role play. First, it is already set up in a role relationship; the letter is written "to" someone, so there has already been a warm-up and the protagonist has identified the person to whom they wish to say something. Second, all you really need to do to make it experiential is read the letter to that person in some form, as represented by an empty chair or a role player.

Letter writing is what we call a "near-psychodramatic technique" that is role-based. It can be a good way to incorporate some small forms of psychodrama into programming in a contained manner. Letter writing is a technique that Moreno originally devised, and it's completely consistent within psychodramatic theory in that the basic form of role interaction is maintained. There are two roles in a letter, the sender and the receiver, so there is your vignette. Someone can be chosen to embody the receiver, or an empty chair can represent them and the protagonist is "leading the way" by choosing the person they wish to speak to.

Adding doubling to this, either by allowing the group members to spontaneously double, by inviting the protagonist to double for themselves, or by the therapist doing the doubling, makes the role play go even deeper and invites group involvement. Reversing roles and allowing the protagonist to respond to themselves, saying what they long to hear or expect to hear, can make this an even fuller and richer process. I often do several letter readings by letting all who wish to do so read their letters, and then inviting the group to share at the end about what came up for them through having done their letter or identified with the letters of others.

Letters can be written to people, to parts of the self, to parts of the body, to a previous self, or to a substance, a behavior, a wished-for self, or, for that matter, a dog or an institution—to virtually anything, in other words. Another way to use letter writing is to write a letter you would like to receive (Wegscheider-Cruse, personal communication, n.d.). In that case someone can be chosen to read the letter to the person who wrote it (the protagonist) or the protagonist can choose someone to stand in or use and empty chair to represent them, and they can read it to themselves as that other person.

Letter writing can be done as homework and brought to one-to-one therapy. Clients can write letters during group. I usually do it after psychodramatic work has been done or sociometrics have brought up feelings. Then they can share them in group—either with the whole group or in small groupings; in Zoom groups; or in breakout rooms—and then return to the group to process the experience.

From Page to Stage: Experiential Letter Writing Full Process

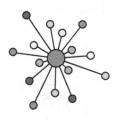

Goals:

1. To process feelings toward someone or a part of the self in a therapeutic way.
2. To provide a contained form of role play.

Steps:

1. Invite participants to make themselves comfortable, either in their chairs or somewhere in the room. If you wish, you can play soft, ambient sound or instrumental music while letters are being written. Ask participants to write their letters by beginning with "Dear So and So" and ending with an appropriate closing and signing their name. *Note: I would do this when clients are warmed up either by a sociometric process or sharing that has taken place.*

2. Encourage group members to write anything that comes to mind. This letter is not meant to be sent but to release feelings. It works best to write quickly, not thinking about how it sounds or imagining that anyone will read it. *Note: these letters are not to be sent to the person they are written to or to anyone; they are for therapeutic use only.*

3. Check in to see if anyone needs extra time. Seven minutes or so is generally sufficient.

4. Letters can be read out loud in the group, in dyads, in small groupings, or you can make them experiential. If used on Zoom, letters can be read in the open meeting or in breakout groups.

Making Letter Writing Experiential by Reading
a Letter to an Empty Chair or Role Player

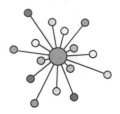

Goals:
---

1. To provide a safe format for doing a piece of experiential work that is deep and meaningful.
2. To work out unfinished business from the past.

Steps:
---

1. Ask group members to get their letters.
2. Set up two chairs facing each other, one for the person reading the letter and one to represent the person or part of the self to whom the letter is written.
3. Invite the group member to imagine that the person, object/entity, pet, or part of the self to whom the letter is written is sitting in the empty chair or to choose a role player to represent them.
4. Invite the group members to read their letters. Protagonist can double for themselves at any point they wish. You can also double as the director, or let group members jump in and double.

    a. Doubling: In the case of doubling, the protagonist stands behind their own chair and articulates their own "inner life," or what is going on inside them that remains unspoken. Or, group members stand behind the protagonist's chair and give voice to the protagonist's inner life—what they may be feeling but not speaking out loud.

    b. Role reversal: In the case of role reversal, the protagonist changes chairs and actually sits in the chair of the other person, momentarily taking on their role and responding to the letter as that other person, entity, pet, or part of the self to whom they wrote the letter.

    c. Doubling for the other person: Once the protagonist has reversed roles, anyone, including the protagonist, may also double for that

---

role, articulating the inner life that they imagine is going on inside that other person; this can help with empathy and understanding. The protagonist is always free to correct or reject doubling.

5. When one group member's letter is finished, the group member returns to their seat and someone else can read their letter.

6. Sharing can occur after the reading of each letter or after several letters have been worked with.

Variations:

The following are some examples of letters that can be written:

- A letter of forgiveness to the self.
- A letter asking forgiveness from someone else.
- A letter forgiving another person.
- A letter to some aspect of the self, for example, the hurt self, the successful self, the child self, the angry self, the addict, the codependent self, or the wished-for self.
- A letter expressing anger toward someone.
- A letter telling someone about a hurt.
- A letter to "the disease" or to a substance or behavior that one is letting go of, thanking it for what it has given, talking about what it has cost, and saying good-bye.
- A letter to an aspect of the self or the self at a particular time in life, for example, child, adolescent, or the self after a break-up or traumatic moment.
- A letter to someone expressing a desire for reconciliation.
- A letter to some part of the body: a part that has been removed, a despised part, a cherished part, a part in transition (aging), a sore part, and so on. *Note: These can get quite hilarious as well as deeply emotional.*
- A "gratitude letter" thanking someone for being there for them or doing something for them or being a good model.
- A letter to a time of life, a job, youth, older years, childhood, etc.
- Role Reversal Letter: A letter from someone expressing sentiments the writer wishes that person had expressed.

A letter of any kind that you wish to receive.

- A letter from someone who has hurt the writer asking the writer for forgiveness.
- A letter from someone expressing understanding of what the letter writer went through.

- A letter from an aspect of the self or the self at a particular time in life, to the self today, for example a letter from the child, adolescent, or the self after a break-up or traumatic moment, or after something wonderful happened.

Variation:

This is a great exercise for a large workshop or a Zoom group. In a large workshop, people can work in small groupings and read letters aloud to each other, or to an empty chair. Or to a role player if the subgroups are large enough. On Zoom, they can read letters aloud if the group is small, or in breakout groups. Then they can return in each case to the larger group and share about the experience.

CHAPTER ELEVEN

Spectrograms and Locograms: Becoming Present in the Room

Tomorrow is tomorrow. Future cares have future cures, and we must mind today."
—Sophocles, *Antigone*

Spectrograms and locograms are oriented in the here and now. Clients are not role playing, they are encountering themselves and each other in real time. As a clinician, I have found the most useful tools and processes of sociometry to be those that can immediately be translated into action, although a social scientist would find great use for them in all forms written and embodied. I often use Moreno's sociometric processes of spectrograms and locograms as experiential check ins and warm-ups. They bring people into the present, into the group, and the work being done.

A **spectrogram** essentially measures degrees of the experience of participants in the here and now: "how much or how little" am I experiencing a feeling, symptom, or anything being explored? It is wonderful for teaching the skills of self-regulation. Spectrograms are also a valuable community check-in in treatment facilities, e.g., "How are you feeling this morning or this evening or both?" One hundred percent being "I'm great," and 0 percent being, "not good."

Think of the spectrogram as a graph that is laid out on a floor. Rather than using lines or dots to represent graphed placement as one would with paper, the spectrogram asks the criterion question and then invites group members to stand in the location that best represents their self-assessment. This moving from one's seat and committing to a standing, choice-making position encourages a greater engagement in the process. Then, as people share, group members express the thoughts and feelings behind their choice. The spectrogram reveals significant information about the group very quickly.

Spectrograms are automatically self-regulating because you are answering the questions asked according to degree. If what you're asking is "How much discomfort are you feeling?" then the answer teaches self-regulation because participants are saying, "I feel 30 percent," and then they share a bit about how that is for them. It's an easy, nonthreatening entry into talking about feelings or issues that is self-diagnostic; no one other than the participant is or should be telling them where to stand or how to feel.

A **locogram** allows group members to articulate their current state of mind. I find they work best as experiential "check-ins" or "ice-breakers" generally at the beginning of group. The therapist can designate four corners of an imaginary box on the floor. They can say something like, "So how are you feeling about being in group this evening? Corner one, I'm super excited; corner two, I can take it or leave it; corner three, I wish I were somewhere else; and corner four, other." We always have the category of "other" in sociometrics and floor checks so that if someone doesn't see anything they identify with they can "write it in." The locogram gives clients a safe way to vent feelings so that they don't linger in group and affect their willingness to do the work of therapy. They make a snapshot as to where the group was at any given moment, an experiential check-in to open the floor for sharing comfort levels for any subject.

Basic Spectrogram: "How Much/How Little?"

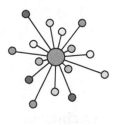

Goals:

1. To teach the skills of self-regulation by providing a floor graph that group members can step into in order to represent the degree and intensity of a particular issue or emotion.
2. To teach and provide practice in the skills of co-regulation as clients share authentically with others and listen as others do the same.
3. To provide a method for exploring issues through sociometry.
4. To create group cohesion and build trust.
5. To give several people in the group a chance to feel involved in experiential work.

Steps:

1. Show participants that each end of the room represents an extreme, for example, zero to 100 percent, or very much and very little. Next, draw an imaginary line bisecting the room down the middle, representing the midpoint, for example, 50 percent or a medium amount. (Visit tiandayton.com/streaming video for a visual example.)
2. Next, ask a criterion question and invite participants to locate themselves at whatever point along the continuum that best describes their response to the question. For example, "On a scale of 1 percent to 100 percent, how comfortable are you feeling about your work life?" The person who was recently fired might go toward 1 percent, while the person for whom work is not an issue might stand closer to the midpoint or toward 100 percent.
3. When each person is standing at the point that represents their response to the question say, "Share a sentence or two about why you're standing where you're standing." Allow people to share with the full group. Or if the group is large, group members can share in small groupings, dyads, triads, and clusters with those

standing around them. This automatically aligns them sociometrically, that is, they are standing next to people who have answered the question similarly to them.

4. After the group has explored as many questions as it wishes to or because it has reached its saturation point, you can do a role play by asking who feels warmed up to do work. Or group members can return to their seats and continue to share.

Variations:

Use criterion questions that are relevant to anything you wish to explore in the group, for example: "How comfortable do you feel in this group? How comfortable are you beginning this program? How comfortable do you feel about your body? How good do you feel about your recovery? How good do you feel about your work life/personal life/family relationships? How comfortable are you in your own skin?" Such questions bring up information for processing and also allow people to discover shared feelings. The therapist can begin asking the questions then ask group members to come up with questions that they, as a group, feel like exploring, or the therapist can come up with all the questions.

In treatment, spectrograms can also be used at the beginning of the day as check-ins or the end of the day as closure check-ins. This can happen in the large community and any questions that the therapist or team feel would be useful can be used. The group members can also suggest questions.

Self-Medication Spectrogram:
Understanding the Impact of Addiction

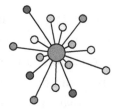

Goals:

1. To bring a relationship with a substance or behavior into greater awareness.
2. To allow secrets and hidden emotions and thoughts to come to the surface.

Steps:

1. Using the spectrogram format, designate one end of the working space to represent "very much" or 100 percent, the opposite wall to represent "very little" or 1 percent, and the middle of the floor to represent 50 percent. Using a few of the criterion questions below, or those you have formulated on your own, ask the group to answer by locating themselves along an imaginary line in the place that best describes or shows where they feel they are at the moment.

   - How much do you feel this substance or behavior has affected your life?
   - How much sadness do you feel relative to this?
   - How much anger do you feel relative to this?
   - How much shame do you feel around self-medication?
   - How much confusion do you feel relative to this?
   - How derailed do you feel your life has been because of this?
   - How much regret about the past do you feel relative to this?
   - How much anxiety about the future do you feel?
   - How much hope or faith do you have that you can change?

2. Allow group members to share if and when they wish to in response to each criterion question. Limit the sharing so that there is plenty of time for all who wish to share to do so. Use only as many questions as the group can handle; generally four or five are plenty.
3. Use this as a warm-up to psychodrama, or a springboard for sharing.

This can be done for anyone who feels that a substance or addictive behavior has influenced his or her life.

ACAs or family week: Addiction can change the life not only of the addict but for everyone surrounding an addict. This is a good family member spectrogram to do for all impacted parties. The group leader can come up with the questions and/or the group can decide together what questions they would like to explore, or there can be a combination of both. Use a mix of positive and negative questions. Use the questions above, or the group members can be allowed to double for each other throughout the process if desired.

An example of a positive question might be "How much do you feel you have grown as a person through coping well or meeting the challenge of living with addiction?"

Basic Locogram Experiential Check-in:
Which One Feels Like Me?

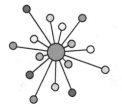

Goals:

1. To break the ice in the beginning of group.
2. To allow group members to announce preferences.
3. To create group bonding and cohesion.

Steps:

1. Identify the issue that the group wishes to explore.
2. Designate four or so areas on the floor to represent possible responses to the issue, including one area representing "other" so that group members aren't limited to only the available choices. For example, if you wish to explore how people are feeling about working on their issues, the director might say: "This corner of the room or stage will represent 'I feel ok about doing this work; this corner, 'I am not sure but willing to be around it; this corner, 'I feel resistant to doing this work; and this corner, 'other.'" Then say, "Please stand in the area that best represents how you feel about working on your issues." "Which skill are you learning to use lately and how does that look in your life?"
3. Once group members are standing in the area that best describes what they're feeling, invite them to share a sentence or two about why they are standing where they are. Group members may also want to stand between two areas if they feel ambivalent or between feelings. Group members may spontaneously double for each other if this seems useful to the process.
4. If you feel that the group wants to make another choice, the leader might say something like "Has anything changed for you since you shared just now? If so, change places and share from where you have shifted to."
5. The director can invite the group members to extend sharing by saying, "Walk over to someone who shared something with which you identify and place your hand on

his or her shoulder. Now share with them why you chose them or how you identify." Or the director may ask people to simply return to their seats for further sharing or move into other processes like floor checks, timelines, social atoms, or role plays.

Variations:

I use locograms primarily in the beginning of groups or as icebreakers. They give people a chance to move through any resistance they might have in a way that is easy and spontaneous. The director might also use it as a mood check at the beginning of group: my day has been good, my day has been challenging, feels like just another day, other.

Adapt for DBT: You can adapt locograms for DBT by putting "wise mind" in the first corner, "emotional mind" in the second, "reasonable mind" in the third, and "other" in the fourth. Then simply use criterion questions like, "Where are you right now?" Or clients can use the DBT skill locogram to process where they go when they get triggered. For example, if they get triggered, the therapist can ask questions like, "Which skill are you learning to use lately and how is that working for you?" or "Which skill do you wish you could use at this moment but can't quite get there?"

You can design your own locogram to explore anything relevant to the group you're working with, as you can with floor checks, by changing the information on the floor and the criterion questions or prompts being asked by the therapist or group leader.

CHAPTER TWELVE

The Tracks of My Tears: Working with Unspent Grief

So take a good look at my face, you'll see my smile looks out of place,
if you look closer it's easy to trace, the tracks of my tears.
—Smoky Robinson, Warren Moore, and Marv Tarplin

When I wrote *Heartwounds: The Impact of Unresolved Trauma and Grief on Relationships* in 1997, the publisher's research showed that "no one wants to buy books with the word *grief* in the title"; they preferred that I keep words like *grief* and *trauma* in the subtitle. Elisabeth Kübler-Ross had beautifully opened up the subject of grief for losses through death. I wanted to open up the subject for losses through life, because this is what I was seeing all the time. Those whose lives had been turned inside out because of trauma and addiction needed to go through a deep grieving process for the life losses they had experienced. For the addict, the losses are numerous and bone-chillingly painful. First, they lose their substance, which was their way of managing their inner pain that they are now expected to manage in some other way. Then, as they sober up and become aware of all the life situations and relationships that they have been sabotaging, they have to mourn lost years, lost opportunities, lost career-building, lost relationships, lost healthy time with their children, and lost time in general. If that weren't enough, they likely have several people whom they care deeply about furious with and/or hurt by them.

Then there is the grief of ACAs, of all that happened in their childhoods that burdened them and took away their safety, play, and comfort, that made them sick with worry at such a young and vulnerable age. Not only did they need to grieve what happened; they needed to grieve what never got a chance to happen.

And the pain of the spouse of an addict who has taken over dropped parenting roles and felt alone and angry. Divorce often went ungrieved as well; it became a hidden wound, as if having your family torn apart was something normal and not a life loss needing to be mourned, even if it was for the best given the situation.

When there is a death, there is a dignity about it and a sense of closure, the community understands that the family is in unusual pain and they take measures to console them.

But there are no black armbands that we can wear to let the world know that we just lost another piece of ourselves to trauma or another part of our parent to addiction. Or that our experience of home has become riddled with secrets and unspoken losses because our family can't talk about their pain and grieve together. Nothing to signal to the world, "I hurt, I need attention." These kinds of losses that surround addiction have no such closure, they live in unmarked graves in our hearts, surrounded by shame and silence. And all too often they go unrecognized and unmourned. They are referred to as disenfranchised losses, or the kinds of losses that society tends not to recognize.

As it became clear to me that those I was treating had a deep need to grieve, it also became clear how few vehicles in our culture, and even in our therapy world, really allowed for that full expression. I became interested in how best to use psychodrama, almost in the way that religion has used ritual, to facilitate a grief process.

It was palpable in my work that embodying the lost object was therapeutic gold.

Through psychodrama, the lost person, part of life, part of self, family group, or even medicator can be concretized and talked to in the here and now. There is simply no substitute for being able to reengage with lost loved ones through role players, or even an empty chair, and say all of what you long to have said but perhaps never did. Or to talk to the substance that has been your life companion that you are being asked in treatment to live without. Or to address the part of the self that you have ignored or medicated or left to fend for itself and then reembrace it as a part of the self. Or to let the child, teenager, young adult, or frozen part within have a voice.

If I could count the relief that I have seen in protagonists who have finally found a way to talk to their lost spouse, child, inner child, parent, part of self, pet, time of life, or friend through imagining them in an empty chair or embodying them through a role player, I could paint a picture of what it does for them. The weight that visibly lifts from their shoulders, the brightening and muscle relaxation on their face are moving. And how many times has the protagonist then reversed roles and talked as their deceased parent back to themselves or disowned part of the self, offering themselves advice, support, or connection?

When We Can't, Don't, or Won't Mourn

When we don't grieve, that pain doesn't disappear, rather it leaks out in a variety of ways that can complicate our lives and our relationships. We talk a lot about growth and learning in therapy, but part of healing is also getting good at falling apart and allowing grief to reshape us. There are a lot of things that happen when we can't grieve. Here are some of them:

Replacement: This is when we replace the lost person or circumstance without mourning the previous loss first. For example, the divorced person who immediately marries again may feel he or she has solved the pain of loss when, in fact, the loss has not been processed and learned from. In the case of divorce, the same issues that led to one loss tend to reappear in the next relationship.

Displacement: This occurs when mourners cannot connect their pain to what is actually causing it and instead displace the grief, upset, anger, and sadness onto something or someone else—*displacing* the pain, or putting it where it does not belong. It becomes difficult to resolve the grief because it is projected onto and experienced around the wrong subject or object. It needs to be owned as our own.

Pseudo-resolution: Pseudo-resolution is a false resolution that occurs when a person fools themselves into feeling that grief has been resolved, when it actually has not run its course.

Spiritual bypass: This involves using spirituality to give someone a false sense of overcoming the pain that they have trouble owning as a way to hide from their very real feelings of say sadness or anger. There is a "tendency to use spiritual ideas and practices to sidestep or avoid facing unresolved emotional issues, psychological wounds, and unfinished developmental tasks," says John Welwood, a Buddhist teacher and psychotherapist who introduced the term mid 1980s.

Premature resolution: This is when people try to force themselves to resolve grief without allowing themselves to move through the full cycle of mourning. In these cases, the unresolved feelings tend to come out sideways in the form of projections, transferences, bursts of anger, simmering resentments, excessive criticism/rumination on negative subjects, bouts of depression, self-medication, and so on.

Types of Grief Reactions

The following is an overview of the forms that grief can take.

- *Normal grief* tends to run its own course and lessen over time, although the time as well as the intensity may vary from person to person and also according to the timing, nature, and intensity of the loss itself. Normal grief doesn't necessarily need therapy, when there is community support, that can be sufficient. And normal grief can surface a year or two after a loss to death. Processing it in therapy immediately isn't necessarily a good idea. This is what can be missing when it comes to unseen losses: the community may not see and support disenfranchised losses.
- *Disenfranchised Grief:* This is a kind of grief that society doesn't tend to recognize or see in its full dimension. Some examples of disenfranchised losses that too often

go ungrieved are the loss of someone to addiction, the loss of safety in the home, the impact of bullying or prejudice, divorce both for the spouse and children, abortion/infertility, dementia of a loved one, death of a pet, job loss or moving to another community. With these losses, society often wants someone to get over their pain quickly or to sideline it and get back to normal life. The grieving process is necessary to get over the loss.

- *Anticipatory grief:* With anticipatory grief, we feel grief in anticipation of what could happen. We grieve in advance. ACAs can experience this kind of grief as kids. We get sad before something bad happens to sort of prepare ourselves for the worst (which we learn to expect) so that it won't hurt as much if, and more likely when, it actually happens.

- *Parental overreaction to their child's pain:* I am naming and adding this category because I see so much of it in my practice. Parents project the unfelt grief of the child that lives inside of them onto the child they are raising. The parent's boundaries become confused as they invade their child's inner world and assign pain to their child that is really inside of them, making their child feel defective or as if there is something wrong with them. Parents need to own and address their own unresolved grief so they can stop making it about their child by overreacting to what may simply be their child's normal pain. This is one of the ways I see pain passing through the generations.

- *Age correspondence reaction:* For a parent, when their child hits the age of a time in their life when they were traumatized, the parent's unconscious pain from that time may get triggered. Then they make their pain from the past about the child's present. The parent may go to one extreme or the other. They may experience extra worry and anxiety for their child. They may want to overprotect their child because the child *in them* felt underprotected or unsafe. Or they may want to distance from their child, because the child in the parent wants to go numb, or doesn't want to touch or feel that old wound.

- *Complicated grief:* Complicated grief is the kind of grief that doesn't seem to resolve itself over time and becomes prolonged or chronic. This can occur due to the nature of the loss being sudden, violent, or hidden (e.g., prison or addiction), or where we are ambivalent about the loss. Being the child of an addict is a receipt for complicated grief. Some warning signs of this kind of complex mourning could include self-medication, sexual acting out, self-harming behaviors, chronic and disabling feelings of guilt, worthlessness, suicidal thoughts, violence, rage, or radical lifestyle changes. The age correspondence reaction may be seen as a form of complicated grief.

- *Inhibited grief:* When a person does not let their grief show, whether it's because they want to keep it private or because they have hidden it even from themselves, their grief becomes inhibited. When someone cannot allow themselves to grieve, their body may do their crying for them. They may have physical symptoms like muscle stiffness, back pain, migraines, or illnesses that are directly connected to deep, emotional stress. Or they may act out, redirect their grief or self-medicate.
- *Cumulative grief:* Cumulative grief occurs when losses accumulate because they occur on top of each other. PTSD and cPTSD can be forms of cumulative grief and hurt has accumulated over time but has gone unidentified and unmourned.
- *Collective grief:* This a form of grief felt by a group. It might be race-related grief, class-related, the death of a public figure, a school shooting, or the result of a natural disaster.

My Own Adaptation of Stages of Loss in Addicted/ Dysfunctional Family Systems

My first attempt at integrating research with sociometry and psychodrama was to use British psychiatrists John Bowlby and Colin Murray Parkes's outline of the four stages of loss that center around attachment figures. Elisabeth Kübler-Ross adapted and added to these in relation to death, but Bowlby's outline pertained to life loss as well, which was what I saw in the addictions field. Because warm-up is a crucial part of role play, I naturally wondered if using Bowlby's research in a locogram would be a way to warm up the group to grief work and individuals to feeling ready to do psychodrama. I put Bowlby's stages of loss into a locogram, **e.g, shock and numbness/ yearning and searching /disorganization, anger, and despair/reorganization** /other. Then I said, "I'm going to designate four spots on a floor in a sort of square so we can explore how to process grief. Walk over to any stage that you're grappling with at the moment, and when you get there, share about why you chose it." (The therapist can ask another question that can be anything that continues the process.)

I began trying it out in my training groups, then in therapy groups, and then with my students at New York University. While it proved to be a great warm-up or check-in to see where the group "was at," it didn't seem to allow for many criterion questions, which meant that the process wasn't rich enough and didn't access enough inner states; it was educational but not sufficiently evocative. Because there are limited choices in a locogram, the process is self-limiting and reaches a saturation point quickly. It can also feel unnaturally divided up, as people may feel many conflicting feelings that don't fit into a neat order.

I eventually put this aside because it didn't work to my satisfaction. However, I have now made my own stages of loss, informed by the work of Bowlby, Kübler-Ross, and Rachel Naomi Remen, and my own clinical work in the addictions field. I use them as a floor check because there is so much more opportunity for choice and member-to-member connection and support. A floor check allows for the complexity of grief to emerge in the process.

Stages of Loss Experienced in Alcoholic Families (Dayton 2022)

Numbness/Shock: The trauma of living with a loved one who is addicted is deeply disturbing and frightening, and the family becomes initially shocked, and then, over time, inured to pain, numb.

Denial/Enabling: The family tries to change the channel, to hide their pain and shame from themselves, each other, and the world. They make excuses, "Mom has the flu again," "Dad is tinkering in his garage."

Hypervigilance/Anxiety: As the problem gets worse, the family becomes hypervigilant, constantly preoccupied with the addict's behavior, scanning the addict and even others in the family for signs of danger, slipping, secrecy, lying, using/abusing as they wait for the other shoe to drop.

Avoidance/Withdrawal/"Factioning": Because the family cannot grieve openly and together, they may avoid subjects, people, places, or activities that are now painful, avoid or withdraw from each other, or separate into factions (J. Collins-Stuckert, personal communication, 2022).

Yearning/Returning: The family is trapped in the yo-yoing pattern of addiction. There is a repetitive pattern of yearning for the addict to return to normal, having them back momentarily or seeing glimpses of "normal" and then losing them to their substance or behavior, over and over again. "Will mom sober up for my birthday?" "Will my dad be sober for parents' night?" Grief is ongoing; there is no clear beginning, middle, and end.

Helplessness/Despair/Hopelessness: Family members feel that nothing they can do will make things better; they come to feel hopeless and despairing of ever returning to normal again.

Anger/Blaming/Mistrust: These feelings become internalized by each family member, then they act them out in their relationships. Anger and resentment get projected around the family and create free-floating pain and scapegoats.

Chaos/Cathexis: Family factions form; some people gain power while others become marginalized. Bonds become dysfunctional, traumatic bonding and codependency develop, and there can be a preoccupation with a person or a family that borders on obsessive.

Intervention/Mobilization: Something in the environment intervenes on the family disease directly or indirectly, for example, a child who is acting out, a DUI, getting fired, an intervention, or a family member reaching out for help. There is a dawning of recognition of the sickness in the family and the need for help.

Reorganization/Recovery/Decathexis: Family members begin a process of decathexis from the disease, and they learn both intrapersonal and interpersonal strategies for dealing with it.

Acceptance/Gratitude/Posttraumatic Growth: Family members realize that they too have become disease carriers and that they need to take individual responsibility for an extended process of recovery. The process of recovery itself becomes a "new design for living," and they come to appreciate their deepened and more meaningful experience of life.

Grief Spectrogram

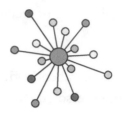

The Grief Spectrogram is a good way to help groups warm-up to the subject of grief. It helps with emotional regulation and increased understanding of the many ways that grief might manifest. It can be the first process used to create awareness of how much or how little one is experiencing any one feeling.

Goals:

1. To educate clients about grief symptoms.
2. To help clients to self-identify as to how much of any one symptom they may be experiencing, and then connect them to each other through identification and sharing.

Steps:

1. Draw an imaginary line dividing the room down the middle, showing group members where the line is as you do so.
2. Explain to the participants that each end of the work area represents an extreme and that the bisecting line is the midpoint: for example, in depression work, one side of the room can represent very much and the other side very little. (See Spectrogram/tiandayton on YouTube or on tiandayton.com/innerlook.)
3. Now choose some of the questions from the list below that are relevant to your particular group and ask participants to stand at whatever point along the continuum that feels right for them in response.
   - How much yearning do you feel?
   - How much sadness do you feel?
   - How much anger do you feel?
   - How much unresolved emotion do you feel surrounding this loss?
   - How blocked are you from getting in touch with your genuine feelings involved in this issue?
   - How disrupted in your daily routines do you feel?

- How much fear of the future do you feel?
- How much is your sleep affected?
- How much trouble are you having organizing yourself?
- How uninterested in your life do you feel?
- How much do you feel your grief has contributed to your becoming a deeper person?
- How much old, unresolved grief is being activated and remembered as a result of this current issue?
- How tired do you feel?
- How much hope do you feel about your life and the future?
- How much regret do you feel?
- How much self-recrimination do you feel?
- How much shame or embarrassment do you feel?
- How much depression do you feel?
- Other

4. After each question, allow people to spontaneously share feelings that come up for them while doing this exercise, either with the entire group or, if the group is large, in subgroups with those who are next to them on the spectrogram. You can do a mixture of forms of sharing; that is, on one question you can let the group share in the large group and on another they can share in subgroups with those who are standing near them along the spectrogram. I generally allow the group to choose however they would like to share by simply asking, "Would you like to share in the large group or subgroups on this one?"

5. Repeat this process for as many questions as can be absorbed. Generally three or four will be plenty, but you can do more if the group wishes.

Variations:

Grief is on a continuum; individuals will vary considerably as to how they experience loss. Consequently, their level of grief, sadness, anger, disruption, and so on will depend upon the individual. The spectrogram allows clients to assess themselves.

Simple role plays can be incorporated into the spectrogram or empty chair work; experiential letter writing or role play can follow it.

Floor Check: Stages of Grief and Loss Experienced with Addiction and Relational Trauma

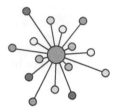

Goals:

1. To offer an experiential way to heal grief.
2. To bring group members to an awareness of the many stages that one can pass through while grieving.
3. To help those overwhelmed by unconscious grief to become more focused as to what part of grief they may be stuck in.
4. To bond and engage group members.

Steps:

1. On large pieces of paper, write these stages of grief that alcoholic families may go through:
   - Numbness/Shock
   - Denial/Enabling
   - Hypervigilance/Anxiety
   - Avoidance/Withdrawal/"Factioning"
   - Yearning/Returning
   - Helplessness/Despair/Hopelessness
   - Anger/Blaming/Mistrust
   - Chaos/Cathexis
   - Intervention/Mobilization
   - Reorganization/Recovery/Decathexis
   - Acceptance/Gratitude/Posttraumatic Growth
2. Place the stages a couple of feet apart from each other, scattered around the floor.
3. Ask participants to stand on or near the stage that best describes their experience of the moment.

4. Say, "Whenever you are warmed up, share in a sentence or two why you are standing where you're standing."

5. After all who wish to have shared, ask another question from this list or come up with your own that work for your group:
   - Where do you feel you are now with your grief?
   - Which stage do you avoid going into or shut down around because it makes you feel too vulnerable?
   - Which stage did your family of origin or your current family avoid?
   - Which stage do you feel stuck in?
   - Which stage do you have trouble tolerating when someone else is going through it?
   - Which stage do you feel you have moved through successfully? Share your new understanding.

6. Next, if you want to extend the process you can invite the group members to "Place your hand on the shoulder of someone who shared something with which you identified." Group members can share directly with the person why they chose him or her. The entire group can do this at once.

7. Next, you can sit down and share about the entire process and what came up for the group throughout, or move into role plays that became warmed up during the process. You can also do the experiential letter writing exercise and invite group members to write a letter to a part of yourself or anyone else that this process warmed you up to talking to.

Variations:

You can put two chairs on the stage and invite group members to talk to a chair representing their loss, or choose a group member as a role player to represent it. The loss can be of a person, a part of the self, or a period in one's life. Grief for addicts and ACAs might be for a lost parent or period of childhood; for the addict it might be years of lost productivity or relationships due to addiction. For addicts who are also ACAs, it might be both.

Note: These are general instructions for all floor checks.

Disenfranchised Losses Floor Check

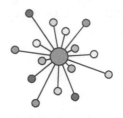

Goals:
---

1. To help clients to understand the types of losses that often go unrecognized and unmourned.
2. To give clients an opportunity to begin to identify and mourn these types of losses in a supportive container.

Steps:
---

1. On large pieces of paper write triggers for relational trauma and scatter them on the floor a few feet apart from each other:
   - Loss of a connection to self, due to trauma
   - The grief of the inner child who lives inside of the adult
   - For the addict, the loss of potential or a part of their life
   - For the adult child of an alcoholic (ACA), the loss of a sober parent or a period of unencumbered childhood
   - For the ACA, the loss of a functional family
   - For the spouse of an addict, the loss of a trusted and dependable partner
   - Divorce abandonment/visitation changes related to divorce
   - Socially stigmatized deaths (AIDS, suicide, murder, DUI, overdose, death)
   - Adoption — either being adopted or placing a child up for adoption, adoptive parents whose child seeks a biological family
   - Death of a pet
   - Miscarriage, infertility
   - Disabling conditions, health issues
   - Moving to a new home, job loss, retirement
   - Mental illness or cognitive deficit
   - Other

2. Ask the following criterion questions or make up your own:
   - Walk over to one of these manifestations of loss that is pulling you now, whether or not it is the loss you are here to work on, share.
   - Walk over to a word that describes the kind of loss you feel your family experienced (family of origin or progenitive), share.
   - Walk over to a manifestation of loss that you have long denied, share.
   - Walk over to a manifestation of loss that your family denied.
   - Walk over to a manifestation of loss that you think you are here to work on (it can change or include more). Share.
3. Next you may invite the group members to "Walk over and place your hand on the shoulder of someone who shared something with which you identified." Group members can share directly with that person as to why they chose him or her. The entire group can do this at once. This step is not always necessary, but it teaches reaching out.
4. Next you can sit down and share about the entire process and what came up or move into role plays, experiential letter writing, or other processes.

Variations:

The group can do role plays by putting two chairs together facing each other and talking to an empty chair or role player or to whomever this process warmed up for them.

This can also be a warm-up to a social atom depicting a relational "snapshot" of the "frozen grief" of the family of origin or current family.

For each question, group members can share so that the entire group can hear them or, if the group is large, they can share with those who are standing on the same word that they chose. If they share on the same word they are sociometrically aligned and sharing with those who are feeling the same as they are, this allows clients to heal through identification, take in sharing and support, and learn the skills of translating emotion into words (emotional literacy) then sharing with others and listening with attention, all of which reduce isolation and trains people in the skills of emotional literacy and emotional regulation in a relational context.

Signs and Symptoms of Unresolved Grief Floor Check

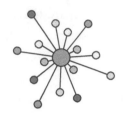

Goals:
---

1. To educate clients as to the ways that unresolved grief might play out without awareness.
2. To provide a process through which clients can identify which ways they might be playing out their unresolved grief.
3. To enable feelings of loss to be felt.

Steps:
---

1. Place these signs/symptoms a couple of feet apart from each other, scattered around the floor.

   - Caretaking/fixing: trying to give another or "fix" in another what you want for yourself or what needs fixing in you
   - Sudden angry outbursts
   - Rage
   - Emotional numbness, shutting down
   - Survival guilt
   - Memorialization: keeping everything about the lost person or a time in life just as it was . . . or do you do the opposite and change everything too fast?
   - Self-mutilation/self-harming behaviors
   - Ghosting: thinking you are seeing the lost person everywhere
   - Anticipatory grief: anxiety over losses that you fear may happen
   - Easily triggered: shooting from zero to ten with no speed bumps in between
   - Irritability/anger/negativity
   - Continued obsessing/rumination
   - Fears of abandonment/rejection/being scapegoated
   - Hypervigilance/free-floating anxiety/fear of another loss or rupture
   - Addiction/self-medication

- Apathy/low-grade depression
- Other

2. Choose among the following criterion questions according to the needs of your group, or make up your own:
   - Walk over to a symptom that draws you, and share why.
   - Walk over to a symptom that you have struggled with the most inside yourself.
   - Walk over to a symptom that you fear could get bigger.
   - Walk over to the symptom that gets in your way the most in close relationships.
   - Walk over to a symptom that you feel has gotten better.

3. Next, you may invite the group members to "Walk over and place your hand on the shoulder of someone who shared something with which you identified." Group members can share directly with that person as to why they chose him or her. The entire group can do this at once. This step is not always necessary, but it teaches reaching out.

4. Next, you can sit down and share about the entire process and what came up for the group.

Variations:

You can follow up with role play or another exercise of your choice, such as the next one in this series.

Group members may have come in touch with parts of themselves they want to talk to, or other people they feel grief around. This exercise creates awareness about how grief has manifested in their lives, as well as in their families, that they may not have recognized as grief.

Talking to the Loss through Empty Chair, Role Player, or Picture

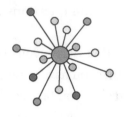

Goals:

1. To embody a lost person, part of a person, part of self, time of life, substance, or behavior.
2. To help the client to clarify, articulate and grieve the loss openly.

Steps:

1. Set up two chairs, one that the protagonist sits in and across from and one that a role player representing the loss sits in or use an empty chair.
2. Invite the client to either enrole a person or part of self to talk to, or use an empty chair to represent them. *Note: Photographs can also be used, simply put the photo on the chair/ bench and talk to the picture and when you role reverse, you become the person in the picture.*
3. Invite the client to say or do all that they wish to, using doubling and role reversal as needed.
4. Bring closure by saying, "Say the last things you want to say for now"; end the role play from the self of the protagonist.

Variations:

If you're using photographs, protagonists can talk to one person or a family photo, they can double for what they imagine anyone is feeling by simply standing behind the chair where the picture is placed. Photographs can be remarkably evocative. Also talking to photos of one's self at any age is a great way to bring those periods of life alive. It can be resilience building to talk to photos that represent strong relationships or happy times of life.

Family photos can also function as a social atom. The protagonist can enrole all family members including themselves, place them on the stage, and proceed with a psychodrama.

CHAPTER THIRTEEN

The Meadows and Newport Academy: Adapted Floor Checks for Special Populations

> *When you're born a light is switched on, a light which shines up through your life. As you get older the light still reaches you, sparkling as it comes up through your memories. And if you're lucky as you travel forward through time, you'll bring the whole of yourself along with you, gathering your skirts and leaving nothing behind, nothing to obscure the light. But if a Bad Thing happens part of you is seared into place, and trapped for ever at that time. The rest of you moves onward, dealing with all the todays and tomorrows, but something, some part of you, is left behind. That part blocks the light, colors the rest of your life, but worse than that, it's alive. Trapped for ever at that moment, and alone in the dark, that part of you is still alive.*
> —Michael Marshall Smith, *Only Forward*

The following adaptations are done by the many therapists who devote their passion and creativity to help others learn to feel, talk, trust, and play. They are floor checks for specific populations, done with staff and by therapists at The Meadows for their specific programs and with Newport Academy staff for adolescents/teens and young adults. Each therapist has entered symptoms or words that their clientele wish to explore that fit their population's needs. They have also come up with criterion questions that move the process in directions that they feel will be useful.

Emotional Difficulties Floor Check

Adapted for and from the Meadows IOP curriculum that incorporates the work of Pia Melody
(Founder and Senior Fellow of The Meadows), with Debra Mayo, LPC, CCTP

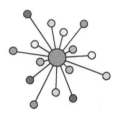

Goals:

1. To create a psychoeducational approach to explore the overview of trauma effects.
2. To engage and bond groups over issues that they are all working on.

Steps:

1. Scatter cards/papers with the "emotional difficulties" written on them, one on each paper, around the floor.
   - Inability to self-soothe
   - Self-hatred
   - Numbing behaviors
   - Chronic anxiety
   - Poor boundaries
   - Seeking attention in inappropriate ways
   - Efforts to control as a response to trauma and triggers
   - Acting out helplessness/powerlessness
   - Problems with authority figures
   - Lack of relational trust
   - Constant demand that others prove they can be trusted
   - Impulsivity
   - Poor conflict management
   - Do not read social situations and cues well
   - Poor transitions from situation to situation
   - Low frustration tolerance
   - Other

2. Ask some of the questions from this list and allow time for whoever would like to share a couple of sentences on whatever question they want to explore.
    - Walk over to one of these difficulties that is pulling you now, whether or not it is the loss you are here to work on, share.
    - Walk over to a word that describes the kind of difficulty you feel your family experienced (family of origin or progenitive). Walk over to something you feel you have come a long way in mastering.
    - Walk over to a difficulty that you have long denied.
    - Walk over to a difficulty that your family denied.
    - Walk over to a difficulty that you feel you have made progress in.
3. Next if you want to extend the process you may invite group members to:
    - Walk over and place your hand on the shoulder of someone who shared something with which you identified.
    - Walk over to someone who said something that moved you and share with them what it was.
    - Walk over to someone you feel you learned something from and tell them what you learned from them.
    - Walk over to someone with whom you have something special you'd like to share and share with them what it is.

Group members can share directly with that person as to why they chose him or her. The entire group can do this at once.

4. Next you can sit down and share about the entire process and what came up or move into another process or simple role plays in which you can set up two chairs and invite group members to talk to a person or part of themselves that this process warmed them up to want to talk to.

Variations:

Add a strength-based approach ask questions like, "Which manifestation do you feel you inherited but doesn't really belong to you? Which manifestation do you now have some recovery around or which manifestation are you glad you don't identify with?"

Shame Circle

Adapted from the Claudia Black, PhD, Young Adults curriculum

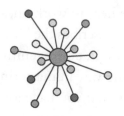

"Don't talk, Don't Trust, Don't Feel" are the "rules of an alcoholic family" created by Claudia Black, PhD, author of *It Will Never Happen to Me* and *Unspoken Legacy: Addressing the Impact of Trauma and Addiction within the Family* (Black 1982).

Dr. Black goes on to expand on other rules that often germinate and grow in families that cannot feel, share, or trust. They are as follows:

- Don't think (just don't think about what is going on)
- Don't question (don't question what is happening)
- Don't ask (don't ask for anything or expect anything)
- Don't play (be mature)
- Don't make a mistake (mistakes are not tolerated)

Goals:

1. To provide an experiential way of exploring the ways that shame can play out.
2. To engage group members with each other over subject matter that is part of their recovery process.

Steps:

1. Scatter cards/papers with the manifestations of shame written on them, one on each paper, around the floor.
   - Control
   - Perfection
   - Addictive disorders
   - Rage
   - Victimization
   - Suicide
   - Depression

- Procrastination
- Others

2. Ask the following **criterion questions** or make up your own:
   - Walk over to one of these manifestations of shame that is pulling you now, whether or not it is the loss you are here to work on, share.
   - Walk over to a word that describes the kind of shame you feel your family experienced (family of origin or progenitive).
   - Walk over to one manifestation you feel you have come a long way in mastering and share a sentence or two about that.
   - Walk over to a manifestation of shame that you have long denied, share.
   - Walk over to a manifestation of shame that your family denied.
   - Walk over to a manifestation of shame that you are here to work on or think you are here to work on (it can change or include more). Share.

3. Next you may invite the group members to "Walk over and place your hand on the shoulder of someone who shared something with which you identified." Group members can share directly with that person as to why they chose him or her. The entire group can do this at once. This step is not always necessary but it teaches reaching out.

4. Next you can sit down and share about the entire process and what came up or move into simple role plays talking to a manifestation of shame.

Variations:

If you want to add resilience building questions ask, which manifestation are you really motivated to work on? Or which manifestation is the biggest piece of new learning for you? Or which manifestation do you feel the most optimistic that you can make positive changes in?

Cognitive Distortions Floor Check

Adapted for and from the Claudia Black, Young Adult Center at
The Meadows curriculum with Claudia Black, PhD

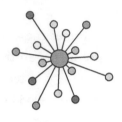

Goals:

1. To provide an experiential way to become more aware of the kinds of cognitive distortions that become our self-talk.
2. To allow protagonists to self-diagnose which cognitive distortions they use and how they use them.
3. To teach the skills of emotional literacy and self-regulation.
4. To facilitate group cohesion in a manner that can include self-reflection, listening to others, and playfulness.

Steps:

1. Write these cognitive distortions on sheets of paper and scatter them around the floor a couple of feet apart from each other.
   - Catastrophizing: Making everything worse than it is. "The repairman didn't come on time, and that means I'll be late to pick up the kids. Then dinner will be late, my husband will be mad, the kids will miss soccer practice, and then they will be mad. Why do I even bother?"
   - Personalizing: Making whatever is going on with anyone about me. "My coworkers were laughing when I walked into the group room. I know they were making fun of me."
   - Mind reading: Imagining you know what another person is thinking about a situation or about you.
   - Shoulds: "I should be doing this" or "I should never have brought this up . . ."
   - Blaming: "If only they would change." "It's because of them that I . . ." "I wouldn't have lost my temper if she just would have . . ."

- Overgeneralizing: "My husband didn't fix the sink faucet right" goes to "My husband never does anything right."
- All-or-nothing thinking: "I didn't score as high on the test as I wanted. I'll never graduate."
- Disqualifying the positive. "Thank you, but ..."
- Mental filtering: Picking out the single negative piece and focusing on it; choosing the one bit of negative feedback and making it everything you think about.

2. Ask participants to stand on or near the cognitive distortion that they identify as a sort of "go to" for them.

3. Say, "Whenever you are warmed up, share in a sentence or two why you are standing where you're standing."

4. After all who wish to have shared, you can explore another question such as "Which cognitive distortion can you really spin out on that gets you into trouble or a dark place?"

5. If the group wants to continue to explore, you can further vary criterion questions by asking, "Which cognitive distortion starts a cascading effect for you, either in your own head or in your relationships?" A next question might be: "Which cognitive distortion do you use that surprises you the most, that you were unaware of?" or "Which cognitive distortion have you made some improvement on managing lately?"

6. If you'd like to extend the process, you can invite the group members to "Walk over and place your hand on the shoulder of someone who shared something with which you identified." Group members can share directly with that person as to why they chose him or her. The entire group can do this at once.

7. Next, you can sit down and share about the entire process and what came up for the group members.

Variations:

If you want to add some variety to this try asking, "Which issue are you the most irritated by when you encounter it in someone else?" or "Which issue do you feel you have gained some clarity around lately?"

Silver Linings Floor Check

Created for Meadows for Rio Retreat with Jean Collins-Stuckart, MSW

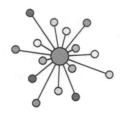

Steps:

1. Write these deep changes on large pieces of paper and scatter them on the floor a few feet apart from each other.
   - I have a deeper appreciation of life.
   - I feel lighter inside.
   - I feel a greater sense of spontaneity.
   - My relationships with others feel more natural and fulfilling.
   - I have learned that I am stronger than I thought I was.
   - I can feel on a deeper level and share more of myself with others.
   - I have reconnected with parts of myself I thought I had lost or never knew I had.
   - I have a sense of my own power.
   - I have more compassion and acceptance for myself.
   - I am braver than I thought I was.
   - I have learned what it means to let go of resentment in the service of my own personal growth.
   - I can do things I thought I couldn't do.
   - I am open to new things.
   - I have grown in a sense of spirituality.
   - I am more mindful and aware.
   - I am learning to take life a day at a time.
   - Other

2. Ask the following criterion questions or make up your own:
   - Walk over to one of these sentences that draws you and share a sentence as to why it does.
   - Walk over to a sentence you feel you have come a long way in mastering.
   - Walk over to a sentence that represents your growing edge.

- Walk over to a sentence that you feel trauma took away from you and you are getting back.
- Walk over to a sentence that used to be a challenge for you and share about how you grew.
- Walk over to a sentence that you look forward to expanding in the future.

3. Next, you may invite the group members to "Walk over and place your hand on the shoulder of someone who shared something with which you identified." Group members can share directly with that person as to why they chose him or her. The entire group can do this at once. This step is not always necessary, but it teaches reaching out.

4. Next, you can sit down and share about the entire process and what came up for the group, or move into future-projection psychodramas, talking to yourself in the future after having moved forward in some of these areas.

Variations:

For each question, group members can share so that the entire group can hear them, or, if the group is large, they can share with those who are standing on the same word that they chose. If they share on the same word, they are sociometrically aligned and sharing with those who are feeling the same as they are.

Sexual Compulsivity Floor Check

Adapted for and from The Meadows, Willow House curriculum, with Havi Kang LPC, CSAT, CPTT

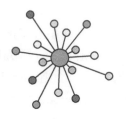

Goals:

1. To make the issues related to sex and love addiction for women more teachable and relatable.
2. To allow the group members to become comfortable identifying, articulating, and sharing issues around sex and love addiction that they struggle with in their recovery.
3. To allow the group members to engage, bond, and connect with each other.
4. To normalize behaviors and feelings that may be surrounded by secrecy and shame.
5. To build resilience, autonomy, emotional literacy, and emotional regulation in a supportive community of healing.

Steps:

1. On large pieces of paper, write issues such as:
    - Sexual fantasy
    - Obsessive sexual thoughts
    - Excessive masturbation
    - Eroticized shame
    - Eroticized fear
    - Seduction
    - Objectification
    - Sexually intrusive thoughts or urges
    - Porn use
    - Using social media to send or receive nude photos
    - Sugar baby/sugar daddy
    - OnlyFans app
    - Webcamming
    - Risky or inappropriate sexual behaviors

- Infidelity/cheating
- Emotional affairs
- Other

2. Ask participants to stand on or near a thought process or behavior that can preoccupy them in significant ways.

3. Say, "Whenever you are warmed up, share in a sentence or two why you are standing where you're standing."

4. After all who wish to have shared, you can ask another question such as "Which preoccupation or behavior is the slipperiest slope for you?" "Which one leads to the most unmanageable behaviors?" "What does this behavior do for you?" "How does this preoccupation/behavior impact your other relationships (with your family/ friends/partner)?" "Which behavior is the toughest to let go?"

5. After sharing has slowed down, if the group is game to continue, you can ask something like "Which preoccupation or behavior have you made progress with in improving in your recovery process?"

6. Next. invite the group members to "place your hand on the shoulder of someone who shared something with which you identified, and tell them what it was." Group members can share directly with the person they chose or the entire group can do this at once.

7. Next, you can sit down and share about the entire process and what came up for the group throughout the process.

Variations:

Questions for exploration: "What would your life be like without these preoccupations or behaviors?" or "What skills do you need to develop in order to better manage these behaviors?"

To lengthen the process, you can do either of the following:
- Use an empty chair to represent any one of the preoccupations or behaviors, and do a vignette of talking *to* the preoccupation or behavior, then reversing roles and talking *as* it back to yourself.
- Use a role player to represent any one of the preoccupations or behaviors and talk *to* them, then reverse roles and talk *as* it back to yourself. Therapists, group members, and even the protagonist can double for any role the protagonist is in as a way to promote group engagement and deepen the exploration.

Love Addiction

Adapted for and from The Meadows, Willow House curriculum, with Havi Kang LPC, CSAT, CPTT

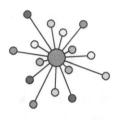

Goals:

1. To make the issues related to sex and love addiction for women more teachable and relatable.
2. To allow the group members to become comfortable identifying, articulating, and sharing issues around sex and love addiction that they struggle with in their recovery.
3. To allow the group members to engage, bond, and connect with each other.
4. To normalize behaviors and feelings that may be surrounded by secrecy and shame.
5. To build resilience, autonomy, emotional literacy, and emotional regulation in a supportive community of healing.

Steps:

1. On large pieces of paper, write issues such as:
   - Serial dating
   - Attention seeking
   - Invulnerability/too vulnerable
   - Needy/clingy
   - Caretaking
   - Intensity seeking
   - Fears of abandonment/rejection
   - Dependency issues
   - Emotional despair
   - Obsessive thoughts of partner
   - Stalking via social media
   - Anxious attachment
   - Falling in "love" quickly
   - Fantasy
   - Denial

- Love withdrawal (extreme emotions, hopelessness)
- Difficulty leaving unhealthy relationships
- Other

2. Ask participants to stand on or near a thought process or behavior that can preoccupy them in significant ways.

3. Say, "Whenever you are warmed up, share in a sentence or two why you are standing where you're standing."

4. After all who wish to have shared, you can ask another question such as "Which preoccupation or behavior is the slipperiest slope for you?" "Which one leads to the most unmanageable behaviors?" "What does this behavior do for you?" "How do these preoccupations/behaviors impact your other relationships (with your family/friends/partner)?" "Which behavior is the toughest to let go?"

5. After sharing has slowed down, if the group is game to continue, you can ask something like "Which preoccupation or behavior have you made progress with in improving in your recovery process?"

6. Next. invite the group members to "Place your hand on the shoulder of someone who shared something with which you identified, and tell them what it was." Group members can share directly with the person they chose. The entire group can do this at once.

7. Next, you can sit down and share about the entire process and what came up for the group throughout the process.

Variations:

Questions for exploration: "What would your life be like without these preoccupations or behaviors?" or "What skills do you need to develop in order to better manage these behaviors?"

To lengthen the process, you can do any of the following:
- Use an empty chair to represent any one of the preoccupations or behaviors, and do a vignette of talking *to* the preoccupation or behavior, then reversing roles and talking *as* them back to yourself.
- Use a role player to represent any one of the preoccupations or behaviors and talk *to* them, then reverse roles and talk *as* them back to yourself. Therapists, group members, and even the protagonist can double for any role the protagonist is in as a way to promote group engagement and deepen the exploration.
- Write a letter to any of the behaviors surrounding love addiction and do the experiential letter writing exercise.

Anger and Addiction Floor Check

Adapted for and from The Meadows Ranch Eating Disorders Program with Billie Church, MC, LPC, CEDS

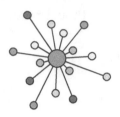

Goals:

1. To allow group members to broaden their concept of the many ways in which anger may manifest.
2. To provide a sociometric exercise for the exploration of anger.
3. To bring awareness of when or how unresolved anger might be fueling addiction.

Steps:

1. On large pieces of paper write or have the group write the many manifestations of anger, such as: cynicism, negativity, criticism, sarcasm, digging in heels, passive aggression, whining, rage, acting-out behaviors, violence, stonewalling, withdrawal, cutting off, coldness, bingeing, restricting, self-loathing, food, purging, overexercising, substances, sex, alcohol, silence, self-harm, depression, gambling, revenge, other, and so on. Always leave a blank piece of paper for writing in any terms that the group may spontaneously wish to add.
2. Scatter these words around the floor and invite group members to stand on or near the manifestation of anger that they identify most as their own.
3. Invite group members to share why they are standing where they are standing.
4. Invite group members to make another choice and repeat the sharing. Most of us have more than one way that we manifest anger. Repeat this process again if desired. Use some of the following criterion questions or make up your own.
   - Which manifestation has cost you the most?
   - Which manifestation did you learn from the home or world you grew up in?
   - Which manifestation do you feel the most shame around?
   - Which manifestation were you most hurt by when someone else did it to you?
   - Which manifestation have you gained some control over?
   - Walk over and stand on or near the type of anger that you have the hardest time with in yourself.

- Walk over and stand on or near the type of anger that you fear most in other people.

5. Next, invite group members to walk over to someone whose sharing they identify with and place their hand on that person's shoulder. Then ask them to share with that person why they chose them or what they identify with.

6. At this point the group may be ready to simply return to their seats and continue sharing, or they may wish to choose a protagonist and move into psychodrama. In either case, always allow plenty of time for sharing.

Variations:

Questions for exploration: "What would your life be like without these preoccupations or behaviors?" or "What skills do you need to develop in order to better manage these behaviors?"

Somatic Floor Check

Adapted for The Meadows Ranch Eating Disorders Program curriculum with Billie Church, MC, LPC, CEDS

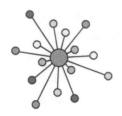

Goals:

1. To allow group members to get in touch with how their bodies may carry the residue of trauma.
2. To provide a sociometric warm-up for the exploration of body/somato-dramas.

Steps:

1. On large pieces of paper, write or have the group write the many manifestations of how trauma might be held in the body, for example: muscle tightness, tightness in the chest, digestive issues, stomach/back aches, feet/toes, organs, legs, arms/shoulders, head/neck, arms/hands/fingers, central nervous system (fight/flight/freeze activation), disease/immune system issues, other.
2. Scatter these words around the floor and invite group members to stand near the body manifestation that they identify as something they grapple with.
3. Invite group members to share why they are standing where they are standing.
4. Invite group members to make another choice by asking other questions. Use these, make up your own, or invite the group to come up with questions that they want to explore:
   - "Which body issue is most unconscious?"
   - "Which body issue gets in your way the most?"
   - "Which body issue do you self-medicate for?"
   - "Which body issue do you feel shame around?"
   - "Which body issue makes you want to cry, and why do you think it does?"
   - "Which body issue makes you angry, and why do you think it does?"
   - "Which body issue do you have the most trouble forgiving yourself for having, and why?"

- "Which body issue is hard for you to hold, and how does that look or manifest?" *Note: The group may well be saturated after a few questions and ready to move on to other work.*

5. If you want to change the vibe, you can invite group members to walk over to someone whose sharing they identify with and place their hand on that person's shoulder. Then ask them to share with that person why they chose them or what they identify with.

6. At this point the group may be ready to simply return to their seats and continue sharing, or they may wish to move into psychodrama.

Variations:

This can be a more fluid exercise than this write-up might indicate. It should feel relaxed and spontaneous, and people should feel free to move around the room. I often do spontaneous role plays during the questioning period if someone looks like they have something inside them that would like to come out. When I do that, I simply walk to that person and say, "Is there someone you'd like to talk to, or would you like to talk to that part of you/your body?" If their answer is yes, I ask them to choose someone to play that part of their body and do a brief role play, then I move back into the process and invite people to share what came up for them.

Another way to introduce role play is to simply put two chairs facing each other in the middle of the room and invite people to go to them and either "put" a part of their body into the empty chair or choose someone to represent that part of their body and proceed with the role play.

Note: At any point in this exercise you can invite people to talk or share as a body part. You can say, "If that part of you had a voice, what would it like to say?" I do this in all of my psychodrama work because the body is so often wanting to talk, and this is a way that trauma held in the body can be metabolized and processed.

Questions for exploration: "What would your life be like without these preoccupations or behaviors?" or "What skills do you need to develop in order to better manage these behaviors?"

Weather Emoji Floor Check

Adapted for Newport Academy Adolescent/Young Adults by Kera Passante, LPC

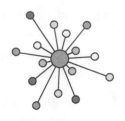

Goals:

1. To get kids up and out of their chairs.
2. To get kids connected to what's going on inside them.
3. To get kids connecting with each other.
4. To teach feeling awareness.
5. To teach kids skills of self-regulation.

Steps:

1. Scatter weather icons on the floor a few feet apart from each other. *Note: you can find examples of weather icons on the internet and download and print them for this exercise. Take care to choose states of weather that represent different moods.*

2. Ask the following **criterion questions** or make up your own and allow time for a "clear, quick" sentence about "why you're standing where you're standing."
   - Walk over to one of weather states that draws you and share a sentence as to why it does.
   - Walk over to a kind of weather that you really hate.
   - Walk over to a kind of weather that you really love.
   - Walk over to a kind of weather that describes how you feel right now.
   - Walk over to a kind of weather that you identify with and share how you identify.

3. Next you may invite the group members to "Walk over and place your hand on the shoulder of someone who shared something with which you identified." Group members can share directly with that person as to why they chose him or her. The entire group can do this at once. This step is not always necessary but it teaches reaching out.

4. Next you can sit down and share about the entire process and what came up or move into role plays and share after that. *Note: If you move into role plays, this process will have served as a warm-up. If you share, it will serve as a full process.*

Variations:

"Empty Chair" Role Plays: One of the kinds of role plays you can do is to put two chairs facing each other and say "Put one of these icons on the chair and talk to it." Group members can "double" as they identify and the director can call for role reversal, etc. Make sure you end the role play from the self-role, "Say the last things you want to say to this part of you."

Soliloquy: Group members can do a soliloquy or a "walk and talk" from one weather state to another or cutting a path through several weather states and narrating that path.

Messages: Floor Check

Adapted for Newport Academy by Caroline Fenkel, DSW, and Heather Monroe, LCSW, of Newport Academy

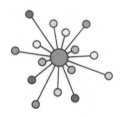

Goals:

1. To provide an experiential way to become more aware of the kinds of messages we tell ourselves.
2. To provide a vehicle for self-exploration and expression.
3. To promote team work and working together.
4. To facilitate group cohesion in a manner that can include playfulness.

Steps:

1. Invite group members to come up with the kinds of negative messages that they tell themselves and write them down on large pieces of paper. *Note: Asking the group to come up with the messages themselves creates a sense of buy-in from the beginning and makes the messages feel specific to their issues/needs of the moment.* If the group would like to mix some positive messages in they can or they can simply do this exercise twice, once for negative message and another for positive messages. Some examples of negative messages are "I can't do anything right," or "I'm just going to screw it up." Some examples of positive messages are "I'm really growing," or "I think I can get better."
2. Place the words a couple of feet apart from each other, scattered around the floor.
3. Ask participants to "stand near" the message that draws them.
4. Say, "Whenever you are warmed-up, share in a sentence or two as to why you are standing where you're standing."
5. After all who wish to have shared, you can explore another question such as "Which message really gets you into trouble or a dark place?"
6. If the group still has energy to continue to explore more questions you can further vary criterion questions by asking "Which message gives you a sense of power,

either dark power or empowerment?" A next question might be, "Which message have you made some improvement on managing lately?"

7. Next invite the group members to "Walk over and place your hand on the shoulder of someone who shared something with which you identified." Group members can share directly with that person as to why they chose him or her. The entire group can do this at once.

8. Next you can sit down and share about the entire process and what came up.

Variations:

For each question, group members can share so that the entire group can hear them or, if the group is large, they can share with those who are standing on the same word that they chose. If they share on the same word, they are sociometrically aligned and sharing with those who are feeling the same as they are—this allows clients to heal through identification, take in sharing and support, and learn the skills of listening all of which reduce isolation. Clinicians and group members can come up with their own criterion questions to move the process along.

If the therapist has enough psychodrama experience, the one protagonist can choose role players to represent each message and make a message sculpture by choosing someone to represent themselves and then placing each "message" where it feels in relation to them. Then the protagonist can talk to each message either from outside or inside the sculpture. Role reversal and doubling can be used. Several group members can take turns doing this or the group can simply derole and then share with the protagonist how they identify and what the sculpture brings up for them.

Messages: Collage

Adapted for Newport Academy by Heather Monroe, LCSW, and Caroline Fenkel, DSW, of Newport Academy

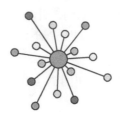

Goals:

1. To provide an experiential way to become more aware of the kinds of messages we tell ourselves.
2. To provide a vehicle for self-exploration and expression.
3. To learn another aspect of an emotional language.
4. To facilitate group cohesion in a manner that can include playfulness.

Steps:

1. Spread many different kinds of magazines on the floor along with scissors, glue and some sort of tag board or large, heavy paper. Select magazines that involve all forms of text and personal, behavioral, and emotional expression with as wide a range of images as possible, i.e., beauty, home, automobile, science, fashion, art, etc.

2. Give the group a specific focus. Ask them to represent themselves in some form somewhere on their page relative to their messages. Then say to the group, "Look for images or word groups that express the negative messages that you say to yourself on the inside and create your collage around that theme."

3. After everyone has more or less completed their collage, ask them to share it. If the group is small, they can share with the entire group. If the group is large, they can have the option of breaking down into small groups. If breaking down, allow people to break down naturally according to where they are drawn to go.

4. Next invite whoever else is warmed up to, to share their picture with the group until everyone has shared.

5. Once the group has shared and felt complete in this part of the process, ask them to paint or create and collage a new picture this time exchanging their negative messages for more uplifting, empowering and self-caring messages, again locating themselves on the page first.

6. Now invite them each to share their picture with the group as they feel warmed up to do so.

Variations:

If the group feels like it, they can hang their message pictures on the wall to refer to them throughout treatment or keep them somewhere for their own use.

Role Reversal Interview as a Parent

Adapted for Newport Academy by Victoria Manik, MA, AMFT, of Newport Academy

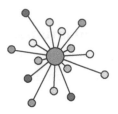

Description: This exercise allows for an exploration of emotions and perspective from a safer "distance" than psychodrama offers. The role of the double allows group members to go a little deeper into the internal dynamics of the role and the sharing after the sociodrama provides further opportunity for personal exploration, if desired. Alternatively, it can be used along the lines of discussion and closure.

Goals:

1. To allow group members to concretize where they feel they are in their recovery process, particularly regarding family systems and family dynamics.
2. To provide group members an opportunity to communicate with caregiver by assuming the role of their own caregiver in an interview with a therapist.
3. Create internal connection, empathy, and understanding with the caregivers who may be absent or disconnected, or with whom their relationship is strained and misunderstood.
4. To create an atmosphere that encourages openness and identification and promotes bonding and support.

Steps:

1. Facilitate group in a safe and secure setting. Make sure all external distractions are mitigated and the group may settle in a private space.
2. Set up two chairs facing each other at the front of the room and encourage group members to sit around the room, much like an audience. Remind group members that the group facilitator will be interviewing using the technique of "role reversal interview," e.g., group members will begin in their role of "self" enrole someone to play their mother, say something to their mother, then reverse roles and "become" their mother and answer questions AS their mother.

3. Ask group members to close their eyes and think of their mother. Ask group members: "Picture your mother, as you picture her, what comes up? What does she look like? How is her hair? How is she dressed? Where is she in your mind? How do you feel as you sit in her presence? Allow for whatever comes up, to come up. Don't judge, label, or make assumptions. Notice what body sensations come up and lean into them as they present themselves. Breathe into the feelings and sensations as you consider your mother as you consider being in the presence of your mother. Now open your eyes and come back into the room, slowly and carefully."

4. Invite group members one by one to "Take the chair whenever you are warmed up, to the role of your mother." *Note: the full group need not participate. In fact, if only a couple of group members participate and the group shares afterward about what came up for them witnessing the role reversal interviews, that is more than sufficient.*

5. The group facilitator can greet mother.

6. Invite the protagonist to say something to their mother, then to reverse roles and answer back to themselves AS THEIR MOTHER.

7. The therapist can then begin to "interview" the group member IN THE ROLE OF THEIR MOTHER. The therapist might ask questions such as "How do you feel about your son/daughter being here in treatment?" or "How would you describe your relationship with your son/daughter," or "How do you feel about your son/ daughter?"

8. Once the group member has answered questions "as their mother," the therapist can ask them to reverse roles back into themselves and either continue with a role play or to end the scene by saying the last things that they wish to say to their mother for now. *Note: As the therapist asks these questions, the group member will answer in role as their mother.*

9. After each group member has been interviewed, close out the group by inviting group members to share any observations (internal and external) about what they witnessed or what they experienced within the role and/or witnessing the work of other group members. Invite group members to journal any insights to bring into individual sessions.

Variations:

Things to Note: due to the sensitive nature of this group for some adolescents, it is suggested that with group members whose caregivers have passed away or whose relationship evokes grief or sadness, the treating clinician briefly describe what's going to happen in the group and encourage self-care activities or individual journaling about the topic, within an individual session prior to the start of the group. Set up two chairs or simply use two chairs that are in the office already. In a private session the therapist can help the group member to get use to reversing roles with another person and answering interview questions as that other person. The client should always begin and the role play in and from the "self" role.

- Do a role reversal interview as your mother.
- Do a role reversal interview as your father.
- Do a role reversal interview as your authentic self.
- Do a role reversal interview as your future self.
- Do a role reversal interview as your past self.
- Do a role reversal interview as your mentor or someone you look up to.

CHAPTER FOURTEEN

Fitting Sociometrics into Your Treatment and Clinical Settings

We don't usually think how we want to think but how we are conditioned to think. Changing our mental paradigms is one of the most important aspects of personal development and one of the cornerstones of lasting transformation.
—Buckminster Fuller

Groups in recovery have a lot they need and long to share, but opening one's mouth and sharing is not necessarily easy to do. In talk-only and even in psychodrama groups, when sharing is done only on the basis of "Who has something they want to say?" a few things may happen. There is a pressure for the therapist to take charge of the process. There can be uncomfortable silences, and more assertive group members get a lot of air time while shyer ones barely open their mouths. Timing is also an issue: it's tough to cut someone off when they are going on too long. This can be discouraging for other group members, and they can see the leader as being unable to manage the group process. On the other hand, if the therapist overmanages the situation, group members can resent them or feel shut down and anxious about opening up themselves.

Sociometrics change this dynamic. The way that they are structured to facilitate multiple moments for member-to-member sharing in dyads and clusters, means that therapists follow a specific process so they don't tend to overmanage, and group members get adequate sharing time so they feel less frustrated and backed-up with emotion. There are countless opportunities built into the processes for anything from casual to intimate exchanges to happen easily and spontaneously. Through attuned criterion questions by the therapist, the process continues to move forward, so that the group doesn't get stuck. The role of the therapist is reduced and the role of the client enhanced and empowered. Group members are on their feet, grounded and oriented in the room and they become stakeholders and choice makers in their own recovery process. Because sociometrics are designed to allow clients to make choice after choice about what feels relevant to them, they help them to take ownership of their own recovery.

Sociometrics teach the research on neuroscience, PTSD, grief, resilience, and post traumatic growth experientially. They operate easily alongside other methods and approaches.

We have rich and enlightening research on trauma and neurobiology that has changed the way we think as clinicians, about healing PTSD and attachment/relational trauma. Translating that research into actionable healing interventions and methods is needed, in order to move the healing from theory into the body, from thoughts into behavior. Sociometrics break that research down and put it into floor checks so that learning can be part of the healing process. This also has the advantage of allowing clients themselves to come up with spontaneous case examples of how any particular symptom might be manifesting in their lives.

Floor checks provide relational vehicles for learning about and processing historical pain, to outline a direct path through our personal history so that we can process wounds, celebrate strengths, and grow.

Sociometrics engage and bond groups and build the skills of emotional literacy, self-regulation, and co-regulation so that clients can convey more accurately how they feel to others. They teach subject matter that helps clients to feel included in and own their recovery process. They teach listening; first tolerating feelings that are stirred up within themselves by what someone says, then staying within the framework of the conversation without fighting, fleeing, or freezing; without exploding or imploding. These intrapersonal and interpersonal skills become portable as clients can take them into the rest of their lives and relationships. They are basic skills of emotional literacy, self-regulation, and co-regulation.

When to Do Trauma Work

Years ago, we felt that it was too risky for addicts who were getting sober from drugs and alcohol to work with their childhood trauma while in treatment. But over time, it became evident that not working with it was also risky, because unresolved trauma can become the pain pump that fuels relapse. In other words, the emotional and psychological pain that may have led someone to self-medicate in the first place was not only still there when they got sober, but it hurt all the more, because they were no longer numbing it with alcohol, drugs, or process addictions. The Band-Aid was ripped off.

One of the beginnings of the ACEs study dates from Vincent Felitti's weight-loss program at Kaiser Permanente in 1985. Frustrated and puzzled by the number of the people in his program who dropped out even though they were losing weight successfully, he began to look more deeply into their personal histories. Upon investigation, he discovered that many people in his clinic—most, actually— had experienced physical and/or sexual abuse growing up. When he questioned his participants further to ask why they dropped out of a program that they were successful in, they reported that their weight felt like "protection." Once they lost weight, they felt vulnerable and exposed; it created a new fear that they'd be attractive, and that felt somehow dangerous. So, they left the program and returned to their medicator, food. Through the lens of addiction, we see that when their medicator was removed, the anxiety and pain that they were medicating, felt all the more intense. Without help in processing those feelings so that they could develop their own skills of mood management, self-regulation, and co-regulation rather than use food to do that for them, they relapsed.

A similar phenomenon can be seen in treatment of any addiction or addictive behavior.

Why Sociometrics Make Trauma Work Safer

There were a few issues that I designed sociometrics to address. While psychodrama was often an important part of a treatment center's programming, it was sometimes done without sufficient knowledge of and training in the method itself. Recall that sociometry is the science of group dynamics and is part of a triadic system that includes psychodrama, sociometry, and group psychotherapy. Without an understanding of sociometry, there was often too much focus on one drama. For example, there was this feeling that all of the healing was taking place in this personal "piece of work." Clients could feel preoccupied about what drama to do then they sometimes regretted their choice of what they did. Therapists and clients alike were seeing one's healing as taking place only when they did their own psychodrama. This is a theoretical error in thinking and reveals a lack of understanding of how psychodrama involves the full group; it leaves out the group dynamics that interface with and contain the process.

Sometimes, for example, there is a deep catharsis through watching someone else's psychodrama—we can be more open and less defended against feeling our feelings if all we are asked to do is watch. Or playing a role in someone else's drama can be a surprising learning experience as we see the world through a different portal, expanding our own ability to perceive. The group, in other words, is always participating in one way or another, through being the protagonist themselves, playing a role, doubling or witnessing, and sharing. As group members share after a drama, they don't give feedback; participants share what comes up for them from their own lives while watching the drama, thus continuing their own healing through identification. This is sociometry in action; it gives the group members a place in the process to make the protagonist's work relevant to them so that they can leave group without carrying their own, triggered history or pain.

Another way sociometry enters the process of psychodrama is when role players de-role. They first share how they experienced playing the role, how they thought and felt as the person they portrayed, then they shake off the role and share from their own lives if they need to.

All of these disciplined parts of the process allow the connections within the group to become grist for the mill of everyone's individual work. If group members give a more traditional form of feedback, such as "I saw you grow," "You did great work," or "You really got to that issue you've been talking about," the drama doesn't get used for group members to process what got triggered or warmed-up in them, so clients wind up taking all of that emotion home with them. And feedback for the protagonist, even if it's positive, can veer into advice and too much mirroring. It can actually feel less supportive than knowing that group members saw and witnessed you at your most vulnerable and raw, that they were there with you identifying with you and vibrating in tune.

Sociometrics eliminate the worry about doing the right "piece of work" because everyone is doing a little work all the time. Additionally, they provide a slow warm-up that can focus not one big piece of work, but many small ones. A therapist might perceive a strong warm-up in a group member and ask, "Would you like to say this to your mom, dad, spouse, or child?"

Much of experiential trauma and attachment work is about the warm-up. If a client is warmed up through the ongoing, engaging experience of doing a floor check, for example, or watching someone else's drama, a part of their work is already being done. If they feel like talking to a part of themselves or someone else through role play, and what they want to say is on the tip of their tongue, their work flows easily and a lot can get done in a short time. It makes the drama more focused and contained, and it's easier to direct.

Another issue I was trying to solve was psychodrama's potential for retraumatization. Therapists worried that psychodrama could get too intense; they were concerned about clients opening up too much. I find that this most often happens if and when the therapist/director isn't following the lead of the protagonist. Or the director is letting role players and group members control the drama through too much "creative" role playing (read: making things up), doubling too far outside the protagonist's framework, or attempting to lead from the double position. Or the therapists themselves are giving too many suggestions, asking too many questions, or being overly goal oriented in the way they direct. Or there isn't enough sharing time for the group, and the sharing is feedback rather than used as an opportunity for the group member's continued processing.

Also I found that having an events-focus associated with trauma work can create problems. It is actually considered a psychodramatic "shock" technique akin to shock therapy to structure a traumatic event on the stage, and it is very rarely indicated because it can cause lasting retraumatization. For example, I wouldn't structure a scene in which someone was sexually abused, raped, or beaten. If you do work with events, there are more subtle ways of working with a frightening one, such as talking to the part of the self that was terrified or to a relationship with a person who the protagonist may feel overwhelmed or controlled by. There is no need to structure an actual traumatic event to heal, and there are other forms of therapy often better suited to this kind of healing. Peter Levine does wonderful work using his Somatic Experiencing (SE) in freeing the body from the residue of, say, an accident. Psychodrama in my opinion is best suited to relational healing and the restoration of spontaneity and creativity within the self-system and life relationships. Certain concepts from SE can be incorporated into psychodrama beautifully by allowing the protagonist to slow the moment of relating down, become aware of what's going on in their bodies, and let the body have a voice.

Still another concern I had was that healing was often seen as having a large catharsis. While catharsis can be important, it is just a part of the picture. Too often, blame and a catharsis of abreaction were becoming the whole therapy. It's easy for anger at someone to become a "go to" in structuring a psychodrama, but discharge shouldn't be a goal or a finishing line. It is helpful sometimes, but if the drama is structured around it, you're giving role training to the protagonist in large emotional discharges. No doubt the bitterness, rage, and anger that we may carry toward our parents, spouses, coworkers, ourselves, or others who have hurt us needs to be explored and expressed in therapy. But we need to move from a catharsis of abreaction to a catharsis of integration; to add new insight and meaning to the past issues we're exploring and reintegrate the split of affect or emotion back into our mind with new understanding. If we stay stuck in blame and anger, remnants of the painful experience and the feelings surrounding it remain split off and unexamined. They live, little landmines waiting to go off when stepped on, lost in the mind/body.

It's important in therapy to give permission for feeling what we have told ourselves we shouldn't or can't feel. It's part of healing unconscious pain from the past so we can stop recreating it in present day relationships. But when permission becomes license, we can start to think that getting angry and expressing all of our negative emotions is what we need to do to be authentic. When we only discharge but don't process our pain, we continue to live in a conflicted inner space, and it becomes harder to internalize all of the good parts of our parents; for example, the parts we modeled and want to keep as our own. Nor can we move past our negative feelings and experience the love almost all children feel for their parents, because we're stuck in our need for or fantasies of revenge.

What good therapy should give us is conscious choice. It should help us to be compassionate with ourselves and empathic with others. Processes like setting up a family-of-origin social atom on stage and talking to the self, inside the moment or system from a safe distance outside of it, help to create compassion for our younger, trapped self. Adding doubling helps to deepen an understanding of the self or any role the protagonist occupies, to bring unconscious emotions to the surface of the mind where they can be thought about. And using role reversal when doing dramas with another helps to create empathy with others and with the self. We can experience ourselves differently, for example, in the system we grew up in. We can reshape the system to reflect our more mature perspective. We can internalize a new experience. It's experiential, embodied, relational healing.

How Can Sociometrics Fit Your Treatment Needs?

I recommend that treatment centers, IOPs, and clinics who want to offer psychodrama as a form of group therapy start with sociometrics either to warm up and focus role plays or as experiential group processes, in and of themselves. Sociometrics are designed so that they can slide into group on an as-needed basis. They work well along with other modalities; they can be a portion of a group or all of a group.

Here is a check list of how to use the various sociometrics:

- **Floor Checks:** Floor checks, along with timelines, experiential letter writing, and social atoms, will form the core of your psychoeducational programming and offer a broad and comprehensive exploration of the material relative to recovery and healing of attachment trauma. They are designed to bond, engage, and educate groups.

- **The Trauma Timeline Process:** The trauma timeline is part of basic trauma work. It can be drawn, done as a group process or one person at a time. Role plays and experiential letter writing can extend the process. And the resilience timeline is an important way of identifying and consolidating strengths, then integrating them into the self so they can be valued and used throughout life. When and where you use this is up to you as the clinician in the room.

- **Social Atom:** The social atom can be used as a diagnostic tool and an experiential intervention. As a diagnostic tool, a social atom can be done upon entering treatment, e.g., an atom of one's relational network, "what network landed me in treatment," can be drawn and shared. During treatment, clients can do a family of origin map/ atom, a frozen moment atom and/or or an atom for any other relational moment or network they wish to explore. Upon exiting treatment, as part of an aftercare plan, clients can do a future projection social atom exploring questions such as, "How do I want my life to look post-treatment," or an atom of their anticipated support network as part of aftercare planning. All of these atoms can be turned into therapy by sharing the social atom on paper and/or turned into sculptures so that clients can experience building, seeing, and even doing role plays of their networks in order to gain a felt sense of its various components.

- **Experiential Letter Writing:** This is the easiest way to add role play to your programming. Letter writing is a tried-and-true therapeutic technique used by treatment centers and therapy venues. Making letter writing experiential extends and deepens the process, and it can also open it to group member participation through casting a role or doubling.

- **Spectrograms:** Spectrograms are great experiential check-ins and can also be easily adapted to explore any issue the group is looking at. The grief spectrogram is an example of this. It gives the therapist information about the group preferences and feeling states and provides the group with easy ways to share. The spectrograms teach self-regulation, as every question is about "how much" or "how little" of a particular feeling or symptom clients are exploring. As they answer those questions experientially, they are called upon to self-regulate by actually standing on the degree of a response to a question that best answers it.

- **Locograms:** Locograms are ice breakers and experiential "check-ins" best used at the beginning of group. They get group members out of their chairs, on their feet and engaged as do all sociometrics. They can also be used to clear the air by giving group members an easy way to express buy-in or resistance to group at any given point in time.

Sociometrics Can Be Broken into Steps for Different Needs and Venues

An advantage to each of the processes is that they can be broken down into steps and/or stages. Each stage can be used as a stand-alone process or it can be broadened into an expanded version, depending on the skill level of the therapist and the needs of the setting, therapist, client, or group. Stages can also be spread throughout the treatment curriculum. A trauma timeline or a social atom done in group can be further processed in one-to-one then brought back into group. Floor checks can slide into existing treatment structures seamlessly, adding an experiential component to both the education and the healing. Letter writing can be done in group or as homework and brought to a group or a one-to-one session. You can even bring artwork into it; floor cards with emotions drawn on them, for example, can be made as an art project and brought into group.

A trauma timeline, as an example, can be done:

- **On Paper and Shared:** The timelines can be done on paper and used as a treatment map, showing where along development a client wishes to begin to take a deeper look. Clients will inevitably add and amend their timelines, as more of their "story" emerges through the process. Timelines can be shared in one-to-one or group. This in itself can be a complete process.
- **As a Group Process:** Timelines can be an experiential group process where numbers are laid on the floor and the entire group stands up and moves to an age, they feel drawn to. This brings sociometric alignment according to age and group members can share meaningfully from or about the age they have in common.
- **One Person at a Time Working in a Group:** Timelines can be done in a group, with one person at a time "walking the timeline" and moving through developmental stages, narrating as they go, and adding small role plays as they feel warmed up to do so.
- **With Role Plays:** As you can see, focused role plays can easily be added to most of these stages. A simple extension of this in one-to-one is that clients can be invited to talk to themselves or anyone else they feel in touch with using an empty chair.

The person walking their timeline can "meet" themselves anywhere along the trajectory of their lives simply by choosing someone to represent them at any age and doing a role play with an auxiliary ego (role player) or an empty chair. They can have an embodied encounter with the self at any point in their development.

The social atom can follow similar stages. It can be done on paper, shared, and used as a treatment map. Role plays can be added in one to one or group simply by inviting clients to talk to anyone including themselves who they feel warmed up to do some work with. Social atoms can be embodied on stage and role-playing added.

Floor checks are primarily a group processes that can have role plays added to them. They might warm someone up to talking to someone in their relational network with whom they have unfinished business. And as the process is warming them up, it is also teaching them about how symptoms of PTSD manifest through spontaneous case studies shared by group members.

On Zoom, timelines, letter writing and social atoms add an experiential component to group. Some therapists put the "floor cards" from floor checks on the Zoom whiteboard and let clients react to them, stamp them, or ask a criterion question and then return to the Zoom room to share about the answer.

Can I Become Certified as a Practitioner of Sociometrics?

Yes, the Association for Addiction Professionals (NAADAC) will be offering a two-level certificate in sociometrics. Visit tiandayton.com for further information. There will be a basic certification that doesn't require a master's degree and a second level that does.

Building a Better Tomorrow

Trauma—at least the kind of relational, addiction-related trauma that I deal with—need not be a life sentence. While the word *trauma* has moved the field forward with a rich body of research, we should remember that pain has ever been the night wind that knocks a door in the soul open so that light can pour in. If an addict is searching for solutions in their drug, they can, if they embrace recovery, recognize a much better solutions for pain in sobriety. If an adult child of relational trauma is working through the unresolved pain from their childhood, it can open the door to consolidating the strengths they exercised and developed along the way that have made them the person they are today. They can gather up all of the rather unique skill sets they have learned from having to solve and rise to unusual challenges and use them in ways that move their own lives forward. Through therapies of all kinds—twelve-step programs and a new design for living that feels connected and nourishing—all involved can live a life they feel good about and proud of, and that is what they can then begin to pass down to the next generation.

Psychodrama and sociometrics are ultimately meant to bring us into the present and unpack the attitudes, frozen emotions, and rigid behaviors that tether us to stale and unexamined ways of living. They seek to transcend psychological, emotional, and spiritual barriers as well as those of gender, race, and culture. They enhance spontaneity and creativity. I find that clients who engage in psychodrama and sociometrics become more confident and self-aware, they feel a greater sense of aliveness, and they learn how to reach out and connect with others because they've learned to connect with themselves.

The notion that healing can only happen in a therapist's office or clinic is becoming increasingly outmoded. Go to any coffee shop or restaurant and you can overhear self-searching conversations filled with language and ideas that were once confined to the realm of therapy. Flip through a magazine, turn on the TV, listen to a podcast, and you'll find people sharing wisdom and personal growth ideas as never before in history. The self-help movement has put information in the hands of the user, and it's being used. So the office or clinic is the starting point, but healing happens through applying the skills learned in therapy (and all sorts of other places) to process blocks as they come up, so that life itself becomes the real teacher.

I always try to support the kinds of activities that research clearly says bring happiness and connection. People don't heal through insight and therapy alone; we need to help them to engage in activities outside of therapy that cultivate well-being, like time for relationships, which are consistently the single best predictor of longevity and good health. Research on exercise and more specifically on the benefits of walking, tells us that walking three times a week for forty or so minutes produces the same benefits as antidepressants. If you can walk outdoors, you add the proven benefits of nature and sunlight, and if you walk with a friend, you have the proven benefits of sharing feelings. I encourage any activities that bring pleasure, produce a flow state, or help clients to expand their social atom. Hobbies are sustaining and creative; they fill time in constrictive self-nourishing ways.

And what you refrain from doing is also very important. It's difficult to have an unhealthy diet or to smoke and expect to reach and sustain positive subtle inner states; the body just gets in the way. Recovery should motivate clients to want more out of life, to become curious about the workings of their inner world and those of others.

It is a rare privilege to be in a group that is vulnerable and open, that is gathered with the intent of healing and growing. Treatment centers and clinics are built around these kinds of groups. Clients are there for many days together, if not weeks or months. They are gathered with the intention of healing and embracing recovery. There are tears and laughter, work and play. There is as much healing happening on the volleyball court and at lunch as in the group rooms. And there are ongoing step-down outpatient, alumni, and twelve-step programs to continue that sense of connection, support, and healing after leaving treatment. The positive limbic resonance in a good treatment center is palpable. It's a beautiful world in which to make deep, personal changes, and those changes gain traction and longevity through an ongoing recovery support network. These settings, with their supportive communities and contained environments, are an excellent place to do psychodrama and sociometrics, to facilitate deep inner change and foster personal, interpersonal and post traumatic growth!

When I have clients in my own therapy groups, I ask them to be in one-to-one therapy and twelve-step recovery. I support hobbies and creative interests and encourage them to embrace exercise and healthy eating. If they do all of these things, alongside the deep healing that happens in an experiential group, they most always make profound life changes. And if they stick with it, those changes become real.

Acknowledgments

In a career that has spanned nearly forty years, I am looking back at as much as looking forward. It is a natural time to want to coalesce what I have learned so that it will serve at least this and the next generation or two below me. By trial and error, I have developed a way that I work with adult relational trauma that I have been researching and honing for decades.

I have always been an experiential therapist and a psychodramatist. As a doctorate in clinical psychology is, at least in part, a research degree, I have had a natural interest in getting psychodrama and sociometry to work better for the population that I serve, which are addicts and family members—in other words, people who have been experiencing adult relational trauma that has its seeds in childhood and/or being addicted or living with addiction. It has always been my feeling that while we used to think that addiction "skipped a generation," trauma does not. And until we treat the trauma, we cannot say we're treating the epigenetics of the addictive thinking, feeling, and behavior that grows out of it. The research into Adverse Childhood Experiences (ACE) certainly supports this thinking. Children who grew up with alcoholism/addiction surfaced in the ACE studies as one of the most at-risk groups for developing PTSD or evidencing symptoms of childhood trauma that impacted both physical and mental health in adulthood. That link is one of the most important to become part of the mental health field in my lifetime.

The other critical research that has shaped sociometrics has been the work of Stephen Porges, Bessel van der Kolk, Stanley Greenspan, Peter Levine, and Daniel Siegel. As it began to surface in the 1980s, their work changed forever the way I saw doing psychodrama and sociometry. I knew intuitively that psychodrama had a power to transform and heal deep pain that no other method I have ever encountered had. But neuropsychology brought the body into therapy, and as such, opened the door for a deeper, scientific understanding of why psychodrama and sociometry, the first western forms of embodied therapy, are so effective and efficient in healing trauma. The task then remained to bring this brilliant research into the methods of psychodrama and sociometry in order to create a trauma informed version on them. This is what my life's work has been devoted to, and that's what this book is all about.

I published my first sociometrics in *The Living Stage: A Step by Step Guide to Psychodrama, Sociometry and Experiential Group Therapy* (2004) and the second in *Relational Trauma Repair:*

Therapist's Guide (2014). I am now gathering some of my most popular processes that I have developed over the past twenty-five to thirty years, ordering them in a way that I feel is the most user-friendly and flexible approach, and calling them sociometrics, a word first coined by J. L. Moreno to refer to his original processes. I have significantly expanded on and created my own sociometrics, e.g., floor checks and timelines, and have added the kind of research to all of them that allow them a targeted and trauma-informed use for treating trauma, addiction, and mental illness. But all of this is only a part of what sociometrics are used for. Their truer objectives, drawn from Porges's research on the social engagement system, are to help clients to resolve pain through meaningful, spontaneous human connection, to build on Moreno's adage that "in a group each person becomes the therapeutic agent of the other" so that clients can absorb the skills of self-regulation through co-regulation. As C. S. Lewis said, "it takes two to see one." As a psychodramatist, mother, grandmother, and even a wife I would say that "it takes two to be one." In other words, successful self-regulation grows out successful co-regulation (Porges, personal communication, 2022).

There are always many people to acknowledge in the making of any book. The truth is that I am always feeling that I am leaving most of the people out. For starters I would like to acknowledge my training groups, staff across the United States, here in New York City and at The Meadows Behavioral Health and Newport Academy, who I have trained, and the clients in clinics, IOPs, and in treatment centers who have used them. The inspiration, interaction, and feedback from these communities are what are really behind the development of sociometrics.

I want to thank Cynthia Moreno-Tuohy, Executive Director of NAADAC, the Association for Addiction Professionals (NAADAC), and Jessica O'Brien, Director of Training and Professional Development at NAADAC, for cocreating a certificate in sociometrics that will roll out in the fall of 2022. I'd also like to thank Samson Teklemariam, Vice President, Director of Clinical Services at Behavioral Health Group and former Director of Training and Professional Development at NAADAC for bringing me to NAADAC.

I would like to thank Sam Quinlan, my friend and colleague, for introducing me to Patrick Hughes who brought me into Central Recovery Press (CRP). Incredibly, every time I hit a wall and Facetimed Patrick full of apologies for interrupting his days, he said, "always time for you, Tian" and proceeded to help me untangle and move through a block. His help in shaping the direction of this book was invaluable.

I would like to thank Stephen Porges for being the embodiment of his work and of co-regulation in offering his expert, creator's eye going over the chapter on polyvagal and psychodrama. No one could ask for more brilliant or kind feedback.

In facing all of the paper shortages and work slowdowns that all publishers have been dealing with throughout COVID, Jeff Speich, Publisher and CEO, and Valerie Killeen, Managing Editor, at CRP have been dedicated to making this book the best it could be. I could not be more appreciative of their support and determination. Valerie's editing, along with the editing of David Fulk, was so very helpful in making sure that thoughts were as clear as they needed to be and the order of the material comprehensible. Valerie's layout is everything I could ask for.

Lastly, thank you to my husband Brandt Dayton, a retired psychoanalyst himself, who listened to every thought and read through the chapters where I needed help, with endless patience. His support and trained eye, as well as simply sharing the sheer joy of writing this along with the inevitable frustrations, I appreciate more than I can ever say.

A Simple Glossary of Terms for Psychodrama and Sociometry

abreactive catharsis. An expulsion of feelings such as anger; an expression of emotions against something

act completion. An impulse for action, or an act hunger searching for completion

act hunger. A hunger for or toward action of some kind

action insight. Insight that occurs as a result of or during enactments

audience. The members of a psychodramatic group

autodrama. A drama that is enacted without a director; that is, the protagonist chooses the auxiliaries and directs the drama him- or herself

auxiliary egos. The group members other than the protagonist who play roles in a psychodrama

catharsis. An expulsion of deep feeling; a releasing of intense feeling that brings about relief

catharsis of integration. A catharsis in which a shift in perception occurs as a result of integrating split or nonintegrated material

cultural conserve. Term first coined by J.L. Moreno; a once-spontaneous act that has become in some way fixed in the culture, for example, Beethoven's Fifth Symphony, a funeral, or a wedding

enroling. Asking someone to play a role; the casting of a role

de-roling. When the auxiliaries let go of the role they have been playing in the protagonist's drama, for example: "My name is Susan. I am not your mother."

director. The person directing the psychodramatic action, usually the therapist

double. The articulation of the inner voice of the protagonist

enactment. The action phase of psychodrama

future projection. A scene that has not actually happened but is anticipated, feared, or wished for in the future

interview. The investigation of a protagonist by a therapist to discover relevant information

locogram. Using the floor as a place to lay out choices that group members can stand on or near in order to designate their preferences

mirror technique. The employment of a double or stand-in for the protagonist so that the protagonist can watch from outside the scene as if in a mirror

monodrama. A drama with a director in which there is only one role player or auxiliary ego representing all the parts

multiple auxiliaries. The protagonist may choose to have more than one auxiliary represent a single role or person

multiple doubles. More than one double may be used for the protagonist

open tensions. Areas within the psyche or self-system that feel unfinished, incomplete, or left in a state of anxious, unfinished closure

present-day scenes. Any scene that relates to the protagonist's present-day life

protagonist. The person whose story is being enacted in a psychodrama

proxemics. A subcategory of the study of nonverbal communication along with haptics (touch), kinesics (body movement), vocalics (paralanguage), and chronemics (structure of time). Proxemics can be defined as "the interrelated observations and theories of man's use of space as a specialized elaboration of culture." Edward T. Hall, the cultural anthropologist who coined the term in 1963, emphasized the impact of proxemic behavior (the use of space) on interpersonal communication.

psychodrama. A therapeutic method that uses action and role playing

psychodramatic trance. A trancelike state that role players may go into while doing a psychodrama in which they actually experience the psychodrama as the real-life situation being portrayed; a healing trancelike state

re-formed auxiliary ego. An auxiliary who, after the conflict or drama has been played out, is offered to the protagonist as the protagonist might wish him or her to be, that is, in a re-formed state

role play. The acting out of an aspect of the self, surplus reality, or a significant person in one's life within the context of psychodrama

role reversal. A technique that allows the protagonist to "reverse roles" and play any role in the drama, in order to experience standing in those shoes and to experience the self from another position

scene setting. The process that the protagonist goes through in setting the scene for the enactment as he or she sees it or wishes to have it

sharing. The portion of psychodrama, after the enactment, in which group members articulate what came up for them as a result of witnessing the enactment and those who played auxiliary roles de-role

social atom. The nucleus of people in a person's life that help that person to remain in social balance and connection

sociometry. The network of connectedness through attraction, repulsion, and neutrality that forms the social grid for all

soliloquy. The speaking out in the first person of the inner goings-on of the protagonist at any given point in a psychodrama or group process

spectrogram. The allotment of personal values, intensities, or definition along a designated line; for example, "On a scale of 1 to 100 percent, how do you feel about . . .?"

surplus reality. What is carried in the psyche as personal history, which affects the whole of who the person is and how he or she relates; the intrapsychic personal material that a person carries within the psyche in reference to the self and to others pertaining to the self **time regression.** Any enactment that represents or concretizes a scene or a metaphor from the past

vignette. A small scene enacted with only one or two role players chosen by the protagonist.

warm-up. A level of readiness and willingness on the part of the client when preparing to do psychodramatic work. The term can be extended into any life activity, for example, "I am warmed -up to writing, seeing someone, sex, painting, cooking," and so on.

References and Bibliography

Anda, R. F. & Brown, D. W. 2010. "Adverse Childhood Experiences & Population Health in Washington: The Face of a Chronic Public Health Disaster." from URL: http://www.theannainstitute.org/ACE%20folder%20 for%20website/44%20Exec%20Summary%20WA%20ACE%20Rpt.pdfAnda, R. F., Felitti, V. J., Bremner, J. D., Walker, J. D., Whitfeld, C., Perry, B. D., Dube, S. R., & Giles, W. H. 2006. "The Enduring Effects of Abuse and Related Adverse Experiences in Childhood. A Convergence of Evidence From Neurobiology and Epidemiology." *European Archives of Psychiatry and Clinical Neurosciences, (256)*(3), 174–86. https://doi.org/10.1007/s00406-005-0624-4

Anda, R. F., Felitti, V.J., Brown, D.W., Chapman, D., Dong, M, Dube, S.R., Edwards, V.J., Giles, W.H. 2006. "Insights Into Intimate Partner Violence from the Adverse Childhood Experiences (ACE) Study." In P.R. Salber and E. Taliaferro (Eds.). *The Physician's Guide to Intimate Partner Violence and Abuse.* Volcano, California: Volcano Press.

Annis, H. M. 1990. "Relapse to Substance Abuse: Empirical Findings Within a Cognitive- Social Learning Approach." *Journal of Psychoactive Drugs (22)*(2), 117–124 https://doi.org/10.1080/02791072.1990.10472537

Anthony, A. 2019. "Stephen Porges: 'Survivors are blamed because they don't fight.'" *The Guardian.* URL: https://www.theguardian.com/society/2019/jun/02/ stephen-porges-interview-survivors-are-blamed-polyvagal-theory-fight-flight-psychiatry-ace

Black, C. 1982. *It Will Never Happen to Me.* Denver, Colorado: M.A.C., First Edition. Printing and Publications Divisions.

Bowlby, J. 1969; 1973. *Attachment: Attachment and Loss* (Volume 1). New York, New York: Basic Books.

Bowlby, J. 1973. *Separation: Anxiety and Anger* (Volume 2). New York, New York: Basic Books.

Brous, K. 2014. "Developmental Trauma: What You Can't See . . ." URL: *http://attachmentdisorderhealing.com/developmental-trauma/*

Carnes, P. 1983; 1992. *Out of the Shadows: Understanding Sexual Addiction.* Minneapolis, Minnesota: CompCare Publications.

Chu, J.A. 2011. "Guidelines for Treating Dissociative Identity Disorder in Adults, Third Revision: Summary Version." *Journal of Trauma & Dissociation,* 12(2), 188–212. doi: 10.1080/15299732.2011.537248

Cozolino, L. 2006. *The Neuroscience of Human Relationships: Attachment and the Developing Social Brain* (p. 120). New York, New York: W. W. Norton & Company.

Csikszentmihalyi, M. 2008. *Flow: The Psychology of Optimal Experience.* New York, New York: Harper Perennial Modern Classics.

Damasio, Antonio 1999. *The Feeling of What Happens: Body, Emotion and the Making of Consciousness.* New York, New York: Harcourt, Inc.

Dayton, T. 1994. *The Drama Within: Psychodrama and Experiential Therapy.* Deerfield Beach, Flordia: Health Communications, Inc.

Dayton, T. 1997. *Heartwounds: The Impact of Unresolved Trauma and Grief on Relationships.* Deerfield Beach, Flordia: Health Communications, Inc.

Dayton, T. 2000. *Trauma and Addiction: Ending the Cycle of Pain Through Emotional Literacy.* Deerfield Beach, Flordia: Health Communications, Inc.

Dayton, T. 2005. *The Living Stage: A Step-by-Step Guide to Psychodrama, Sociometry and Experiential Group Therapy.* Deerfield Beach, Florida: Health Communications, Inc.

Dayton, T. 2007. *Emotional Sobriety: From Relationship Trauma to Resilience and Balance.* Deerfield Beach, Flordia: Health Communications, Inc.

Dayton, T. 2012. *The ACoA Trauma Syndrome: The Impact of Childhood Pain on Adult Relationships.* Deerfield Beach, Florida: Health Communications, Inc.

Erikson, E.H. 1950. *Childhood and Society.* New York, New York: W. W. Norton & Company.

Greenspan, S. I., & Lewis, N. B. 2000. *Building Healthy Minds: The Six Experiences That Create Intelligence and Emotional Growth in Babies and Young Children.* New York, New York: Da Capo Press.

Greenspan, S. & Greenspan, N. T. 1989. *First Feelings: Milestones in the Emotional Development of Your Baby and Child.* New York, New York: Penguin Books.

Greenspan, S. 1999. *Building Healthy Minds: The Six Experiences That Create Intelligence and Emotional Growth in Babies and Young Children.* New York, New York: Da Capo Press.

Hagedorn. 2011. "The Call for a New Diagnostic and Statistical Manual of Mental Disorders Diagnosis: Addictive Disorders." Journal of Addictions & Offender Counseling, 29(2), 110–127. https://doi.org/10.1002/j.2161-1874.2009.tb00049.x

Herman, J.L. 1992. *Trauma and Recovery: The Afterman of Violence – From Domestic Abuse to Political Terror.* New York, New York: Basic Books.

Horowitz, M.J. 1997. *Stress Response Syndromes: PTSD, Grief and Adjustment Disorders (3rd ed.).* Northvale, New Jersey: Jason Aronson Inc.

Horney, K. 1950. *Neurosis and Human Growth.* New York, New York: W.W. Norton & Company.

International Society for the Study of Trauma and Dissociation. 2011. "Guidelines for Treating Dissociative Identity Disorder in Adults, Third Revision: Summary Version." *Journal of Trauma & Dissociation,* 12(2), 188–212. doi:10.1080/15299732.2011.537248

Johnson, S. & Tronick, E. 2016. *Love sense: From Infant to Adult (Sue Johnson and Ed Tronick)* [Video]. YouTube. https://www.youtube.com/watch?v=OyCHT9AbD_Y

Jung, C. G. 1970. *Civilization in Transition: The Collected Works of C. G. Jung, Vol. 10.* G. Adler (Ed.). Princeton, New Jersey: Princeton University Press.

Krystal, H. (Ed.). 1968. *Massive Psychic Trauma.* New York, New York:: International Universities Press.

Krystal, H. 1978. Trauma and Affects *the Psychoanalytic Study of the Child,* 33, 81–116.

Krystal, H. 1984. Psychoanalytic Views on Human Emotional Damages. In B. van der Kolk (Ed.), *Post-Traumatic Stress Disorder: Psychological and Biological Sequetae,* 1–28. Washington, D.C.: American Psychiatric Press.

Landy, R. J. 1996. *Persona and Performance: The Meaning of Role in Drama, Therapy, and Everyday Life.* New York, New York: The Guilford Press.

Ledoux, J. 1996. *The Emotional Brain: The Mysterious Underpinnings of Emotional Life.* New York, New York: Simon & Schuster.

Levine, P. A. 1997. *Waking the Tiger: Healing Trauma.* Berkeley, California: North Atlantic Books.

Levine, P. A. 2010 *In an Unspoken Voice: How the Body Releases Trauma and Restores Goodness (1st ed.).* Berkeley, California: North Atlantic Books.

Linley, A.P., & Joseph, S. 2004. "Positive Change Following Trauma and Adversity: A Review." *Journal of Traumatic Stress* 17: 11–21. https://doi.org/10.1023/B:JOTS.0000014671.27856.7e

MacLean, P. D. 1968. "Alternative Neural Pathways to Violence." In *Alternatives to Violence,* ed. L. Ng 22–34. Fairfax, Virginia: Time-Life Books.

Marano, H.E. 2003. "The Benefits of Laughter." *Psychology Today.* URL: *https://www.psychologytoday.com/articles/200304/the-benefits-laughter*

Marineau, R. F. 1989. *Jacob Levy Moreno 1989–1974: Father of Psychodrama, Sociometry and Group Psychotherapy.* New York, New York: Routledge.

McGrath, J. C. & Linley, P. A. 2006. "Post-Traumatic Growth in Acquired Brain Injury: A Preliminary Small Scale Study." *Brain Injury*, 20(7), 767–773. https://doi.org/10.1080/02699050600664566

Moreno, J. L. 1934. *Who Shall Survive? A New Approach to the Problem of Human Interrelations.* Washington, DC: Nervous & Mental Disease Publishing Co. doi.org/10.1037/10648-000

Moreno, J. L. 1946; 2019. *Psychodrama Volume I.* Ambler, Pennsylvania: Beacon House.

Moreno, J. L. 1969. *Psychodrama Volume III: Action Therapy & Principles of Practice.* Ambler, Pennsylvania: Beacon House.

Moreno, J. L. 1975. *Psychodrama Volume II: Foundations of Psychotherapy.* Ambler, Pennsylvania: Beacon House.

Moreno, J. L. 1993. *Who Shall Survive? Foundation of Sociometry, Group Psychotherapy and Sociodrama: Student Edition.* Roanoke, Virginia: Royal Publishing.

Moreno, J. J. 1999. *Acting Your Inner Music: Music Therapy and Psychodrama.* St. Louis, Missouri: MMB Music.

Moreno, Z. T., Blomkvist, L. D., & Rützel, T. 2000. *Psychodrama, Surplus Reality, and the Art of Healing (1st ed.).* London & New York: Routledge-Taylor & Francis. doi.org/10.4324/9780203770047

Murphy, S. T., Monahan, J. L., & Zajonic, R. B. 1995. Additivity of Nonconscious Affect: Combined Effects of Priming and Exposure. *Journal of Personality and Social Psychology,* 69, 589–602. doi.org/10.1037/0022-3514.69.4.589

Pennebaker, J. W. 1997. *Opening Up: The Healing Power of Expressing Emotions.* New York, New York: The Guilford Press.

Pert, C. B., Dreher, H. E., & Ruff, M.R. 1998. "The Psychosomatic Network: Foundations of Mind-Body Medicine." *Alternative Therapies in Health & Medicine,* 4(4), 30–41.

Porges S. W. 1995. "Orienting in a Defensive World: Mammalian Modifications of Our Evolutionary Heritage." A Polyvagal Theory. *Psychophysiology,* 32(4), 301–318. https://doi.org/10.1111/j.1469-8986.1995.tb01213.x

Porges. S. W. 1998. "Love: An Emergent Property of the Mammalian Autonomic Nervous System." *Psychoneuroendocrinology,* 23(8), 837–861. https://doi.org/10.1016/S0306-4530(98)00057-2

Porges, S. W. 2004. "Neuroception: A Subconscious System for Detecting Threats and Safety." *Zero to Three* (24)5, 19–24.

Porges, S. W. 2011. *The Polyvagal Theory: Neurophysiologial Foundations of Emotions, Attachment, Communication, and Self-Regulation.* New York, New York: W. W. Norton & Company.

Porges, S.W., & Dana, D. 2018. *Clinical Applications of the Polyvagal Theory: The Emergence of Polyvagal-Informed Therapies.* New York, New York: W.W. Norton & Company.

Rando, T. A. 1993. *Treatment of Complicated Mourning.* Chicago, Illinois: Research Press.

Schore, A. N. 1991. "Early Superego Development: The Emergence of Shame and Narcissistic Affect Regulation in the Practicing Period." *Psychoanalysis and Contemporary Thought* 14(2). 187–250.

Schore, A. N. 1994; 1999. *Affect Regulation and the Origin of the Self: The Neurobiology of Emotional Development.* Hillsdale, New Jersey: Lawrence Erlbaum Associates, Inc.

Schore, A. N. 1996. "The Experience-Dependent Maturation of a Regulatory System in the Orbital Prefrontal Cortex and the Origin of Developmental Psychopathology." *Development and Psychopathology,* 8(1), 59–87. doi.org/10.1017/S0954579400006970

Siegel, D. 2011. *The Neurological Basis of Behavior, the Mind, the Brain and Human Relationships.* [Video]. Garrison Institute. URL: *http://www.youtube.com/watch?v=B7kBgaZLHaA*

Stevens, J.E. 2012. "The Adverse Childhood Experiences Study—the largest, most important public health study you never heard of—began in an obesity clinic." URL: *https://acestoohigh.com/2012/10/03/the-adverse-childhood-experiences-study-the-largest-most-important-public-health-study-you-never-heard-of-began-in-an-obesity-clinic/*

Tedeschi, R. G. & Calhoun, L. G. 1996. "The Post-Traumatic Growth Inventory: Measuring the Positive Legacy of Trauma." *Journal of Traumatic Stress,* 9(3), 455–471. URL: doi.org/10.1002/jts.2490090305

Tedeschi, R. G. & Calhoun, L. G. 2004. "Post-Traumatic Growth: Conceptual Foundations and Empirical Evidence." *Psychological Inquiry,* 15, 1–18. doi.org/10.1207/s15327965pli1501_01

"Toxic Stress." 2015. *Center on the Developing Child.* URL: https://developingchild.harvard.edu/science/key-concepts/toxic-stress/

Ungar, M. 2004. *Nurturing Hidden Resilience in Troubled Youth.* Toronto, ON: University of Toronto Press.

van der Kolk, B. 1987. *Psychological Trauma.* Washington, D.C. American Psychiatric Press.

van der Kolk, B. 1993. Group Therapy with Traumatic Stress Disorder. In *Comprehensive Textbook of Group Psychotherapy.* Kaplan, H., and B. Sadock (eds.). New York, New York: Williams & Wilkins.

van der Kolk, B. 1994. "The Body Keeps the Score: Memory and the Evolving Psychobiology of Post-Traumatic Stress." *Harvard Review of Psychiatry*, 1(5), 253–65. doi.org/10.3109/10673229409017088

van der Kolk, B. 2003. Posttraumatic Stress Disorder and the Nature of Trauma. In *Healing Trauma: Attachment, Mind, Body, and Brain.* M. F. Solomon and D. J. Siegel (eds.), 168–195. New York, New York: W. W. Norton & Company.

van der Kolk, B. 2006. [Lecture]. Sponsored by The Meadows. New York, New York.

van der Kolk, B., McFarlane, A., Weisauth, L. (Eds.). 1996. *Traumatic stress: The Effects of Overwhelming Experience on Mind, Body, and Society.* New York, New York: The Guilford Press.

Winerman, L. 2005. "The mind's mirror: A new type of neuron—called a mirror neuron—could help explain how we learn through mimicry and why we empathize with others." *Monitor on Psychology*, (36)(9), 48.

Woititz, J. 1983. *Adult Children of Alcoholics.* Deerfield Beach, Florida: Health Communications, Inc.

Wolin, S. & Wolin, S. 1993. *The Resilient Self: How Survivors of Troubled Families Rise Above Adversity.* New York, New York: Villard Books.

Wong, P. T. P. 2009. Viktor Frankl: Prophet of Hope for the 21st Century. In A. Batthyany & J. Levinson (Eds.), *Anthology of Viktor Frankl's Logotherapy.* Phoenix, Arizona: Zeig, Tucker & Theisen Inc.

Wong, P. T. P. (Ed.). 2012. *The Human Quest for Meaning: Theories, Research, and Applications.* New York, New York: Routledge.

Wong, P. T. P. & Wong, L. C. J. 2012. A Meaning-Centered Approach to Building Youth Resilience. In P. T. P. Wong (Ed.), *The Human Quest for Meaning: Theories, Research, and Applications*, 585–617. New York, New York: Routledge.

Wylie, M. S. 2004. "The limits of talk: Bessel van der Kolk wants to transform the treatment of trauma." *Psychotherapy Networker*, (28) 30–41. URL: https://www.psychotherapynetworker.org/magazine/article/818/the-limits-of-talk

Young, S. N. 2007. "How to Increase Serotonin in the Human Brain Without Drugs." *Journal of Psychiatry & Neuroscience*, 32(6), 394–399. URL: http://www.ncbi.nlm.nih.gov/pmc/articles/PMC2077351

CPSIA information can be obtained
at www.ICGtesting.com
Printed in the USA
JSHW020207231022
31966JS00001B/1

9 781949 481648